IMAGES of America

D'IBERVILLE AND ST. MARTIN

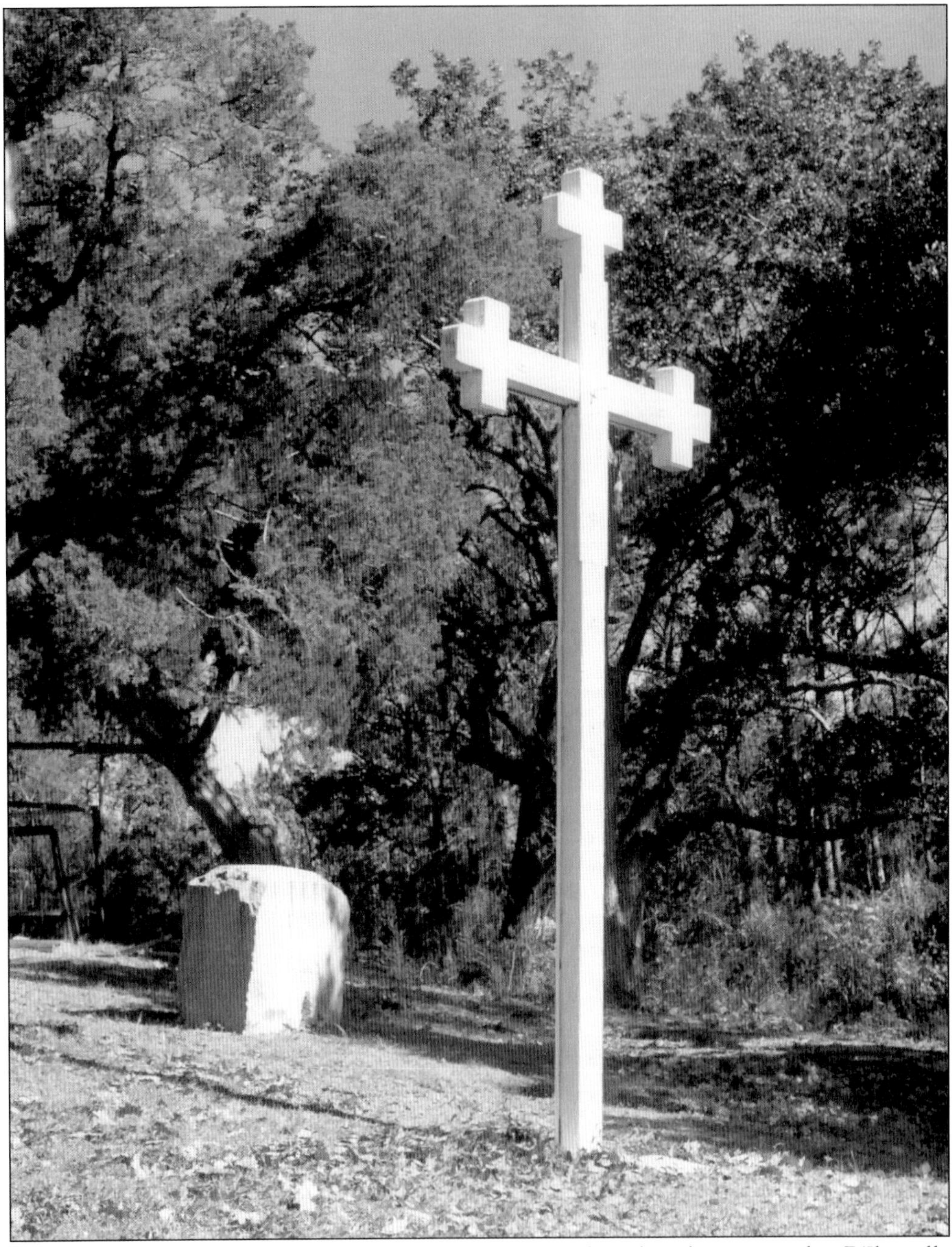

Shown here is the Cross and Boulder. On this terrace, the first chapel was erected in D'Iberville by Emanuel Sanchez in the 1830s. Folklore tells of Pierre LeMoyne's explorers visiting this shore in 1699. The site's history is explained later in this text. (Courtesy Paul Fayard.)

On the Cover: Six of the ten members of Johnny Bosarge's Orchestra are seen in session in the early 1950s. Johnny is on the drums; Ruth Collins is at the piano; John Tiblier is with the bass; Woody James is the trumpeter; and Sidney Kontz is the saxophonist. The guitarist, sitting in for clarinetist Clarence Harder, is unidentified. (Courtesy Laura Thompson.)

IMAGES
of America

D'IBERVILLE AND ST. MARTIN

Dale Greenwell

ARCADIA
PUBLISHING

ISBN 978-0-7385-9424-8

Published by Arcadia Publishing
Charleston, South Carolina

Printed in the United States of America

Library of Congress Control Number: 2012944787

For all general information, please contact Arcadia Publishing:
Telephone 843-853-2070
Fax 843-853-0044
E-mail sales@arcadiapublishing.com
For customer service and orders:
Toll-Free 1-888-313-2665

Visit us on the Internet at www.arcadiapublishing.com

Dedicated to my wife Frances, daughter Michelle, and mother Martha, for having the courage to stand by me through the years

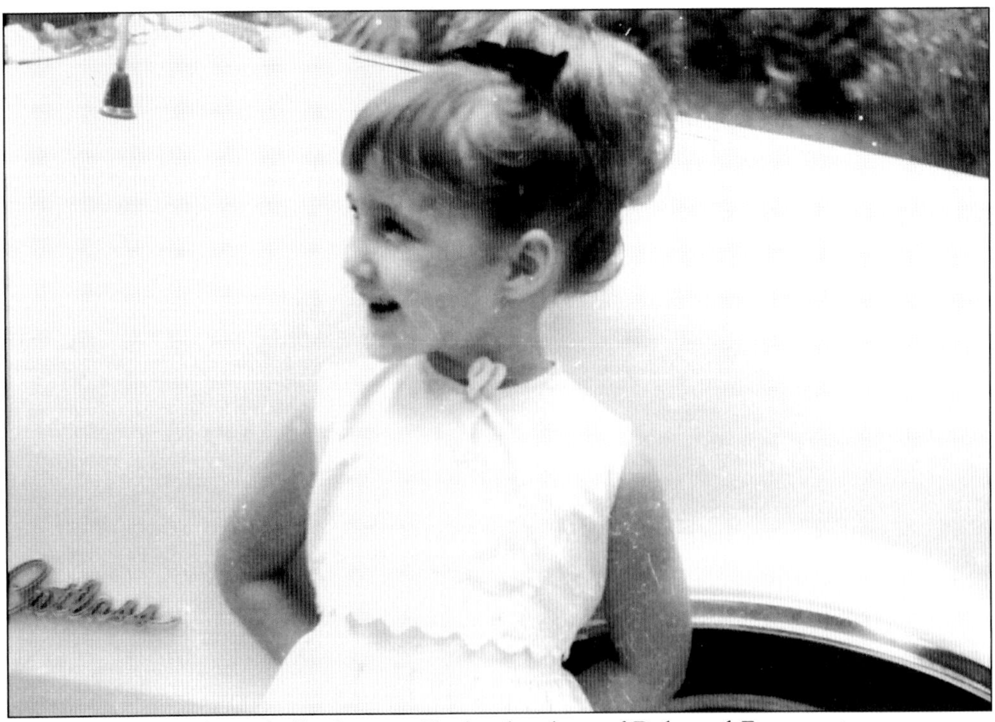

Pictured as a child, Michelle Greenwell, the daughter of Dale and Frances, is now among the angels.

Contents

Acknowledgments		6
Introduction		7
1.	Welcome to the Beginning	9
2.	Pioneers on the Frontier	17
3.	Wars, Railroads, and Reconstruction	25
4.	The Open Range	41
5.	From the Waterfront	51
6.	Searching Family Albums	63
7.	Tour of Duty	77
8.	Faces in the Crowd	87
9.	A Waterfront Town	103
10.	The Birth of a City	111

ACKNOWLEDGMENTS

The project of putting this book together has been a social and personal experience worth fond memories. If not for the destruction of our town and its neighbors by Hurricane Katrina in 2005, the desired photographs would have been readily available. Most photograph treasure troves were swept into oblivion, leaving few in the hurricane's wake. Yet an interesting collection was gradually realized and presented in this volume. From the intense search for surviving photographs, new relationships were born. Many around the Bay of Biloxi joined in the search and are recognized for their assistance, most especially Paul Fayard.

Special thanks are due to Catherine Lawrence, Maxine Ramsey, Bessie Nielsen, Jackie Toncrey, Dana Ferguson, Alice Mae Voght, Kenneth Fountain, Laura Thompson, Dionne Ollier, Janet Derouen, Ralph Borries, Jane Shambra, Linda Hasley, Wayne Creel, Cheri Rowan, Ted Aycock, Caroline Anderson, Billie Ladnier, Tommy Ferguson, Deanna Comer, Mike Mullins, Shirley Santa Cruz, Doty Fournier, Linda Davis, Yvonne Battaya, Betty Duggan, Merle Groue, Alton Richards, Rip Poulos, Lyndell Lepre, Jane Rogers, Edith Moran, Mark Shoemaker, Joe Tomasosky, Oliver Diaz, and Arnie Gollott.

My research of local history began at age 14, as a Boy Scout working on merit badges. Our young scoutmaster, James Moran, encouraged it. In those early years, information was basically gleaned from the memories of our elders, who have all since passed. Those best remembered for their enduring patience are Leontine Beaugez, Alberta Saujon, Emma Harvey, Adolph Santa Cruz, Harry Moran, Nick Seymour, Laura Seymour, Gladys Boney, Davis Fayard, Elvis Fayard, Vernon Santa Cruz, Phillip Trochesset, Ethel Fairley, Arthur Boney, Randolph Santa Cruz, Orey Krohn, Vanna Blackwell, Vada Talley, Effie Seymour, John Brashier, Jake Fountain, Emily Cannette, Julius Cannette, Snooks Batia, Corine Fountain, Albert Fountain, Millie Seymour, Joe Santa Cruz, Clementine Fournier, and my mother, Martha Greenwell.

More recently, gaps were filled by Elvis Fayard, Kitty Husley, Fred Husley, J.W. Fletcher, Buddy Fountain, Walter Fountain, Bill Hubbel, Harvey Saujon, Hunter Grantham, Bill Holland, and Lucius Hengen.

Very special thanks to Leslie Robertson, Chase Foreman, Earl Wetze,l and Cindy Feranda for their assistance. Biloxi Library Archives and record sources of the *Daily Herald* were also valuable sources of information.

My sincere apologies to any contributor overlooked; a tired mind does that.

—Dale Greenwell

Introduction

Looking back through generations of imaginations, the future as it progressed to this day was neither prophetic nor imaginary. What had been the "center" of the small town is now a quiet memorial parkway, no longer Ramsey Road or Central. Along it, citizens saw few strangers, and visitors gathered to pass on the news of the day. Where cattle once ranged, hotels, shopping malls, and subdivisions now crowd the landscape. Where giant forests once towered above briar-free wilderness, folks now groom their lawns and garage their cars.

It all began more than two centuries ago, when related families settled along the northern shore of Back Bay Biloxi. Three were descendants of Christian Maturin Ladner, a native of Pitersene, Switzerland, exiled to the colony of Louisiana in 1719 for having sold salt on the streets of France without the king's permission; the fourth was Elizabeth Boudreau (French and Indian). They were granted land during the Spanish colonial period. When the coast came under the American flag in 1812, all but Elizabeth updated their claims.

Of the three Ladniers, Joseph had initiated his claim in 1793, Jean Baptist in 1800, and Dominic in 1802. Dominic's section, the most practical for connecting both sides of the bay by ferry, was selected for the first bridge span between the two shores in 1901.

The geology of the north shore favored Dominic's section, the plateau, as the most practical convergence of trails into the bay area. That convenience continued through the first half of the 20th century. The eastern third of the plateau, Jean's part, became the community of St. Martin. These original claims are the boundaries for this book. To go beyond these imaginary lines would require a much larger volume. I regret we could not extend the contents beyond Cedar Lake and old St. Martin, but the story of any part reflects the story of all.

Cedar Lake is included because it was the heart of the local timber industry, of which many of the local men and women were involved for half a century. Our pioneering ancestors would just shake their heads if they could see how their lands appear on government maps today.

What was granted to Joseph included the first industrial site and trading post north of the bay, the French colonial brickyard of the 1720s. When the French colonial headquarters was transferred in 1726 to the present-day site of New Orleans, the brickyard lingered, then closed. However, that was not the end; it reopened several times over the next two centuries on the original site—where the bay's channel touches shore. There was no better landing in the days before bridges and paved roads.

There is no point in history that can be identified as the beginning of the town before it was incorporated in 1988. There are suggestions that trappers with Indian wives were on the bay before the colonizers arrived in 1699. Then there is the question of Elizabeth Boudreau's land between the Ladnier strips that records confirm, but so far have not explained how the United States later presented it to L.A. Caillavet. One thought is that she might not have made the trip to Old Augusta, Mississippi, to reregister her title after Mississippi became a state in 1817. There was also an old Canadian wooden fort on her property, mentioned in records. This has always been a topic of discussion among historians and elders.

After the land opened to Americans in 1812, the migration was not immediate. Though Indian trails were not supportive of wagon trains across the southeast, it was different in prairie country. In timber and swamp country, travel was by horse and foot until wagon roads evolved from a lot of hard work by many families and the militia.

To young America, Mississippi was part of the Southwest. People from the original colonies were seeking homesteads in different clines. After the families mentioned above, the next immigrants to the north side of Back Bay were Spanish men married to French women. Then came the German, Croatian, Austrian, Italian, Irish, and English-American immigrants. They bought from the Ladners and settled among them. Many settled north of the old claims and cleared land in the Tchoutacabuffe watershed. Language barriers dissipated as their children merged and married. They, in turn, were the storytellers of the migrations and burials along the way.

The population by the 1840s included boat builders, town builders, ranchers, farmers, merchants, millwrights, brick makers, seamen, and fishermen. As they set up shop, the unemployed and adventurers followed with their saddles, plows, axes, and saws. Mills, stills, and kilns were set up throughout the tall timber. As the forests fell to the axe, an open range evolved, encouraging a new breed: ranchers and range-riders. Sheep and cattle soon roamed the tall grass where virgin pines once towered skyward.

General merchandise stores replaced frontier trading posts; boatyards and oyster shops dotted the waterfront; rough-clad towns grew up around timber mills; schooner transportation of goods and produce to cities along coasts were soon replaced by railroads. After terrible losses in the Civil War Yankee occupation and Reconstruction ended, the railroad arrived in 1870, igniting industry on the coast. Timber, seafood, and other natural resources created an economic boom and population growth to all settlements along the coast.

On the north side of the bay, people could hear the faraway sounds of industry. Their resources and products were essentially different but supportive to the city folks and included cattle, wool, timber, produce, dairy and garden products, and the mechanics and laborers for factories and stores, railroads, and fleets. The wounds of war were healing. Children were going to school and church. Ball games and boat races, staged shows and dance pavilions created social platforms everywhere. The frontier days had ended, and the modern world had arrived.

This book is a sketch of their world. Enjoy it.

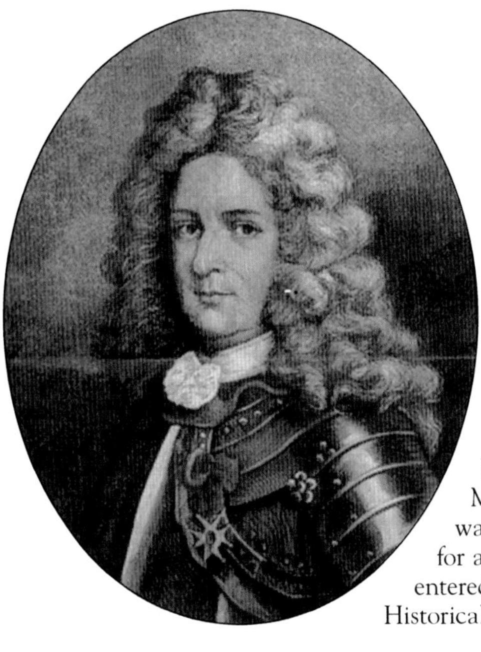

Pierre LeMoyne, le sieur d'Iberville (July 16, 1661–July 9, 1706), son of Charles LeMoyne de Longuiel of Montreal, Canada, was appointed by King Louis XIV in 1698 to explore the Lower Mississippi Valley via the Mexican Gulf. The purpose was to locate a suitable place on the Mississippi for a fort and to initiate a colony. In the process, he entered Biloxi Bay in February 1699. (Courtesy Montreal Historical Archives.)

One

Welcome to the Beginning

The north shore geological formations of Back Bay Biloxi evolved during the Sangamon Stage of the Quaternary Ice Age of 125,000–75,000 BP (Before Present). In the current post-glacial period, the Holocene, beginning more than 10,000 years ago, the Biloxi Bay area evolved to its present form.

The Paleoindian Period, referred to as the period of the big game hunters, more than 8,000 years ago, would have viewed the shores of the Gulf of Mexico many miles south and several hundred feet lower than the coastline today.

During the subsequent Archaic Period (when the hunter-gatherer culture was present) of 8,000–3,000 BP, the rising gulf waters encroached upon the river basin that is today, in part, Back Bay. The Woodland Period (incipient farming and semi-sedentary civilizations) followed from around 1000 BC to 1000 AD. The last pre-Columbian period (c. 1000 AD to 1650 AD) is referred to as the Mississippian (farming and sedentary civilizations).

Along the shorelines are hundreds of midden (debris) sites consisting of discarded oyster and clam shells, animal and fish bones, and volumes of broken pottery, tools and adornments, all confirming the popularity of the coast at least for seasonal procurement of food and materials, such as sea shells. It is also known from the archaeological data that people throughout the Mississippi Valley and adjoining regions were trading, especially what each considered exotic, such as sea shells for copper.

By the time the French arrived in 1699, the Indian settlements were no closer than four miles of the gulf's shoreline. The Acolapisa were four miles up the Pearl River and the Biloxis and Pascagoulas were more than 18 miles up the Pascagoula River. Hurricanes were probably the cause for abandonment of the shores of the gulf and bays except for fishing camps.

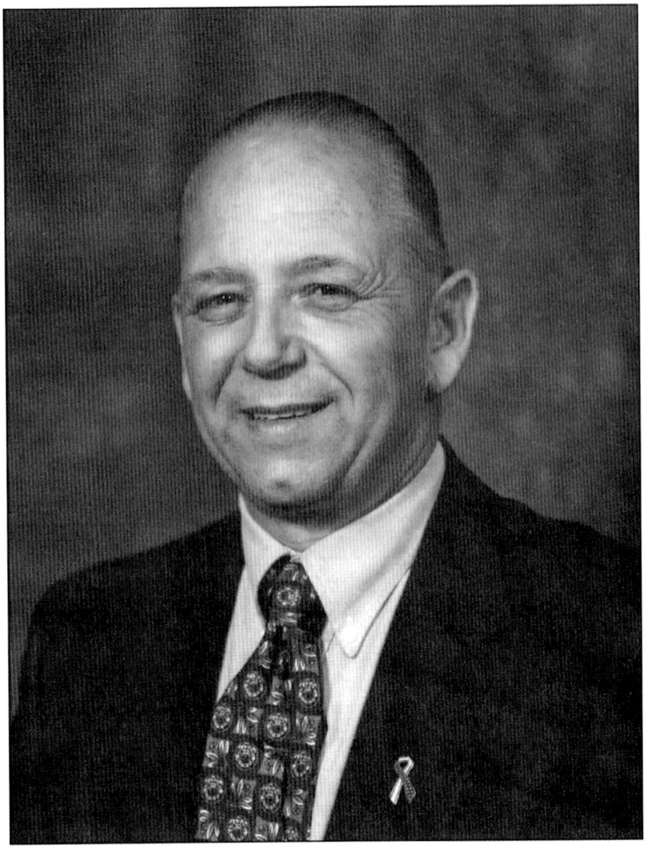

City of D'Iberville mayor Rusty Quave is the son of Russell and Beverly (Ladner) Quave of D'Iberville. He has served the people since 1993 as the second mayor. (Courtesy the City of D'Iberville.)

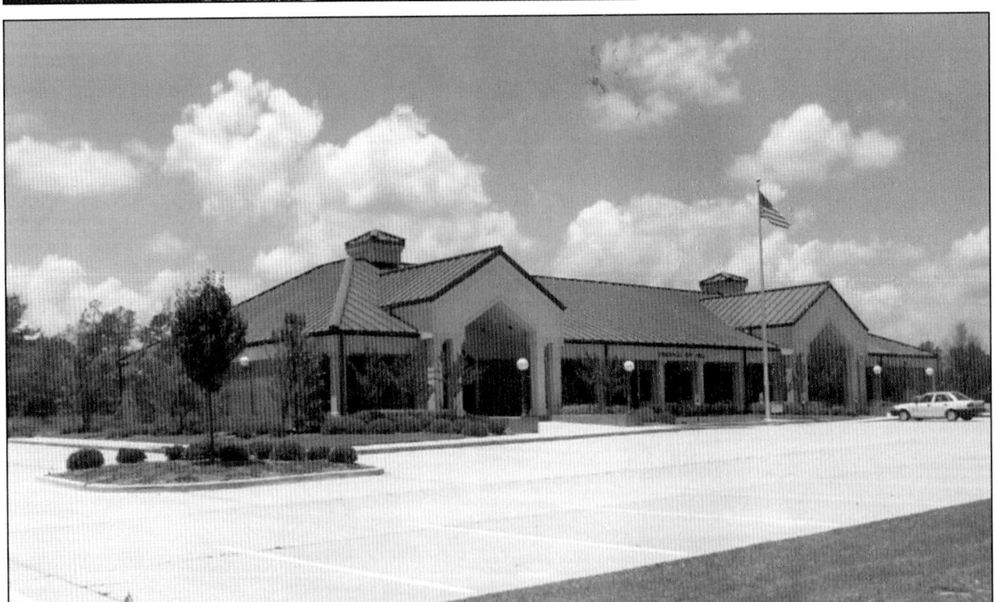

With Mayor Rusty Quave at the helm, the city government, at age seven, moved into the new city hall on Auto Mall Parkway (Old Cedar Lake Road) in 1995. Before the hall, this land was part of a large pecan orchard where cattle browsed. (Courtesy the City of D'Iberville.)

The Warrior's Aim is a sketch by the late Dr. A.R. Galle, a student and expert on southeastern Indian cultures. His reproductions included tools, weapons, dugouts, ceramics, and clothing. The replications were so precise, the Mississippi Department of Archives and History asked him to mark them.

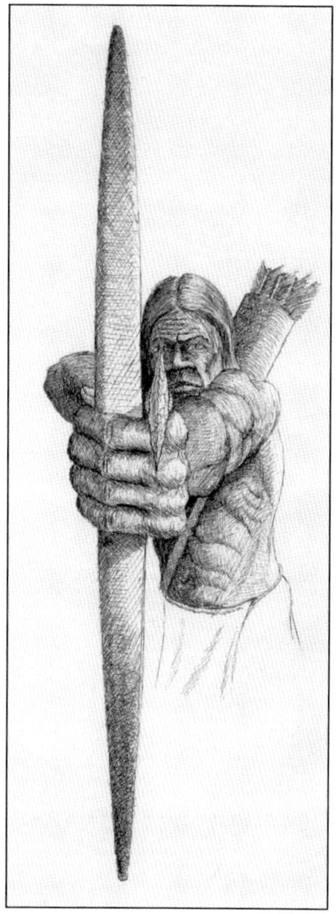

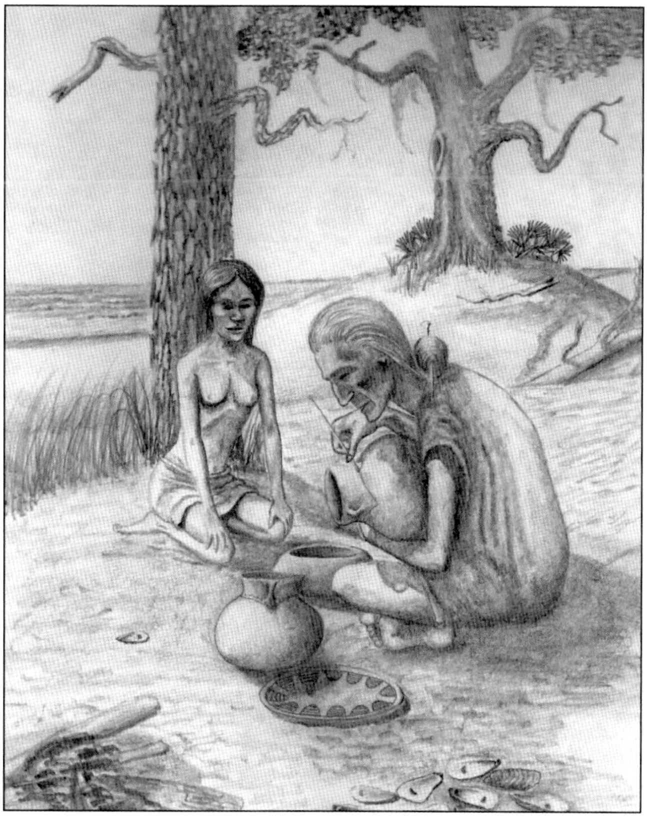

This sketch by Galle is titled *Teaching a Curious Child.* Notice the saltpan's sunburst design. It was a common ceramic of the Mississippian cultural tradition in the Southeast for several centuries before Pierre LeMoyne arrived in 1699. Saltwater evaporation was one of several processes.

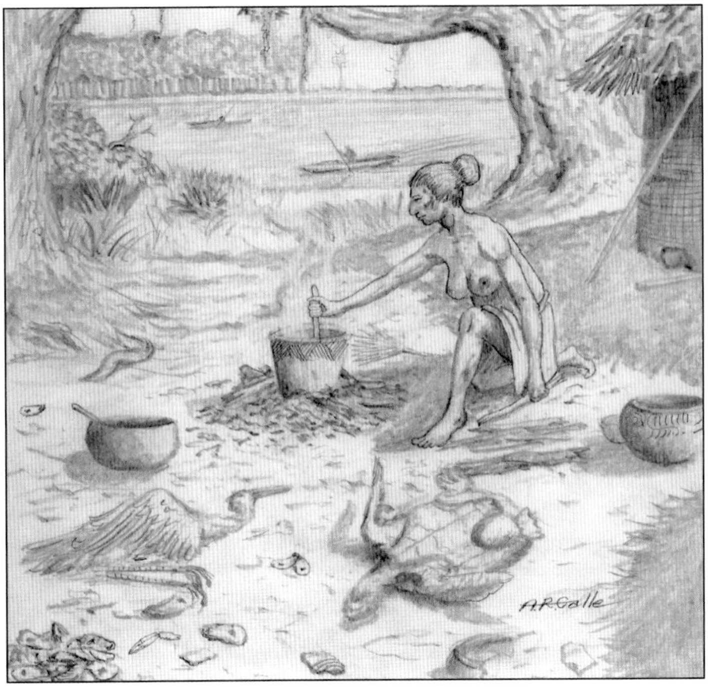

Seen here is a seasonal fishing camp along the bay as envisioned by Dr. Anthony R. Galle, based on accumulated archaeological data from the coast and bay. The hut is suggested from the same and sketches made by early exploration artists during and after Pierre LeMoyne's arrival.

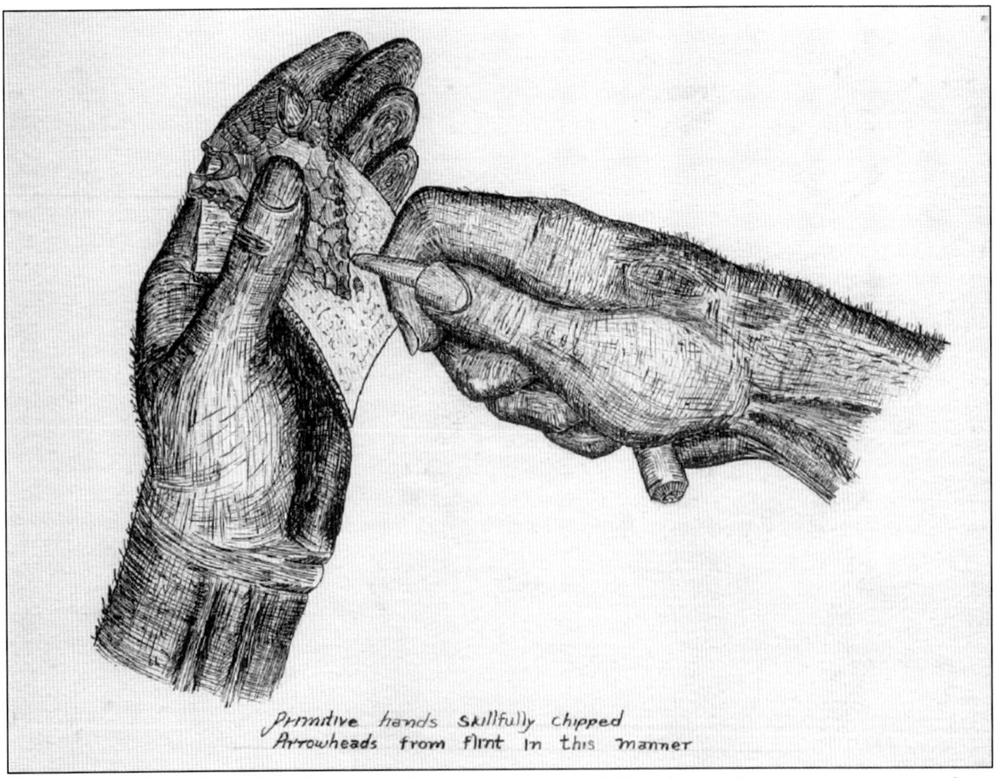

Flint-knapping was a technology brought to the new world by the earliest migrants more than 14,000 years ago. Lithic artifacts included points, blades, scrapers, choppers, drills, beads, and others. (Courtesy Jim Tribble.)

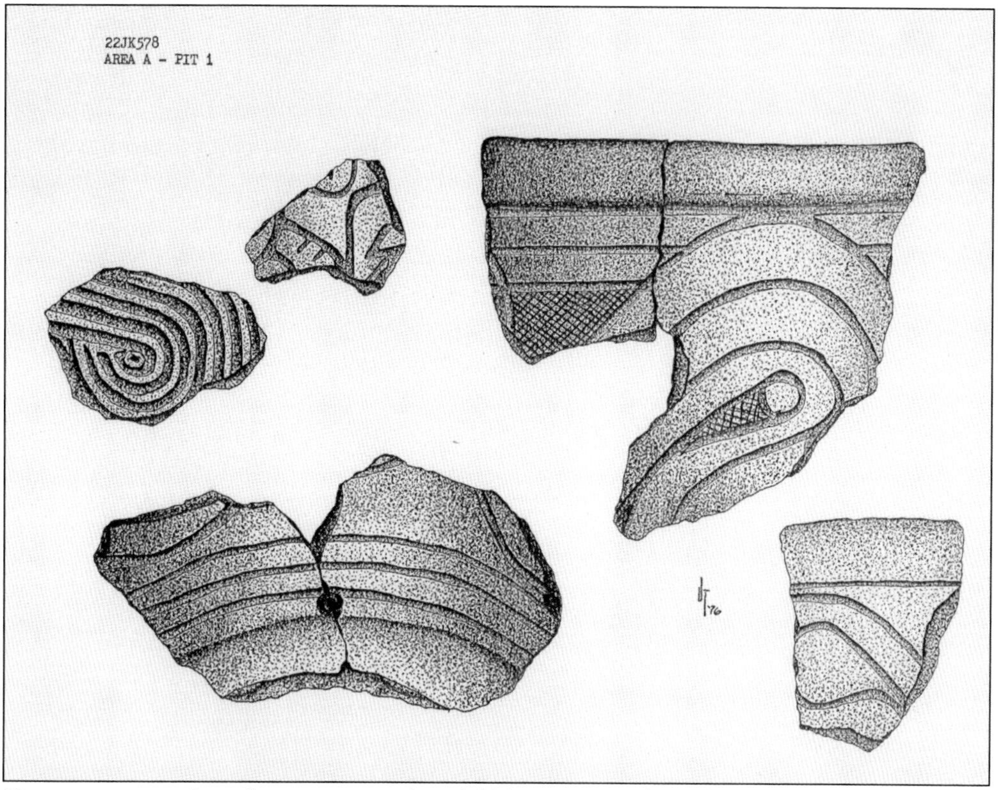

Ceramics appeared on the coast more than 3,000 years ago. These sherds reveal the shape, size, and form of ceramics common on the coast, and are diagnostic criteria separating different cultural periods in time. These are from the Middle Woodland and Late Mississippian cultural periods (from around 400 AD to 1500 AD). (Courtesy Jim Tribble.)

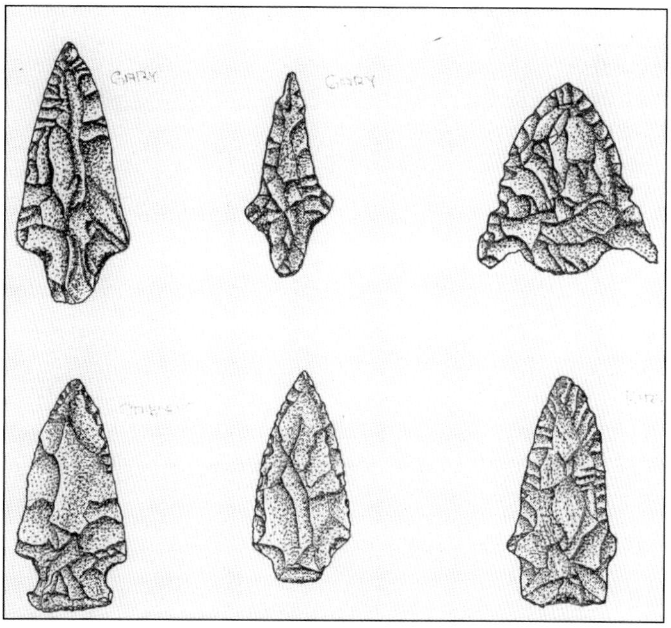

Other than river gravel, stone is not natural to the coastal area. These lithic artifacts from the fields of Brodie's Nursery in D'Iberville were used as points, blades, drills, scrapers, and other tools typical of the Late Archaic and Early Woodland periods (from around 2,000 to 5,000 BP). (Courtesy Jim Tribble.)

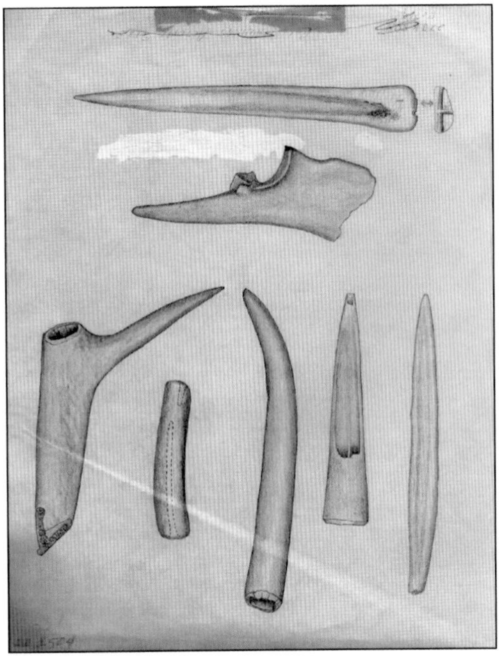

Long before Native Americans had pottery, they were nomadic hunter-gatherers, utilizing every available material resource, including shell, skin, hide, bone of all animals, birds, and fish for weapons, tools, and decorations. These are from bay area sites. (Courtesy Jim Tribble.)

This 1732 map by Le Sieur d'Anville locates Indian villages he had visited and others reported to him. Minor errors in the map indicate his dependence on data from others rather than careful mapping via surveys. Still, it is a valuable source. (Louisiana State Archives.)

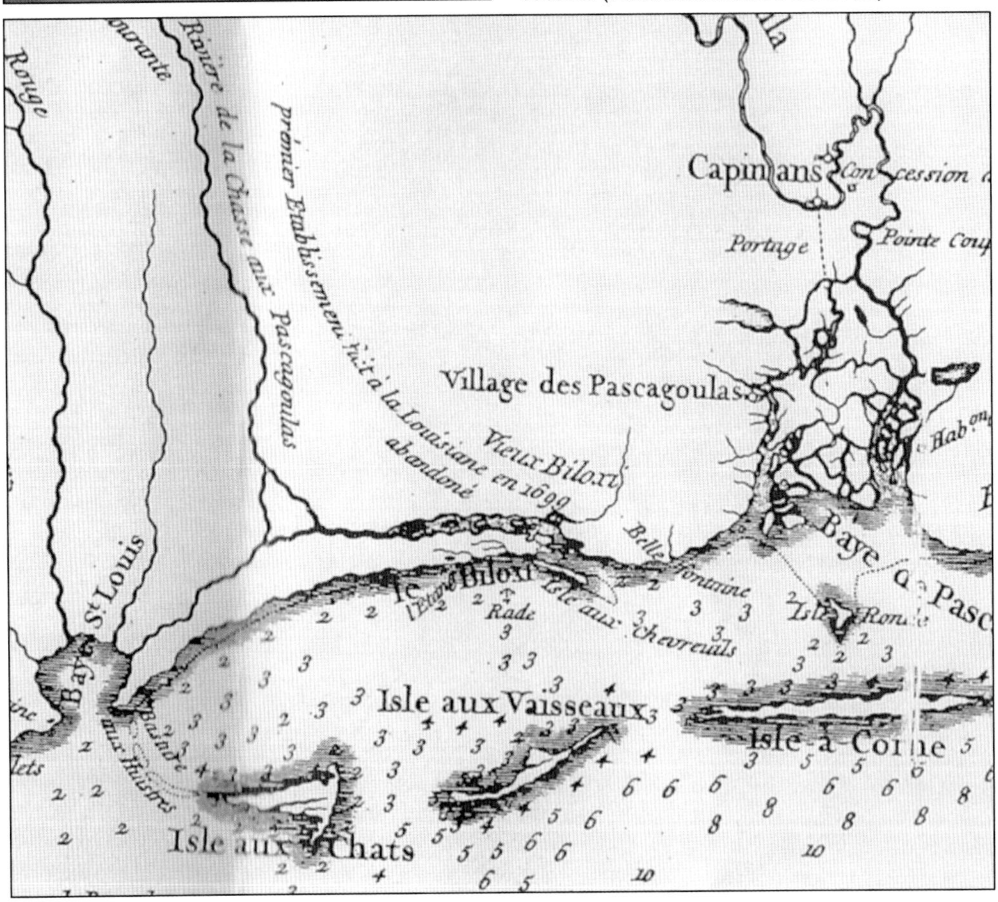

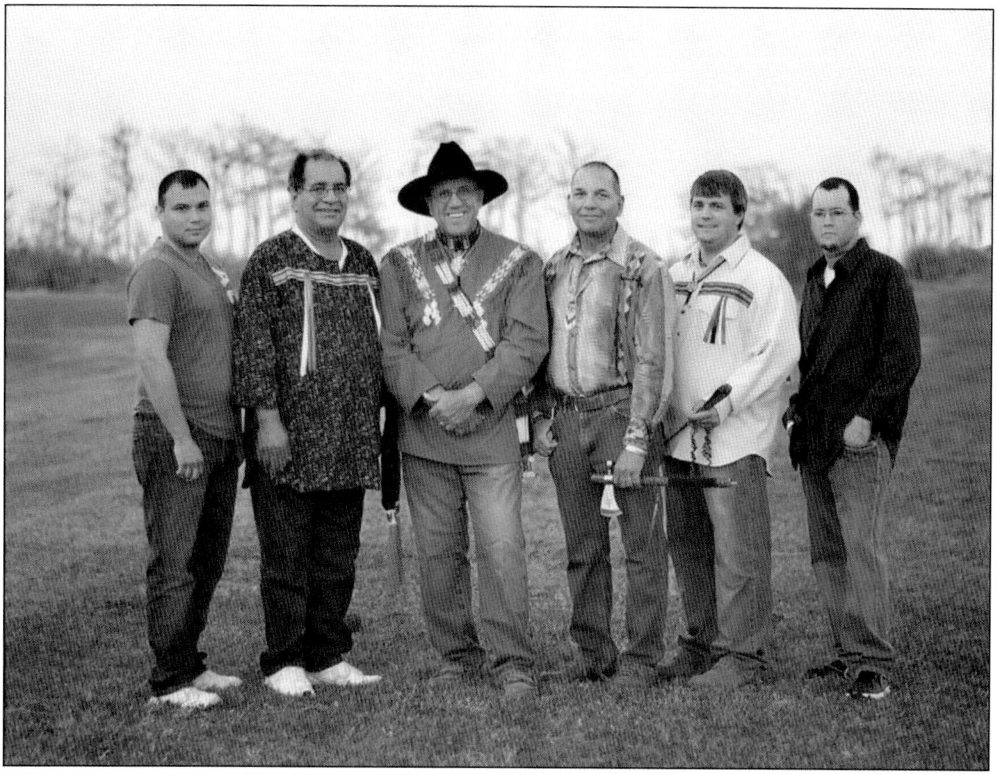

Biloxi-Chitimacha band's traditional chief Albert Naquin is surrounded by other members of the tribe in this 2012 photograph. The tribe and the people of D'Iberville enjoy warm relations. (Photograph by Michelle Lirette Ray of Flashover Photography; courtesy the Biloxi-Chitimacha.)

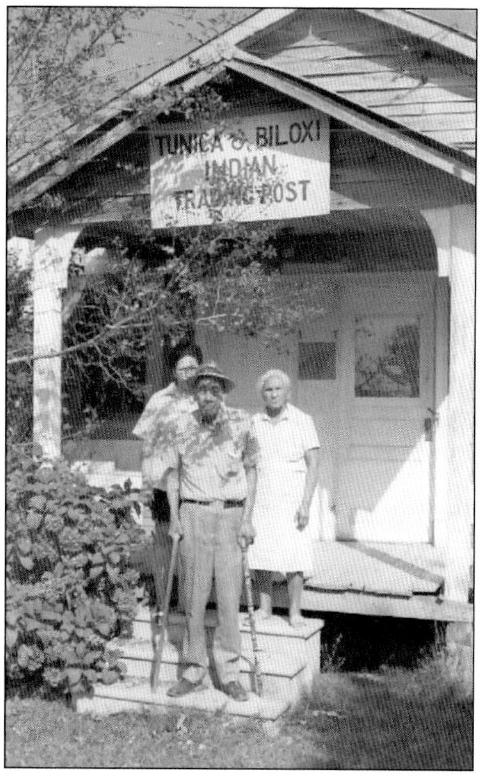

Tunica-Biloxi chief Joseph Pierette and his wife, Rosa, are seen in this 1973 image, taken in the front of the small Tunica-Biloxi Tribal Museum that is next to their home in Marksville, Louisiana. Both are now deceased. (Photograph by author.)

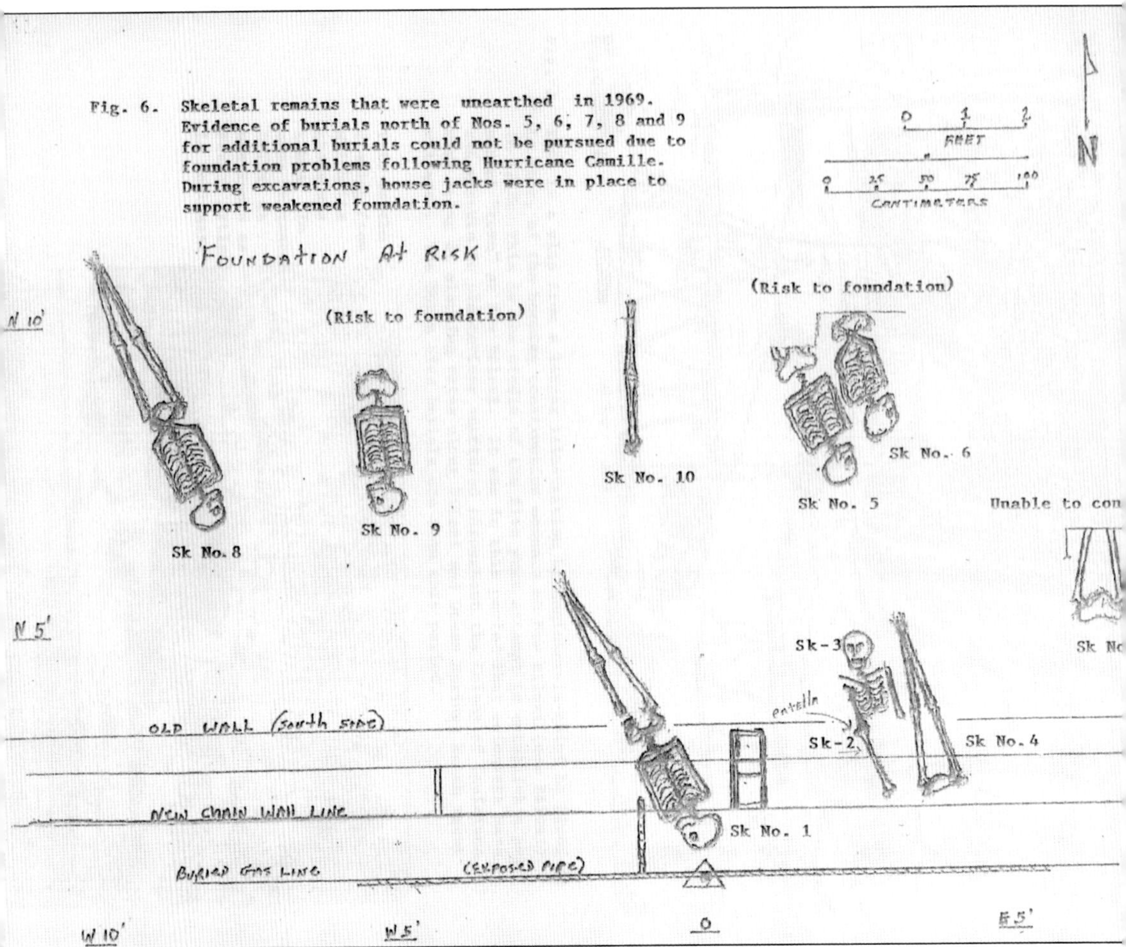

Colonial burials near the present-day Biloxi Lighthouse were identified after Hurricane Camille in 1969. They confirm archived reports of hundreds of deaths around 1720 due to illness and deprivation. Bodies were evidently stripped, as clothing and shoes were needed commodities. The author directed this first archaeology project of the site in 1969. (Illustration by author.)

Two

Pioneers on the Frontier

On February 10, 1699, a French naval squadron under the command of Capt. Pierre LeMoyne, le sieur d'Iberville, dropped anchor at an island they named Ile aux Vesseaux. Three days later, they went ashore on what is now Biloxi's beach. A small group of Indian men and women fled in canoes; they encouraged a meeting with them at a camp on present-day Ocean Springs Beach. They were the Biloxi (Taneks Anya), a recent Siouan tribe to the coast living on the Pascagoula River.

What seemed to amaze the explorers most about the bay was the lack of settlement and the huge "crocodiles" (alligators). Their purpose was to locate the Mississippi and find a suitable place to build a defensive military base to establish control of the river, which had been claimed for France by Rene Robert Cavelier, Sieur de LaSalle, in 1682, for his king, Louis XIV.

The bay was part of an extensive frontier that included the lower Mississippi River and the gulf territory west of Mobile Bay. However, there have been comments in French colonial documents that suggest the area was no secret to the French. Trappers (*coureurs des bois)* from as far away as Montreal were familiar with the rivers and creeks of this part of the world. With Indian friends, they visited the new settlement at the mouth of the bay (Fort Maurepas) soon after it was occupied.

Land concessions were sold to wealthy Europeans beginning in 1719, but the lands on the north side of the bay were not granted until the English period (1755–1779) and Spanish period (1779–1810). In 1812, land south of the thirty-first parallel between the rivers Perdido and Pearl were claimed as part of the Mississippi Territory. On December 10, 1817, Mississippi became the twenty-second state in the Union. The coast was divided into the counties of Hancock and Jackson. The new wave of immigrants began arriving from the old colonies and Europe. First on foot and horse, then, as the Indian trails were worn into wagon roads, by ox-pulled wagons loaded with children, furniture, and tools, with goats and dogs in tow. They were the new generation from different nations and languages, eager to start over and become one. The children mixed, learned a common language, married, and removed cultural barriers.

Towns along the coast had academies for those who could afford attendance, but the rural communities were without schools until the growing populations realized the children had to put education ahead of chores—at least for a few hours a day for a few months of the year. Still, immigrants as far back as the French period included a few literates; they aided the illiterate majority.

There were also missionaries making the rounds to bless children and perform the rites of passage—all part of the records genealogists rely on today. Business communities were in their infancy. In 1841, Harrison County was created from parts of Hancock and Jackson. Literate folks took office and leaders were elected to construct and maintain public properties, especially a courthouse and jail, then bridges and roads—all paid for by money from property taxes and business licenses from such businesses as saloons, mills, and ferries.

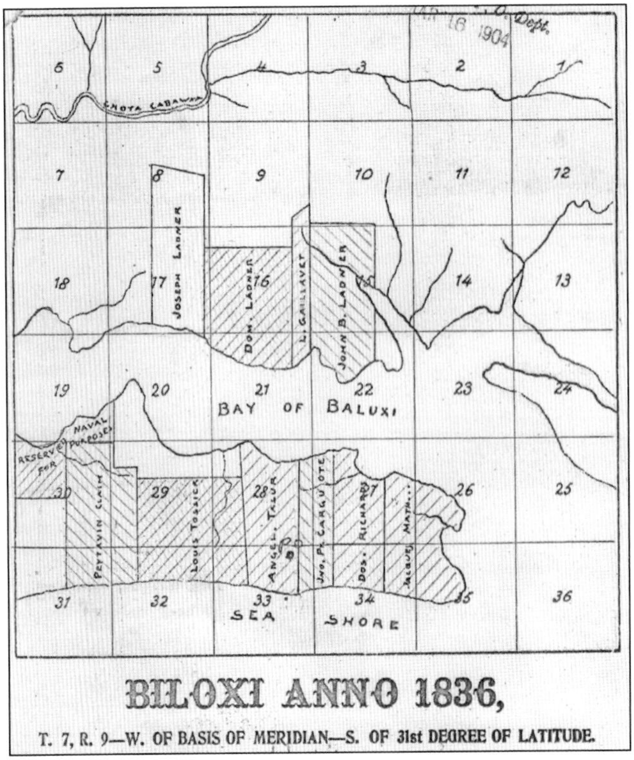

This map identifies land grants on record as of 1842. The Dominic Ladnier Grant became the center of development. Central Avenue centers that land today. All but one grantee settled on the grants. What was granted by the Spanish to Elizabeth Boudreau (born to a French father and Indian mother) is shown as Caillavet's strip; he never occupied it. (US Survey, 1842.)

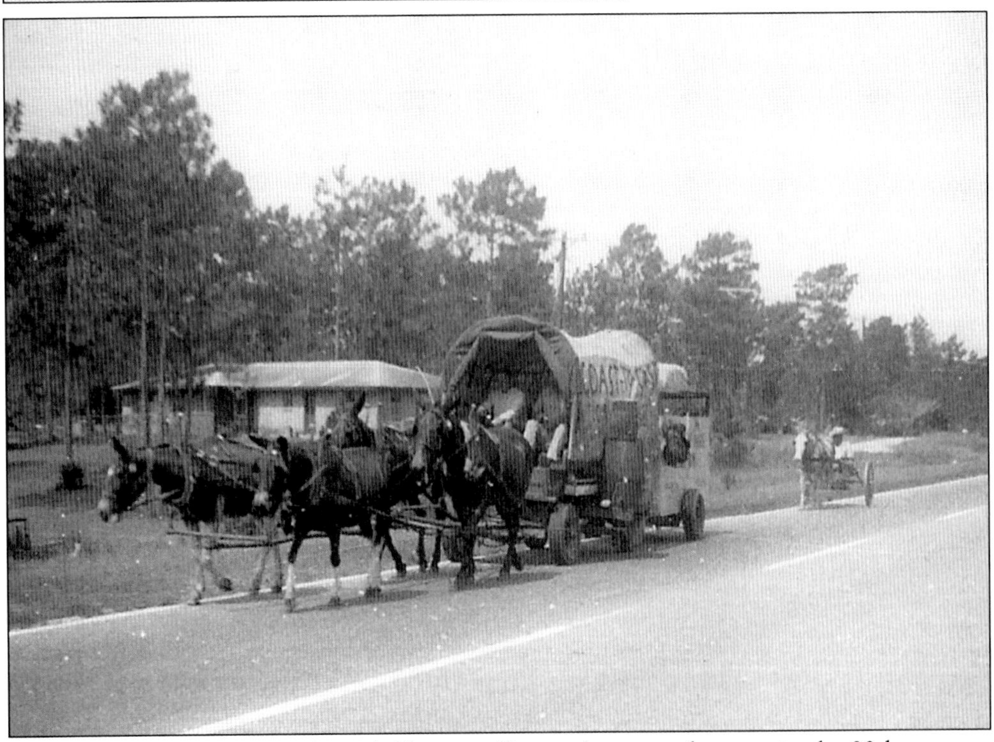

This image shows a journey through Harrison County by covered wagon in the 20th century. (Courtesy the author)

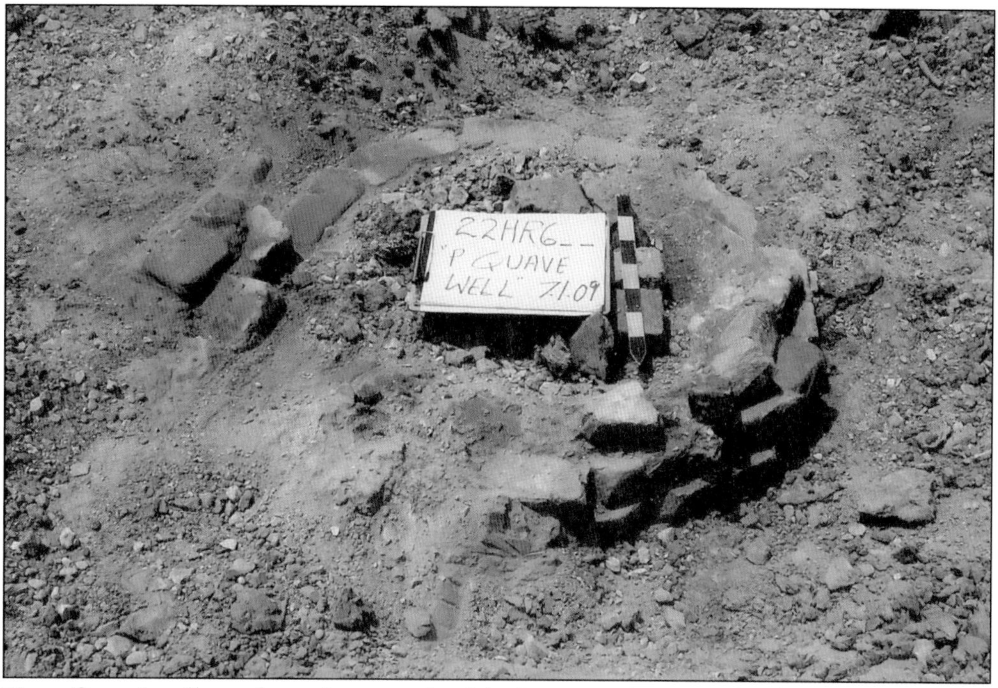

Pierre Quave's well was down slope, north of the house on the west side of Ramsey Road (later Central) in the late 1800s. It was rediscovered in the North Bay Seafood parking lot in 2011. Archaeological efforts were terminated after the well was vandalized. (Photograph by author)

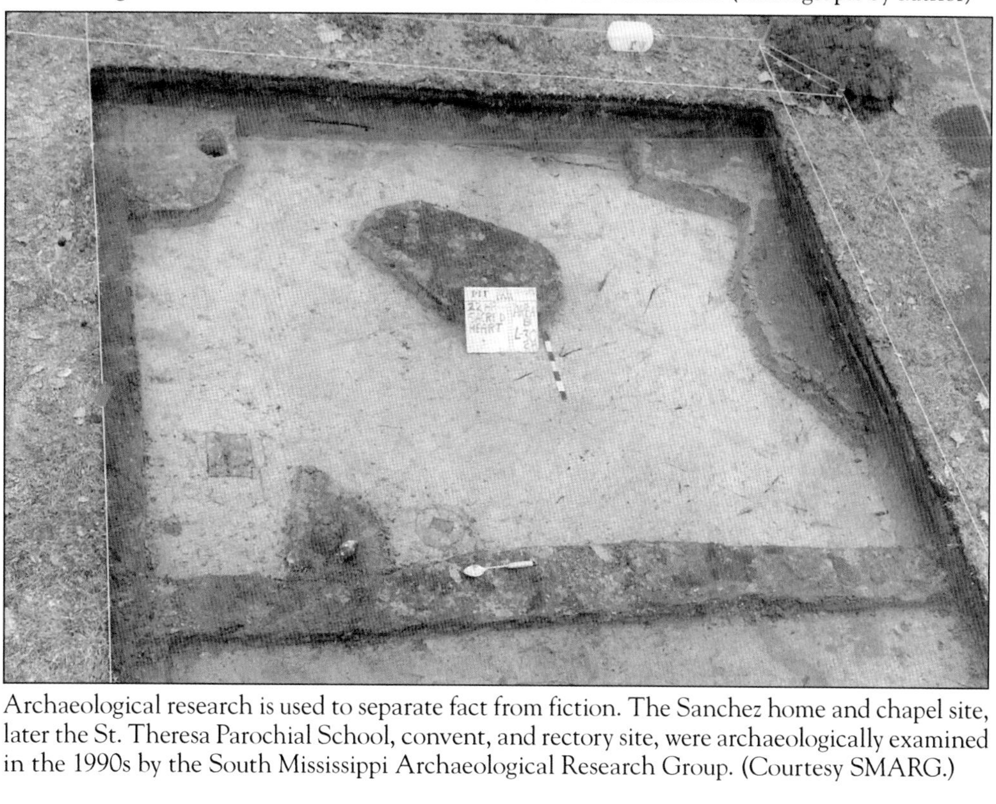

Archaeological research is used to separate fact from fiction. The Sanchez home and chapel site, later the St. Theresa Parochial School, convent, and rectory site, were archaeologically examined in the 1990s by the South Mississippi Archaeological Research Group. (Courtesy SMARG.)

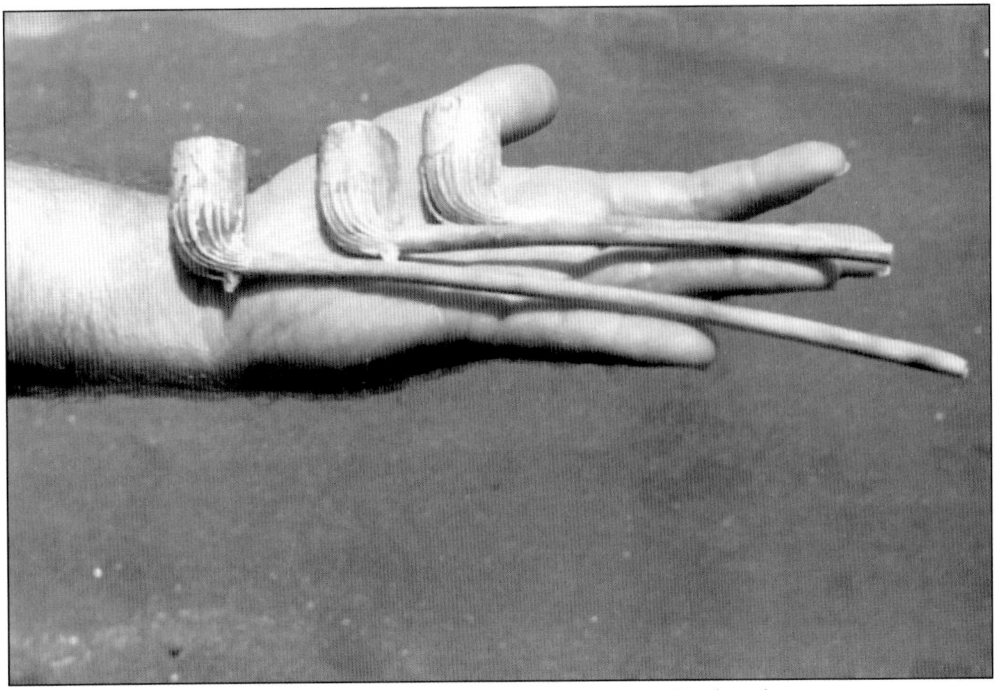

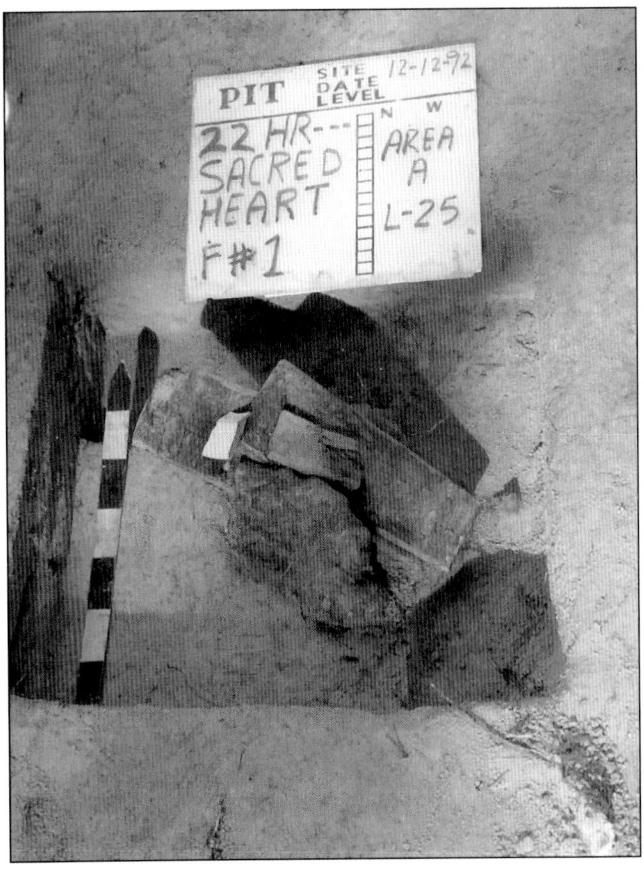

Kaolin-clay pipes were common around Biloxi Bay, especially in Ocean Springs. One of these was recovered at water's edge, below the bluff, at the Sacred Heart site. This style is from the 1780–1820 period. (Courtesy SMARG.)

These wooden bucket staves (with pine resin on inner surfaces) were found 25 centimeters (10 inches) below the surface of where the convent was built in the 1920s. Resin was commonly used for sealing boat hulls. This may have been Emanuel Sanchez's resin bucket. (Courtesy SMARG.)

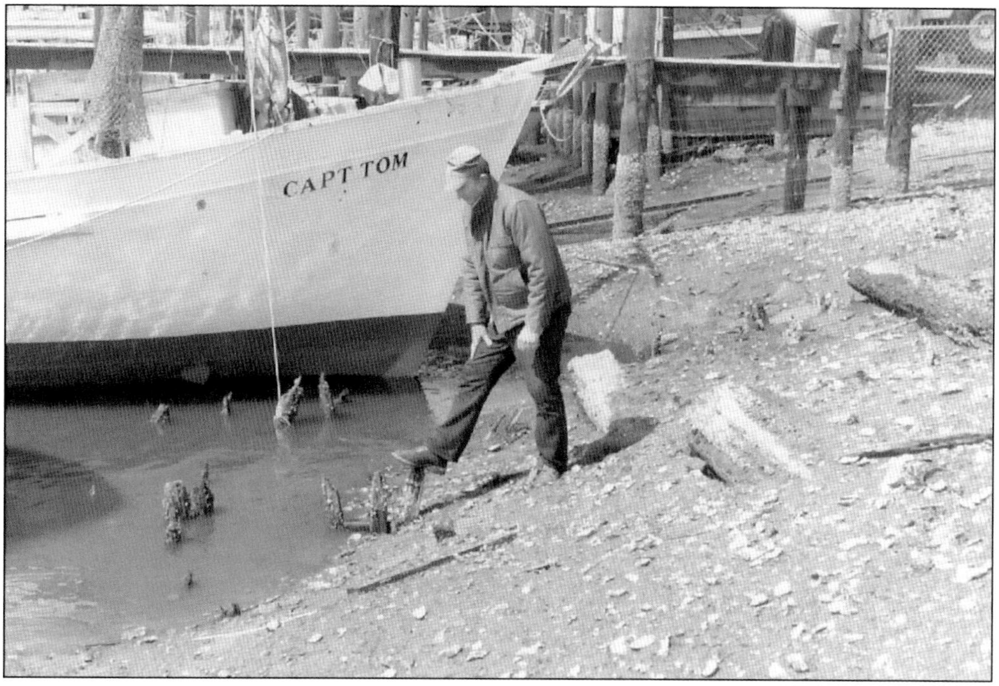

Master boat-builder Bill Holland is studying the remains of the 19th-century boatyard adjoining the Sacred Heart archaeological site. Earlier boatyards of the site were operated by Emanuel Sanchez, then John Foretich, then Ramon Quave into the early 20th century. (Photograph by author.)

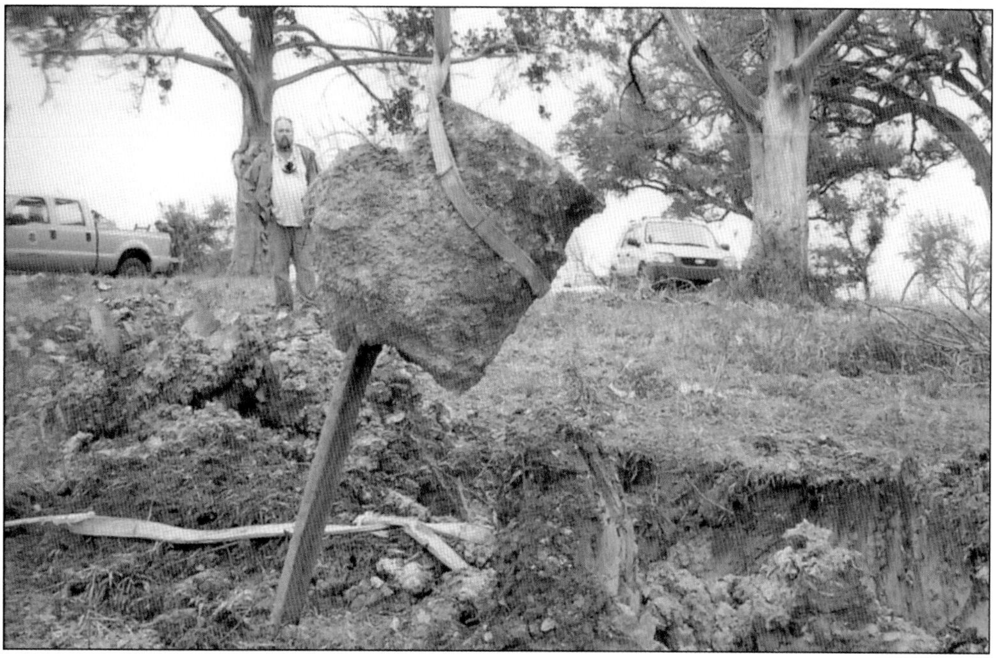

City of D'Iberville's Mike Mullins is directing the removal of the memorial cross base at the site of Philipe Sanchez's chapel, erected for her and opened to the public. The first chapel cross, of iron, was discovered in a field in 1910 and thought by many to have been left by Pierre LeMoyne's explorers. (Photograph by author.)

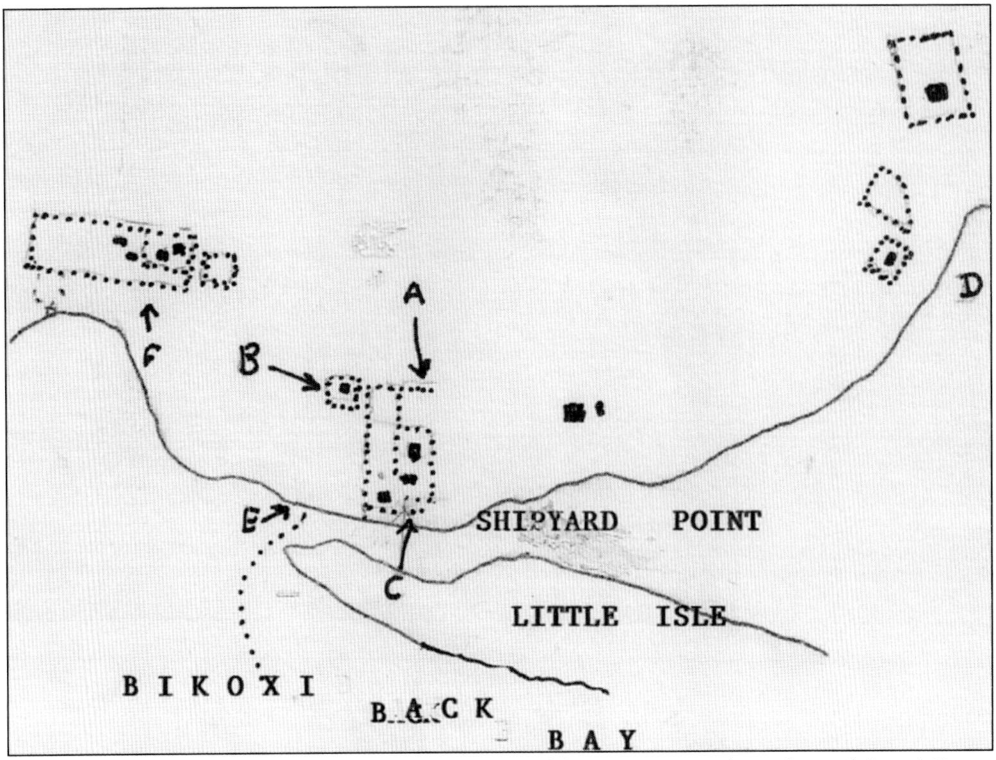

The central settlement on the north side was born of the Dominic Ladnier Spanish Land Grant of 1802, confirmed by the United States in 1812. The areas are identified as follows: A—Sanchez strip (1834); B—Pierre Quave (1834); C—Sanchez chapel site (later convent); D—Boatyard; E—Ferry landing; F—Seymour; G—"Old Canadian Fort" (Fountain's strip, 1839); H—Fountain. (1853 US Map, County Records.)

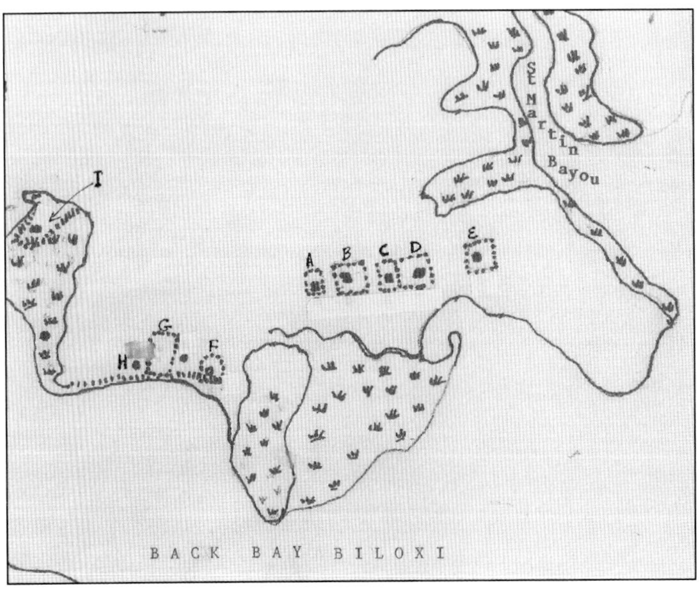

The Point St. Martin settlement grew out of the Jean Baptiste Ladnier Spanish Land Grant of 1790, confirmed by the United States in 1812. By the 1840s, the large tract was divided among his children's families and are identified as follows: A—LaForce, B—Groue, C—Beaugez, D—Ladnier, E—Ryan, F/G/H—LaFontane (Fountain) tract. (1853 US Map, County Records.)

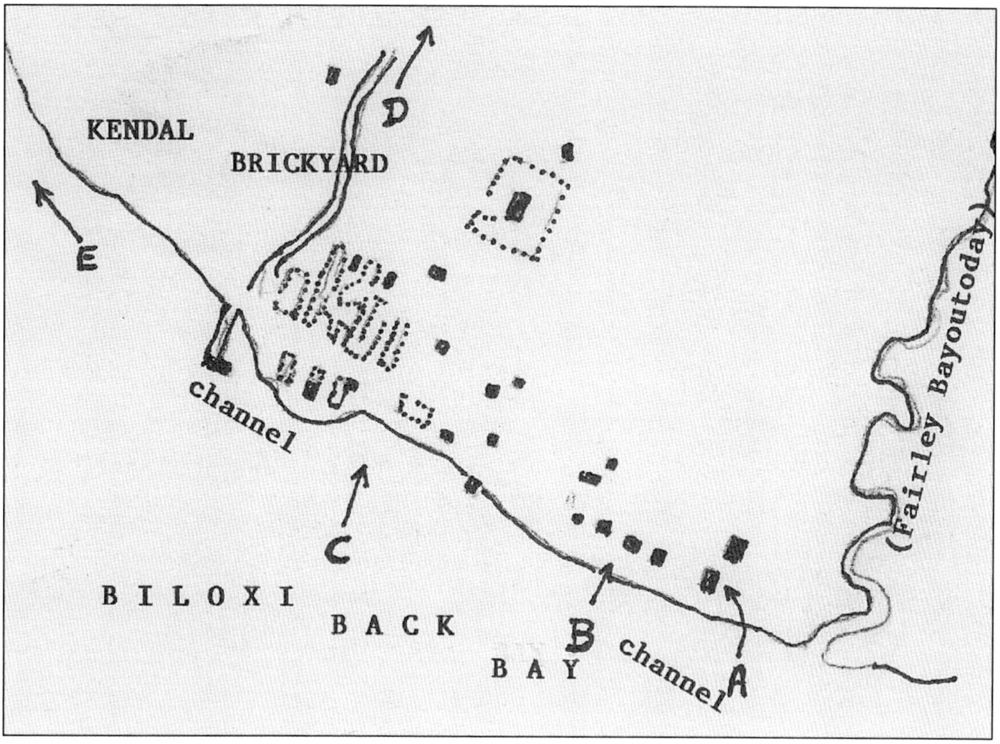

The west settlement included land of the French brickyard of the 1720s that was reopened by Moran (1830s), McRae (1840s), Kendall (1850s), Moran (1890s), and Imperial (1905–1920). Joseph Ladner's Spanish Grant in 1793, confirmed by the United States in 1812, evolved and is identified as follows: A—Jose Santa Cruz home/trading post (1834), B—Moran Hill, C—brick company operations, D—road to clay, and E—direction of Boney and Harvey neighborhood later. (1853 US Map, County Land Records.)

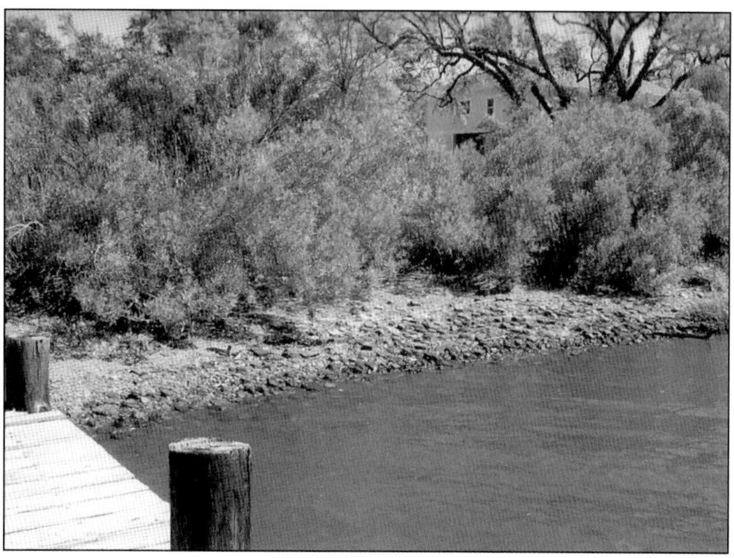

The manmade brick beachfront is composed of brick fragments and discards from the two centuries of production on the property. The clay was surface mined throughout the area. The bricks were used locally and as far away as New Orleans. (Photograph by author.)

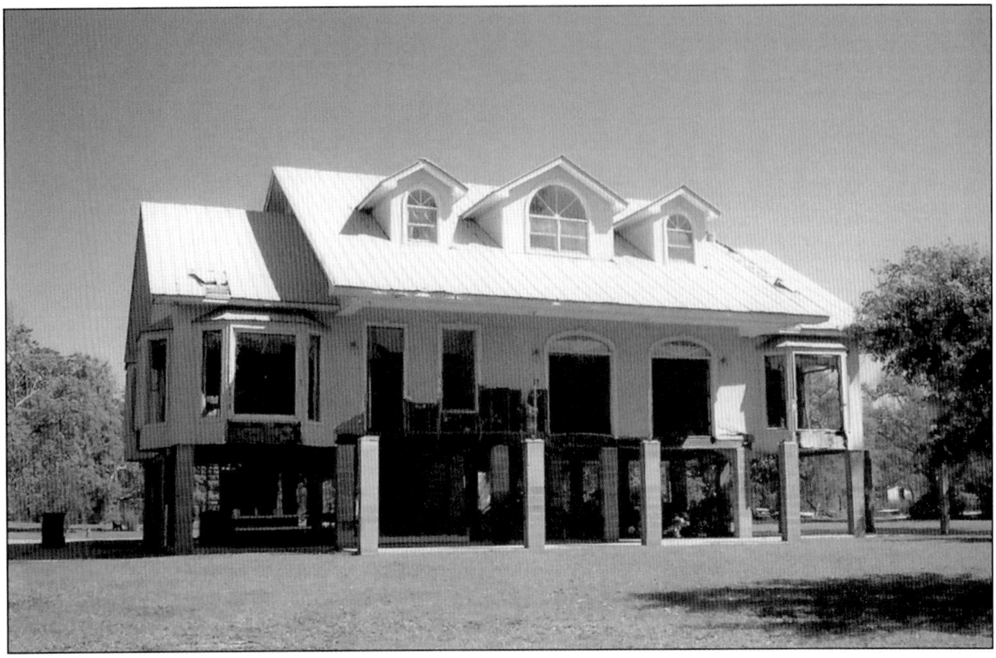

Andy Balius's home occupies the site of the old brickyard offices. It was gutted by Hurricane Katrina and never salvaged. A hundred yards behind it were the brick-making facilities and the cabins for the workers—whites, blacks, and Indians. (Photograph by author.)

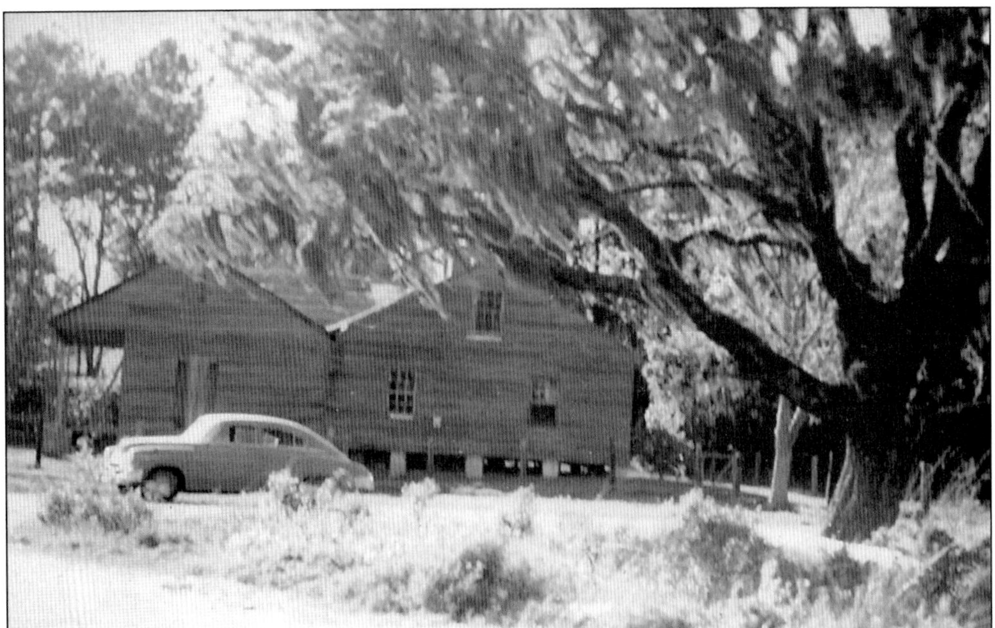

Shown here is a 1958 photograph of Jose Santa Cruz's trading post on the old Brick Yard Road (today's Bay Shore Drive). Around 1890, the family added the north half as a residence, allowing more space for the store and social gatherings. A small warehouse on the wharf served schooners. All were destroyed by hurricanes. (Photograph by author.)

Three

War, Railroads, and Reconstruction

As the county settled into the new order with positive, sensible growth plans, a maelstrom was brewing across the nation. By 1860, the towns of Biloxi, Mississippi City, Ocean Springs, Scranton, and Shieldsboro were in the political fray. Within a year, men formed six companies of infantry and cavalry. The 3rd Mississippi Regiment of Infantry joined other units as far away as Hinds County and became the Army of Mississippi. Many from north of the bay were involved as well. While engaged in a war far from home, the coast was left vulnerable.

After battles across six states, most did not return. Their most notable engagements were at Champion's Hill, Vicksburg, Atlanta, Nashville, Kensaw, Franklin, and Bentonville. In their absence, Yankee troops, scalawags, and carpetbaggers took over for several years. Many widows and children were destitute, often losing their property through schemes.

The idea that slavery caused the war would be argued for generations. Blacks on the coast experienced life quite differently from those in the agricultural areas. Most were cooks, maids, nurses, guardians, handymen, mechanics, masons, blacksmiths, and carpenters. Before the war, many had earned their release from bondage along the coast and were respected by the whites.

Charles Sanchez, son of the Sanchez family slave woman mentioned earlier, was Emanuel's sole beneficiary by will. In a few decades, the Sacred Heart Church and Rectory were erected, followed in 1926 by St. Theresa Parochial Elementary and Convent, built where the old Sanchez home had been. Charles raised several white children who had been orphaned. One became his heir. Whites also took in black children.

The period of military occupation and reconstruction following the Civil War disappeared in less than six years when the New Orleans, Mobile & Ohio Railroad arrived on the coast. Now connected with the rest of the nation, investors poured into the bay area, creating an industrial revolution based on timber, seafood, and tourism. While coast cities raced into the industrial world, the north side of the bay quietly evolved. Rails scattered throughout the forests as villages grew around timber railheads such as Vennie. Boatbuilding, charcoal, and turpentine industries joined the timber companies in their quest to provide cities like New Orleans and Mobile with necessities that had not yet been replaced by petroleum and electricity.

Overall though, the pioneering basics remained apparent.

In spite of earlier predictions, the vast forests of giant pines were not going to last forever. To the surprise of the earlier forecasters, the forests were laid bare by 1926. Trains and rails were moved to other states, where the industries resumed. Vennie shut down, and many of the families engaged in that industry followed with the tools of the trade. But some among them recognized what the deforestation created: open range.

3rd Mississippi Regiment, 1st Brigade, Loring's Division, CSA, Campaigns 1861- 1865

Western Kentucky. Mississippi (Champion's Hill, Edwards Station, Big Black, Vicksburg). Georgia (Resca, New Hope Church, Kenesaw Mountain, Atlanta, Big Shanty, Ackworth).

Tennessee (Franklin, Nashville). North Carolina (Kinston, Bentonville). Stacked arms at Citronelle, Alabama on May 4, 1865, (25 days after Lee's Surrender).

Re: The Third Mississippi Regiment, CSA. Dale Greenwell, 1972

The hard work of clearing land and building homes on a quiet frontier came to a sudden standstill in 1861. All around the bay, able-bodied men joined the Live Oak Rifles (Company A) and Biloxi Rifles (Company E), 3rd Mississippi Regiment, Confederate States of America (CSA). The regiment engaged in some of the bloodiest battles of the Civil War. (Courtesy the author.)

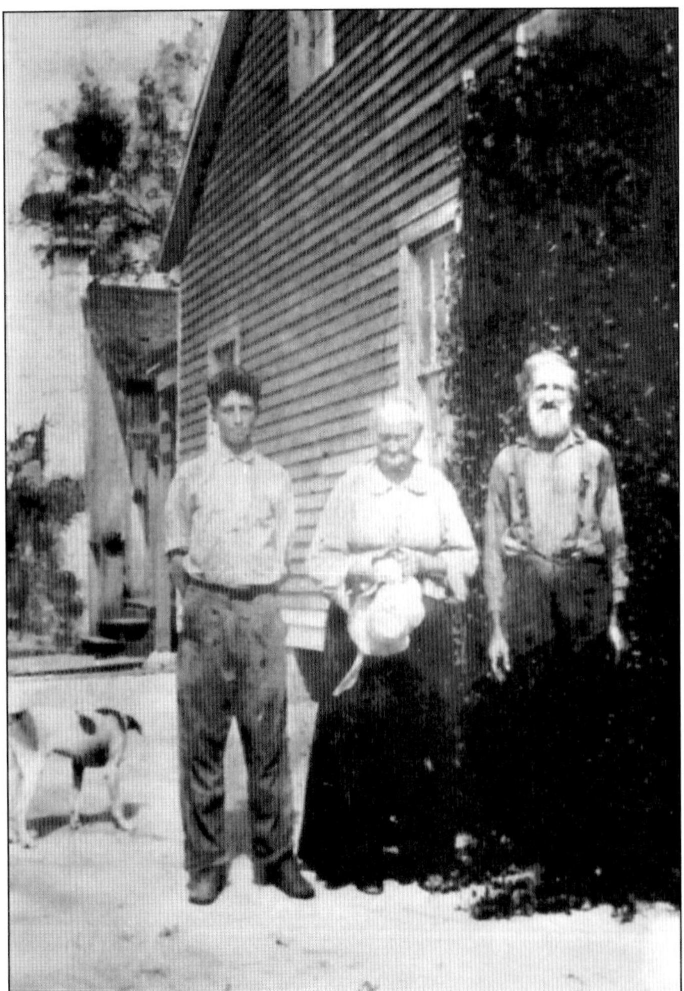

Confederate veteran of Company A, 17th Mississippi Battalion, Steede's Cavalry, Vance Krohn is pictured with his sister Caroline and an unidentified man at Krohn's home near the Tchoutacabuffe River eight years after the war. He and his brothers were in many campaigns across the South from 1862 to 1865. (Courtesy Paul Fayard.)

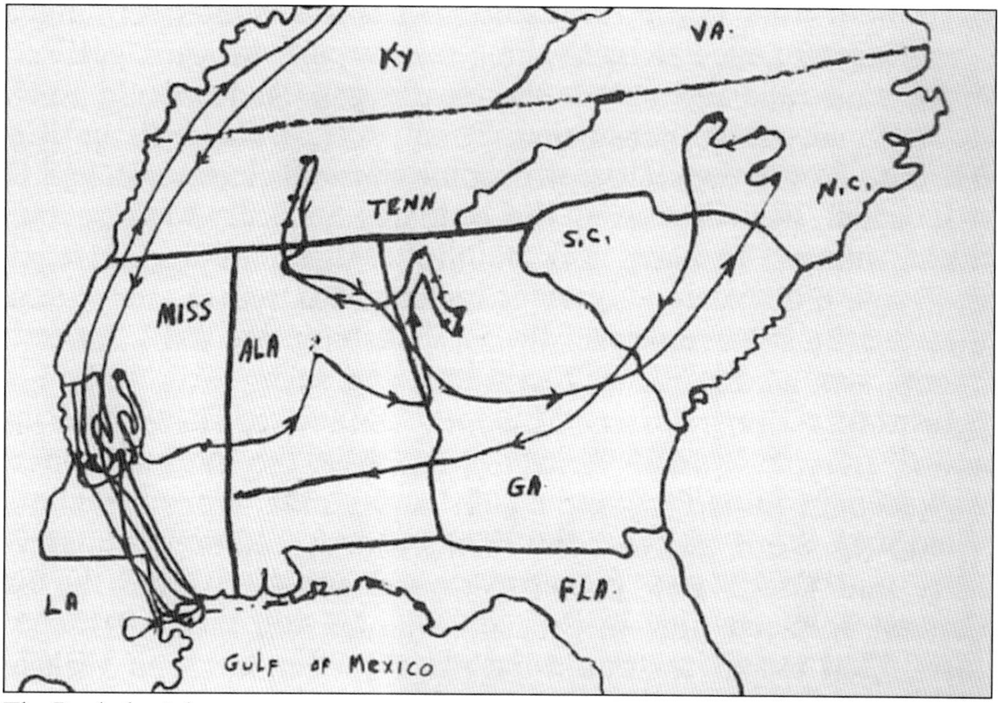

The Battle for Atlanta was one of the bloodiest campaigns for the 3rd Mississippi Regiment, Featherston's Brigade, Loring's Division. Breaking through enemy lines, the regiment lost 615 of its 1,230 men while Tennessee and North Carolina waited for their help. A month after Gen. Robert E. Lee surrendered, the last of the 3rd stacked arms. (US Civil War Archives map.)

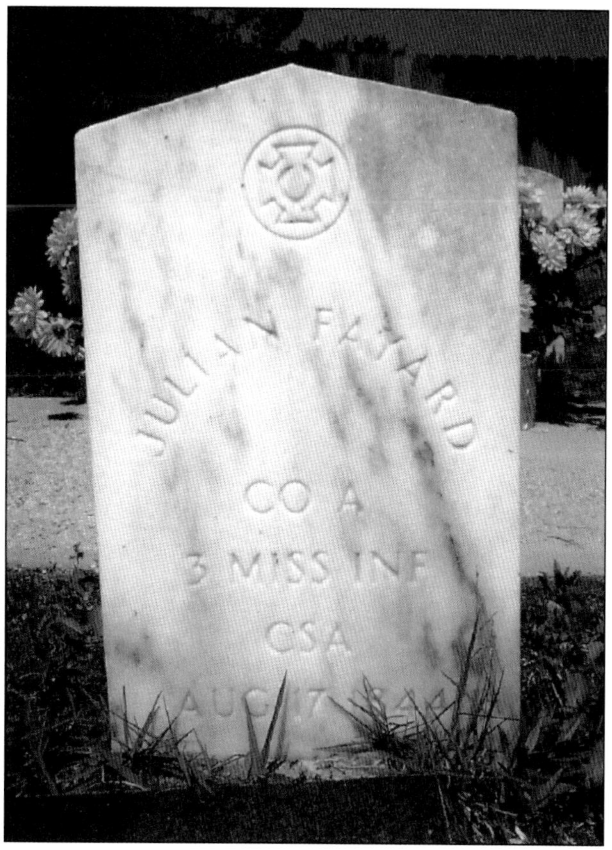

Julian "Jules" Fayard, a veteran of the 3rd Mississippi, is interred in the Fountain Cemetery in D'Iberville. The remains of many are scattered across the southeastern United States. Few of those who returned received CSA headstones. (Courtesy Mike and Paul Fayard.)

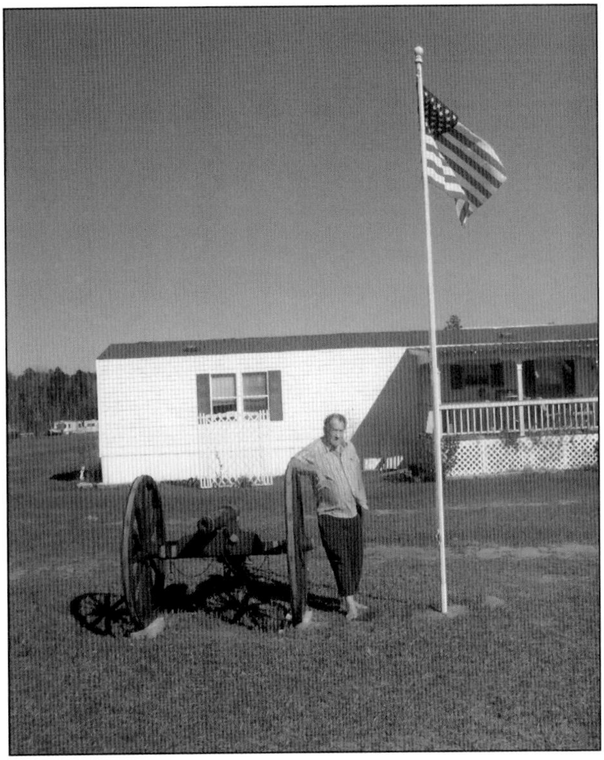

Alton Richard's wooden replica of a Civil War cannon is displayed under the American flag. It had been in his yard in St. Martin before moving into the country after Hurricane Katrina. Until then, it was beneath the "Stars and Bars." Alton served in the US Army. (Photograph by author.)

INVENTORY IN QUAVE'S STORE JUST BEFORE HE JOINED THE THIRD MISSISSIPPI REGIMENT

* * *

Barrels of flour and rice; cans of butter, coffee and lard; sacks of corn and beans; boxes of macaroni, black pepper, flax seed, salt and sugar; slabs of different cheeses; bins of potatoes, yams and onions; kegs of mackerel and cod; bottles of whiskey, "jin" (!), wine, olive oil, castor oil, cream of tartar, sweet oil, turpentine and vinegar; garlic and other seasoning; horse feed.

Among the hardware are guns, gun-powder, shot, firing caps, gunlocks, knives, axes, files, hammers, nails, augers, shovels, spades, chisels, rope, water buckets, pump tacks, campfire buckets, lumber, wrenches, rules, levels Candles, lamps, lamp-wicks, matches and oil, dishes, plates, tin plates, spoons, baskets, coffee pots, pots and pans, cups and saucers, bridles, martigills (?), reins, plows, plow-lines, curry combs, hooks, fishing line, betmendrops(?), brimstone(?), preese legand (?), smoking and chewing tobacco, combs, razors and soap (at 25 cents a bar(!) he didn't sell many).

Bolts of linen, calico, cotton, crape, cottonade, bedticken(?) and hickory; shoes, socks, stockings, shirts and hats. (No washcloths or towels, underwear, dresses or pants—and no sewing machines.

Variety of fresh, smoked, salted beef and fish.

Treats offered: Coltar sundries (?), chocolate and candies. (No ice cream or sodas.)

A sample of prices: Loaf of fresh bread—10cents; Eggs—30cents a dozen; Pound of butter—25 cents; Pound of cheese—20cents; Pound of coffee—14 cents. Coffee mill—75cents; Hogshead cheese—6 cents; Cologne water—75 cents; book—15cents;

Pierre Quave's store, the first store in the central settlement, offered a variety of products in the 1850s. Note the absence of ladies' clothes and men's pants. Via ferry, locals could shop Biloxi for items not in Quave's. The store closed during the Civil War—Most men left home to join the CSA. (Courtesy Rita Dildy.)

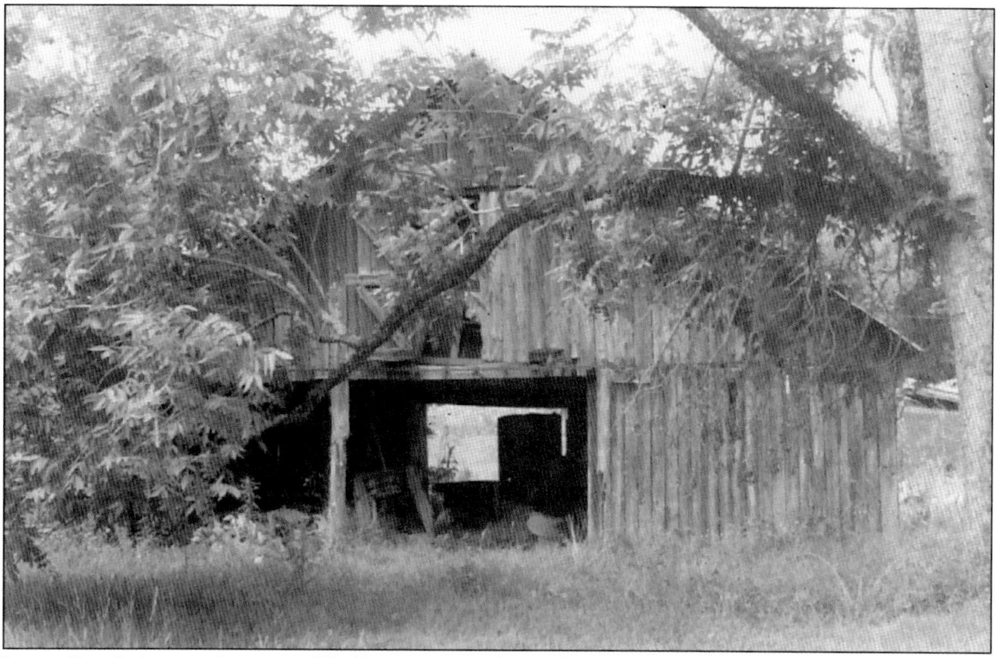

James Brodie's sons, James and Robert, operated Brodie's Biloxi Nursery throughout their lives, employing many locals, black and white, boys and men. This barn and the hothouses (not shown) were the out-of-rain work areas, normally occupied by stacks of sacks, boxes, tools, and tractors. Many local boys were baptized into manhood at this nursery. (Photograph by author.)

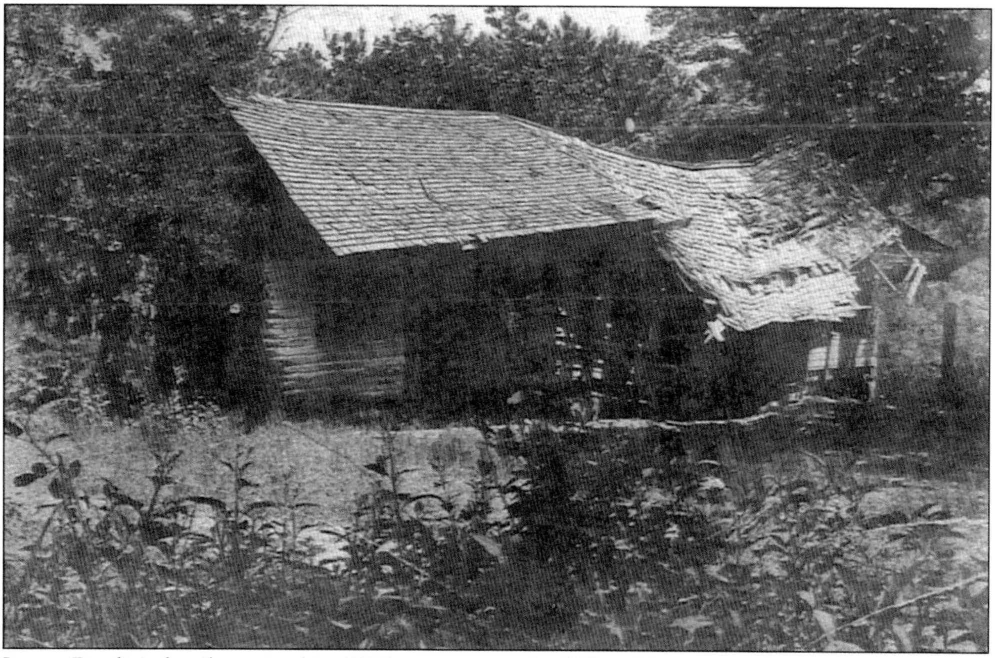

James Brodie's family arrived in 1896 to manage the Biloxi Nurseries. They occupied this log house (perhaps occupied by pioneer Joseph Ladnier's family until completing his own to the east in 1902). He managed the Biloxi Nurseries until he bought it from the owners and changed the name to Brodie's Biloxi Nursery. (Courtesy Paul Fayard.)

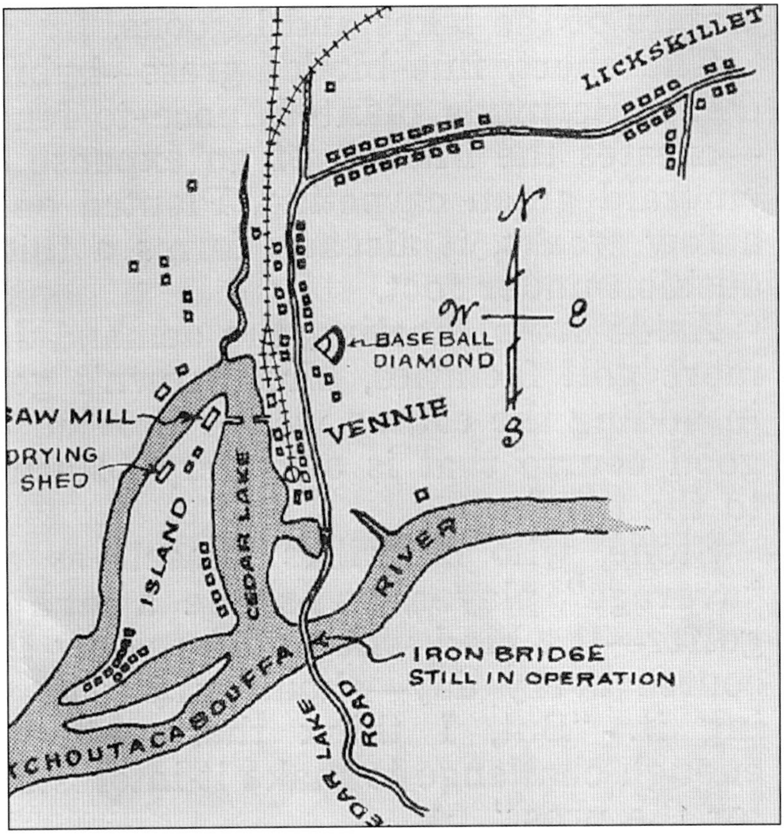

Many men and women worked in and out of the mill villages until 1926, when the forest had been clear-cut and mills shut down. Vennie, owned by Henry Leinhard then L.N. Dantzler, is today the Cedar Lake community. It shared the Tchoutacabuffe River with the Krohn, Morris, Holly, and smaller mills, and they shopped in what is now D'Iberville. (Map by author.)

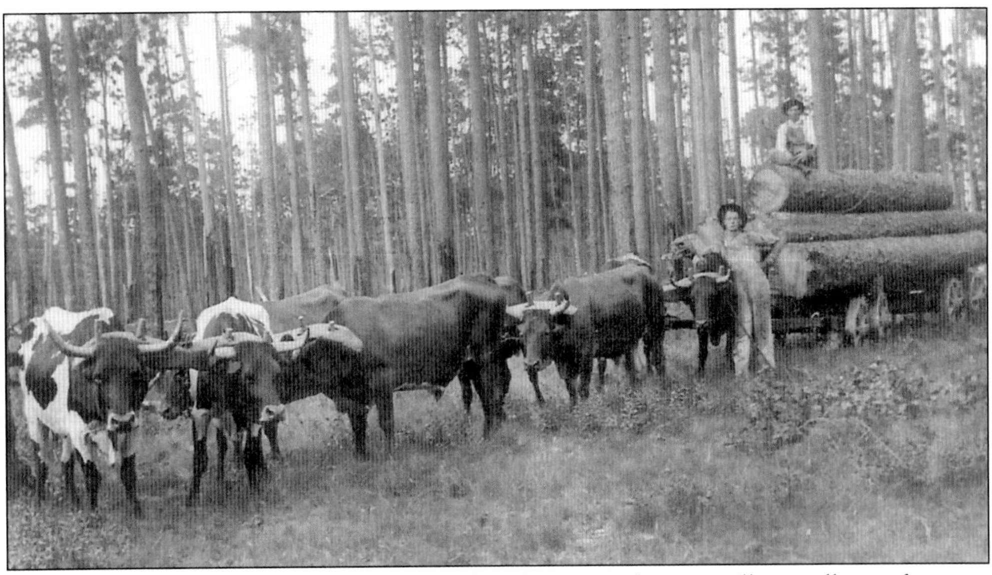

This photograph reflects the standard procedure for getting logs to mills, usually not far away, before the narrow-gauge trains got involved. Even then, oxen were used to haul timber to the rails for transfer to the mills. After the war, trains entered the scene. George E. Mallette is driving this team sometime before 1926. (Courtersy of Debbie Mallette.)

Shown here are timber-jacks with saws. For the last 30 years of the timber boom, most of their travel into the outback was via log trains. When the mills shut down, most timber men headed north and west with their tools; others remained and took up other trades. (Courtesy Fred Husley.)

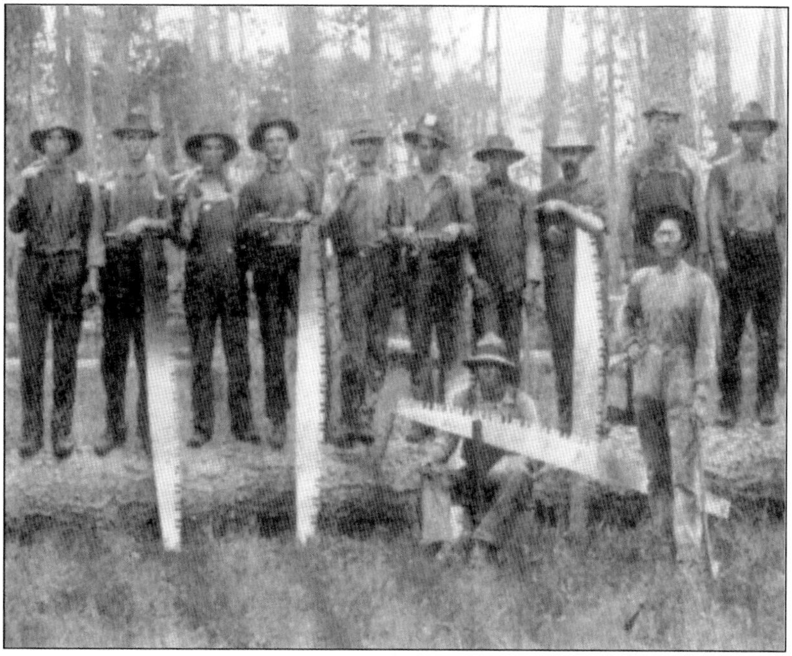

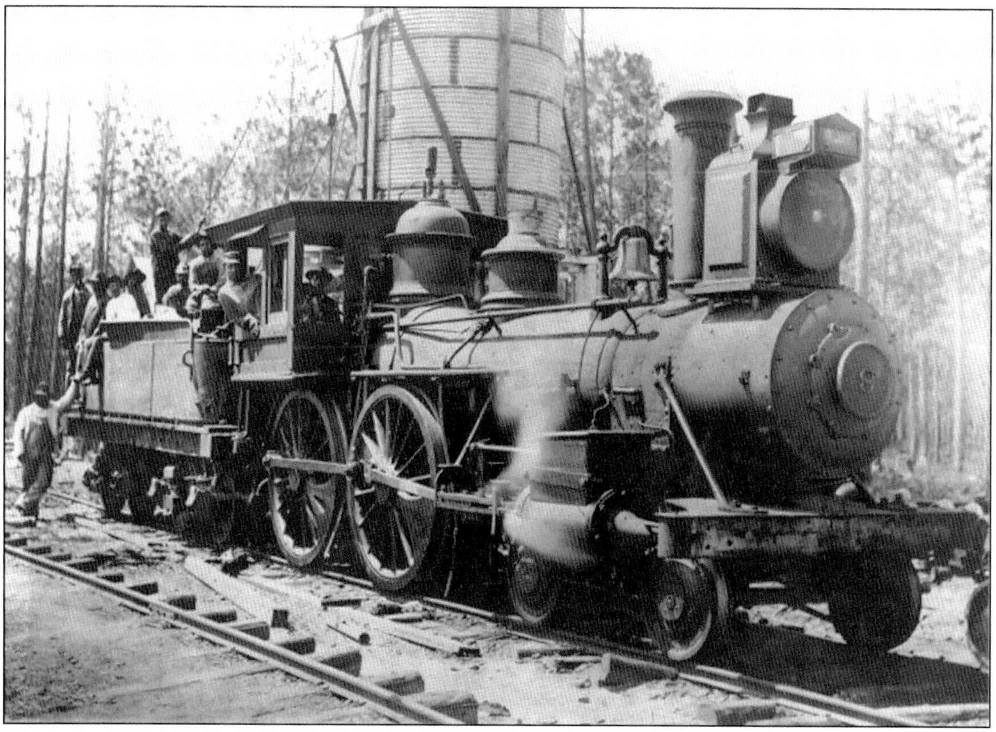

This engine was typical of those employed on the narrow-gauge tracks between the timber mills and the forest around 1926 when the forests were depleted. Three operated out of Vennie at Cedar Lake. (Courtesy Joe Tomasosky's Vail collection.)

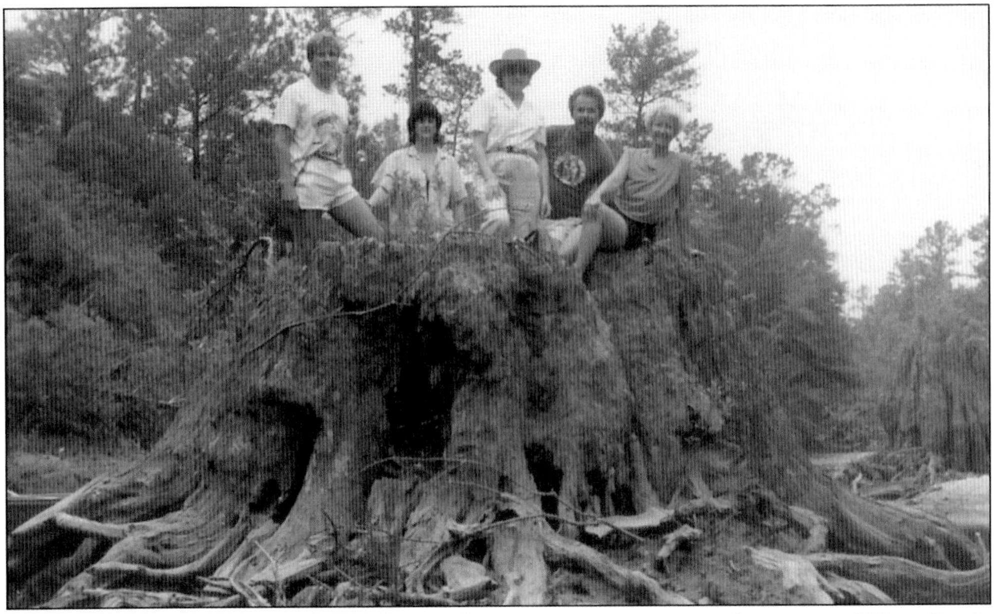

This ancient cypress stump, downed more than a century ago, is in the center of Tuxachanie Creek, near White Plains Church. In spite of the erosion, a small group rests upon it around 1990. They are Ron and Rickie Skrmetta, Murella and Dave Powell, and Frances Greenwell. (Photograph by author.)

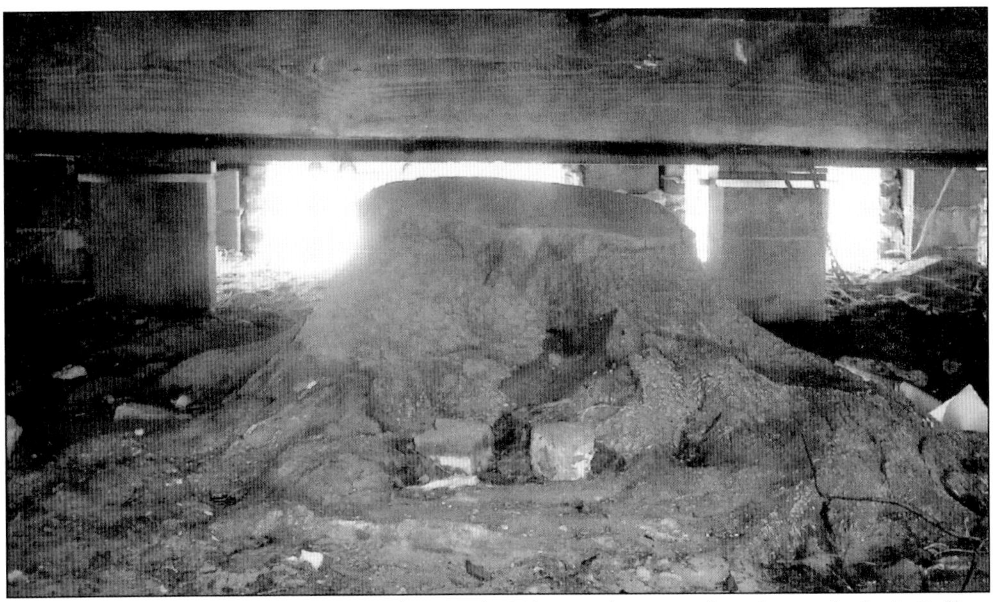

The oak from this stump was removed around 1910 to make room for a house (today's Gollott Lyons Real Estate on Howard Avenue). There is neither decay nor insect intrusion of the stump. (Photograph by author.)

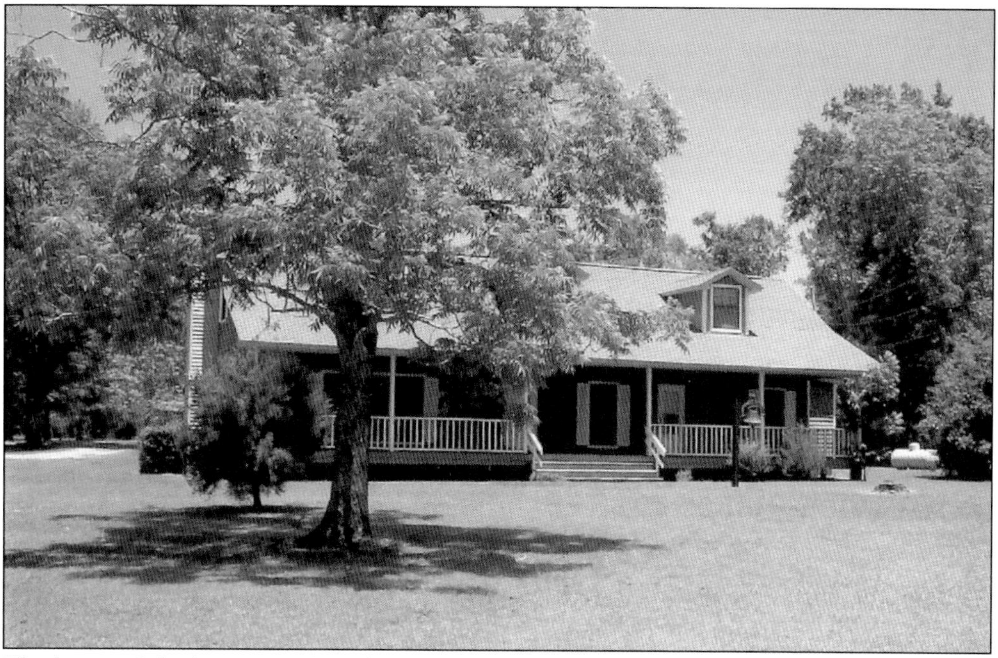

The home of the late Hattie Broadus was west of Cedar Lake Island on the site of her father's (Henry Krohn) sawmill in the late 19th and early 20th centuries. (Photograph by author.)

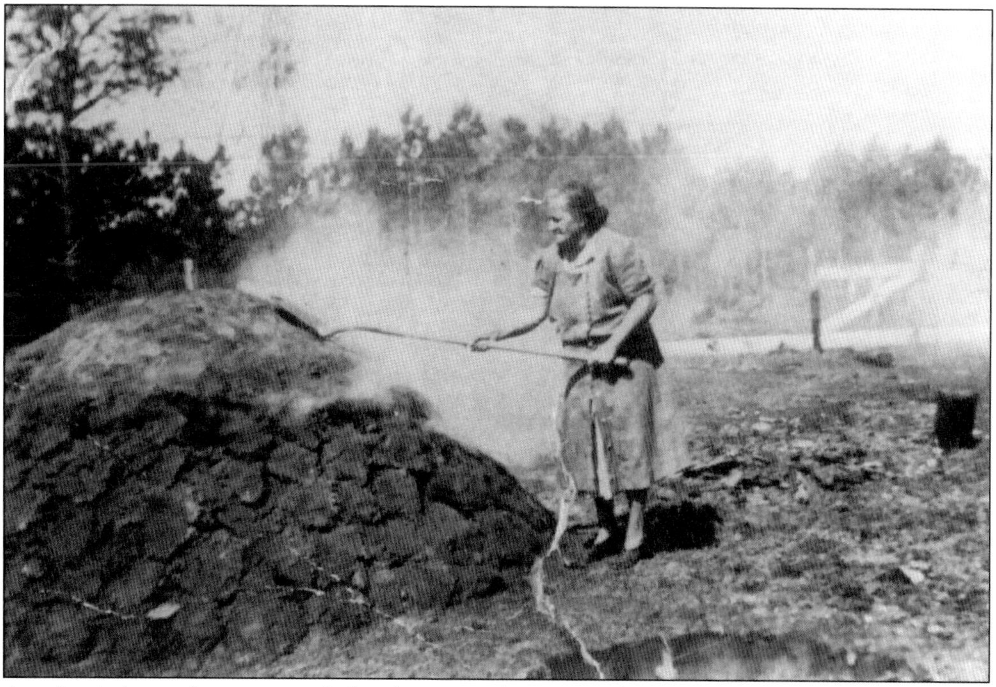

Another industry that continued after the war, and even into the Great Depression, was charcoal. In this photograph, Julia Holley is packing the dirt atop stacked wood before striking the match. After many hours of slow, controlled burning, the charcoal was removed, sacked, and marketed. It was a local company and family industry up to World War II. (Courtesy Biloxi Library Archives.)

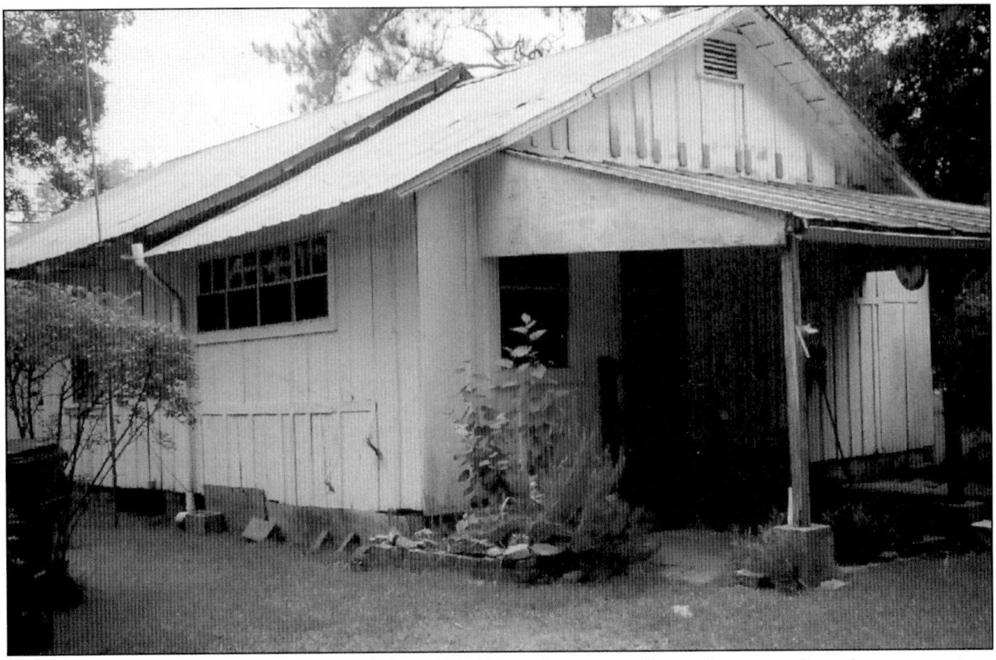

Charles E. Byrd purchased some of the L.N. Dantzler sawmill machinery after that operation closed at Cedar Lake in 1926. He opened a mill at the west end of School House Road (Quave Road) in D'Iberville. Their home, seen here in front of the business, was constructed of boards of various widths, up to two feet wide. It is seen here after Katrina. (Photograph by author.)

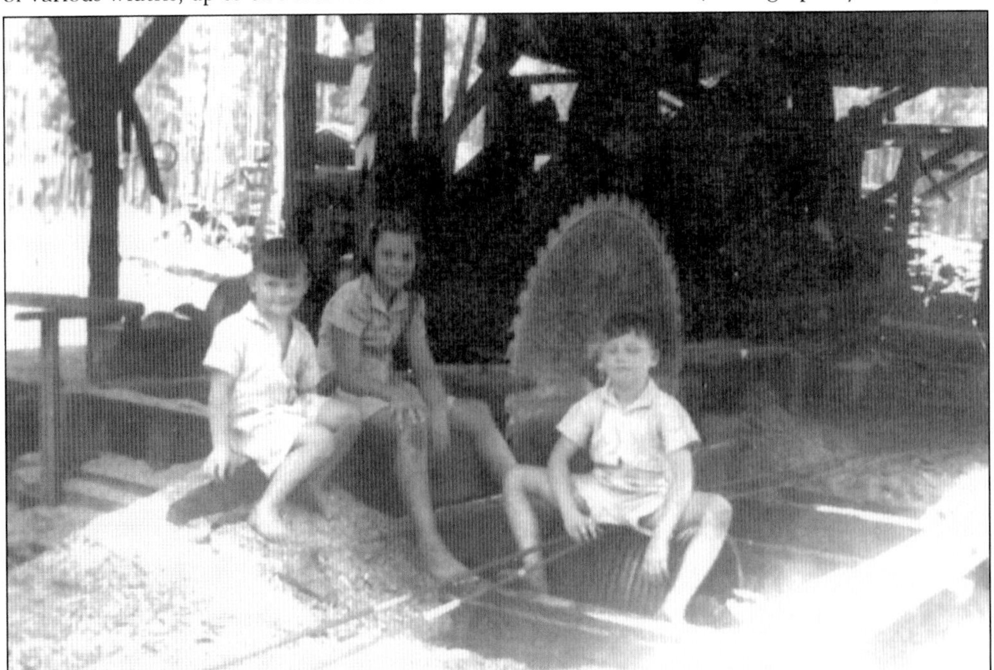

Inside the idled sawmill in the late 1940s are Charles Byrd's grandchildren: Patrick, Margarite, and Curtis. The business included the mill, drying shed, racks, lumberyard, hardware, office, store, and residence on the property. Mike Babuchna's sawmill was near. (Courtesy Pat Byrd.)

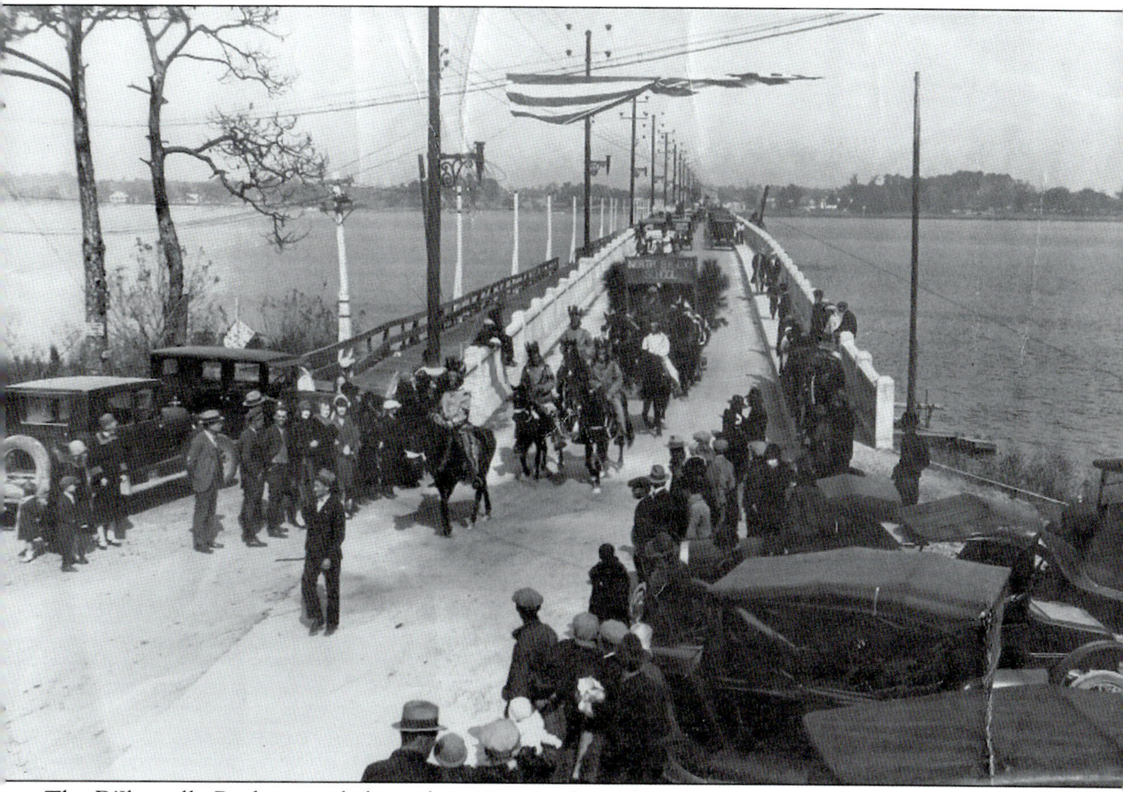

The D'Iberville Bridge was dedicated in 1926. In the colonial period, crossing the Back Bay of Biloxi was accomplished by canoe or small sailboat. A century later, barge-like toll ferries were carrying people, wagons, and livestock across. In 1901, a wooden toll bridge was erected (seen to the left in this image of the new concrete bridge). This was the last link in the new "Old Spanish Trail" highway crossing the United States from Jacksonville, Florida, to San Diego, California. The dedication ceremony included speeches from local, state, and national officials. The bridge was replaced by the interstate bridge in 1979 then destroyed by Hurricane Katrina in 2005. (Courtesy Tay Greenwell.)

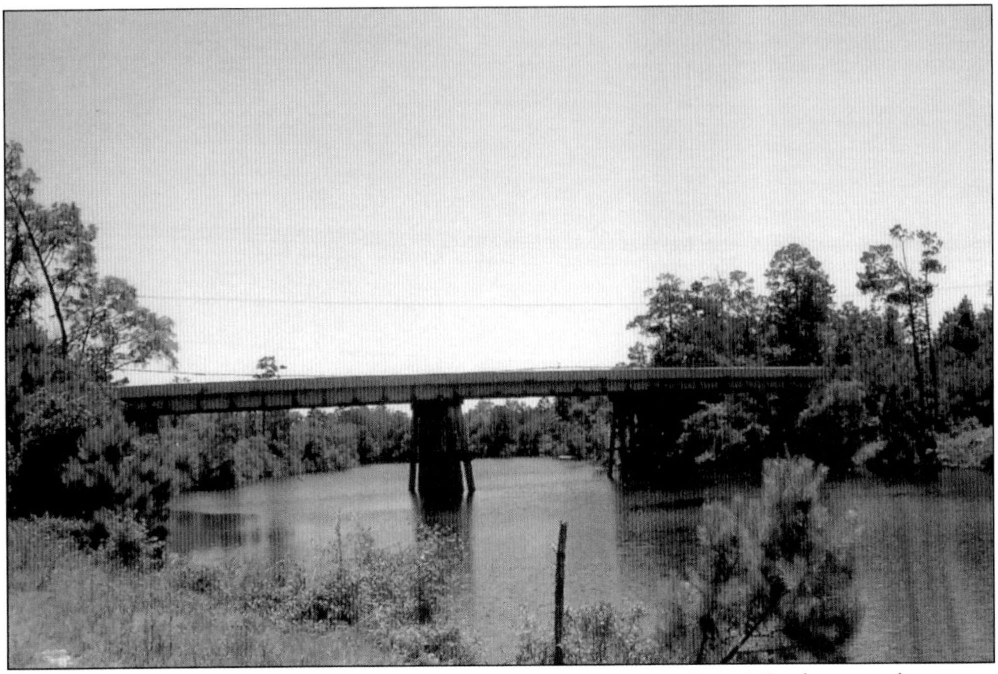

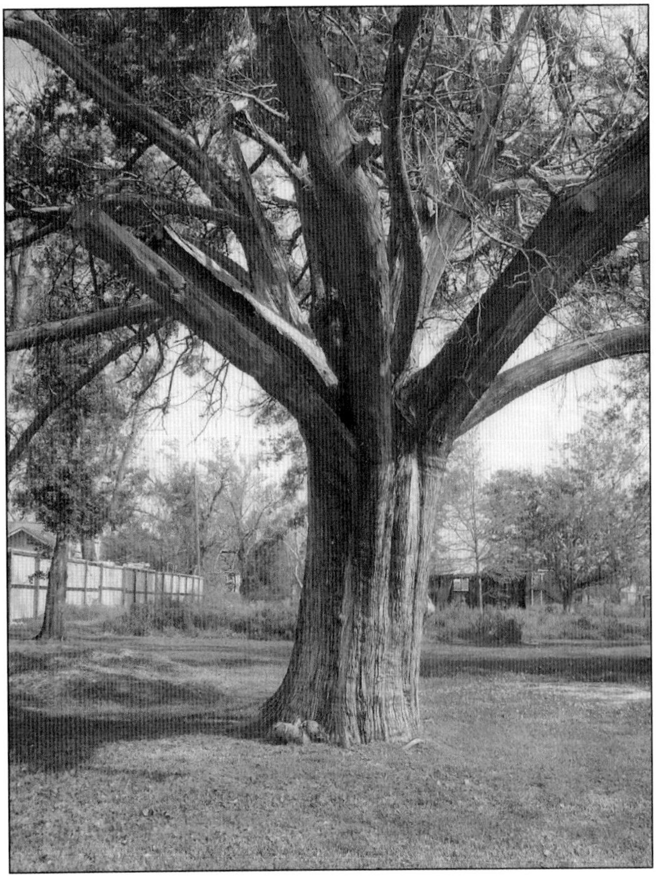

Corso's Bridge over the Tchoutacabuffe River was on the route of Highways 15 and 67 in D'Iberville. Before 1950, traffic depended on Cedar Lake and Lamey Bridges, and before 1926, most auto and foot traffic depended on Wells and Lamey's ferries to cross the river. (Photograph by author.)

In the late 1800s, Lazarus Seymour had a general store with a postal kiosk. Mary "Aunt Sissy" Young, a midwife, nurse, bookkeeper, and postmistress of Seymour (today D'iberville) from 1908 to 1914, had the tree in her front yard. The tree has been removed and preserved elsewhere in the city, thanks to the Roy Anderson Corp. (Photograph by author.)

Tony and William Shoemaker are on break while their load is transferred to rails for transfer to the International Paper Company mill in Moss Point. (Courtesy Burton Shoemaker.)

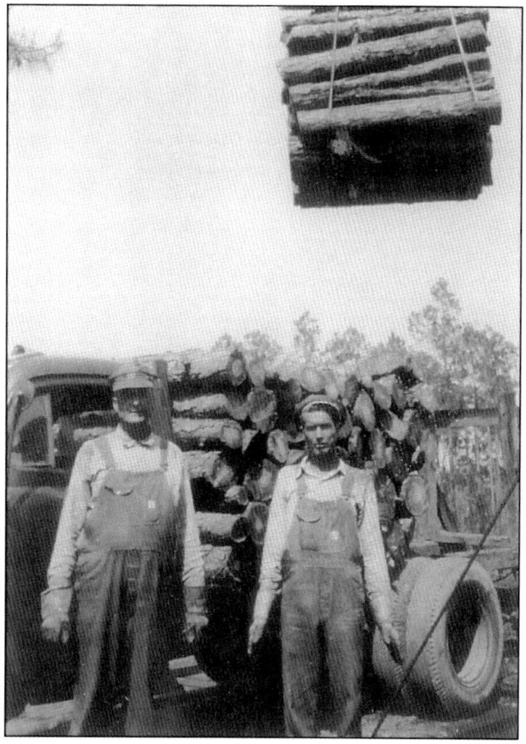

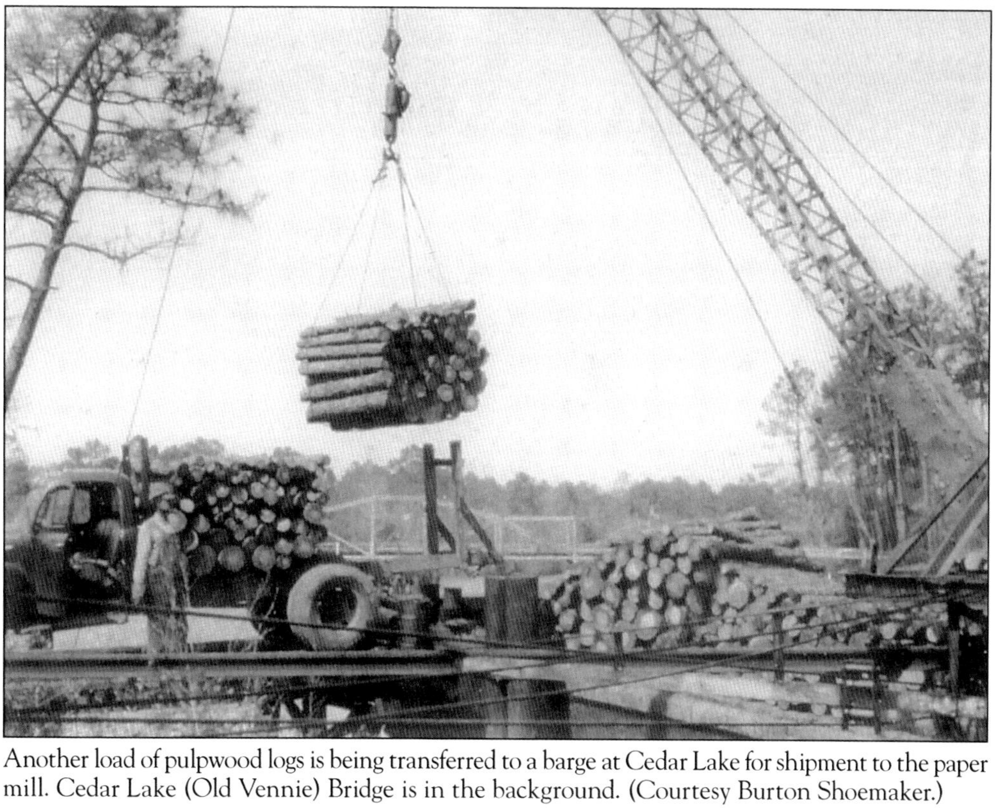

Another load of pulpwood logs is being transferred to a barge at Cedar Lake for shipment to the paper mill. Cedar Lake (Old Vennie) Bridge is in the background. (Courtesy Burton Shoemaker.)

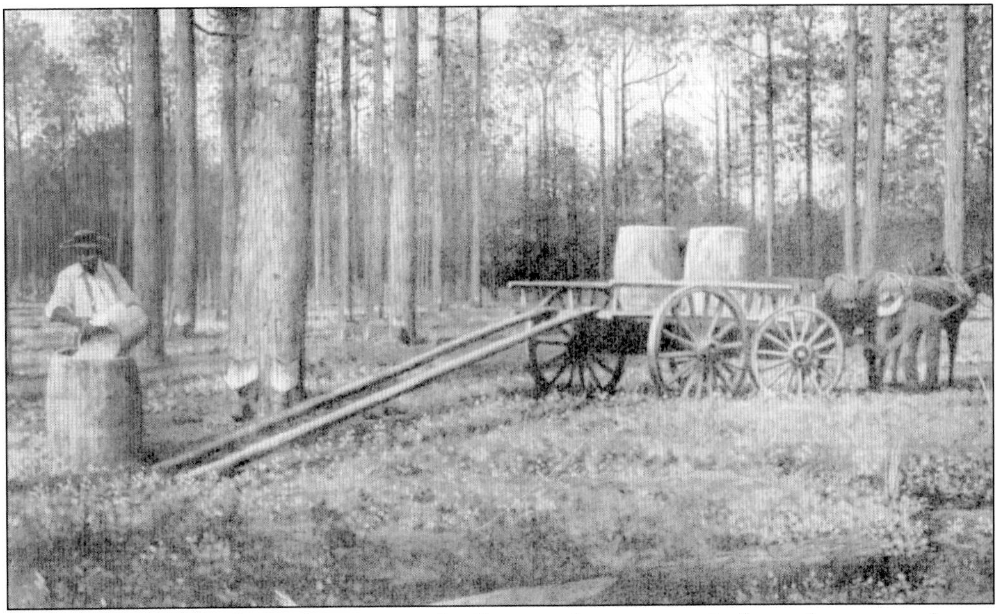

The painting above shows the process of collecting the sap or resin from the cups and trays attached to the trees below the scab, which was hauled to the distilleries by ox-drawn wagons before trucks arrived in the 20th century. Resin was used in the boat, paint, and pharmaceutical industries. (Courtesy artist Ken Brauner.)

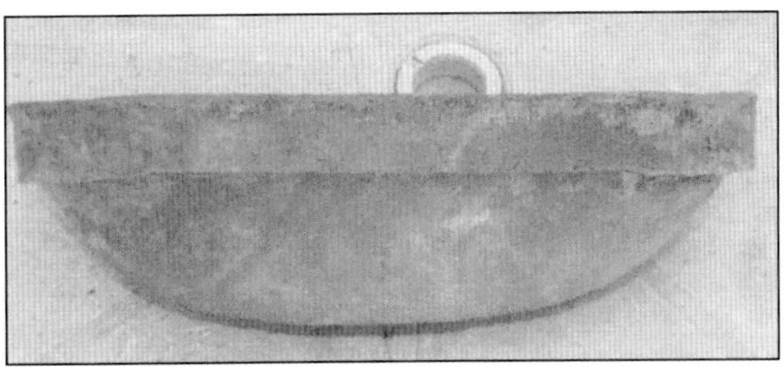

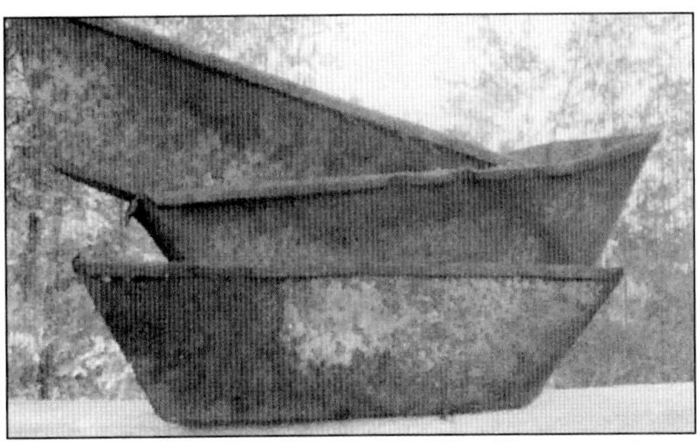

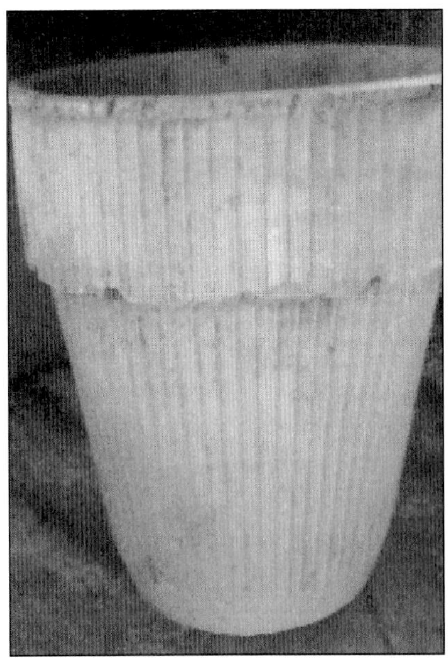

These three types of turpentine "pots" were used to collect resin, sap, or pitch from pine trees. The clay one on the right was common in the late 19th century; the top left followed; and the tin replaced both in the 20th century. (Photographs by author.)

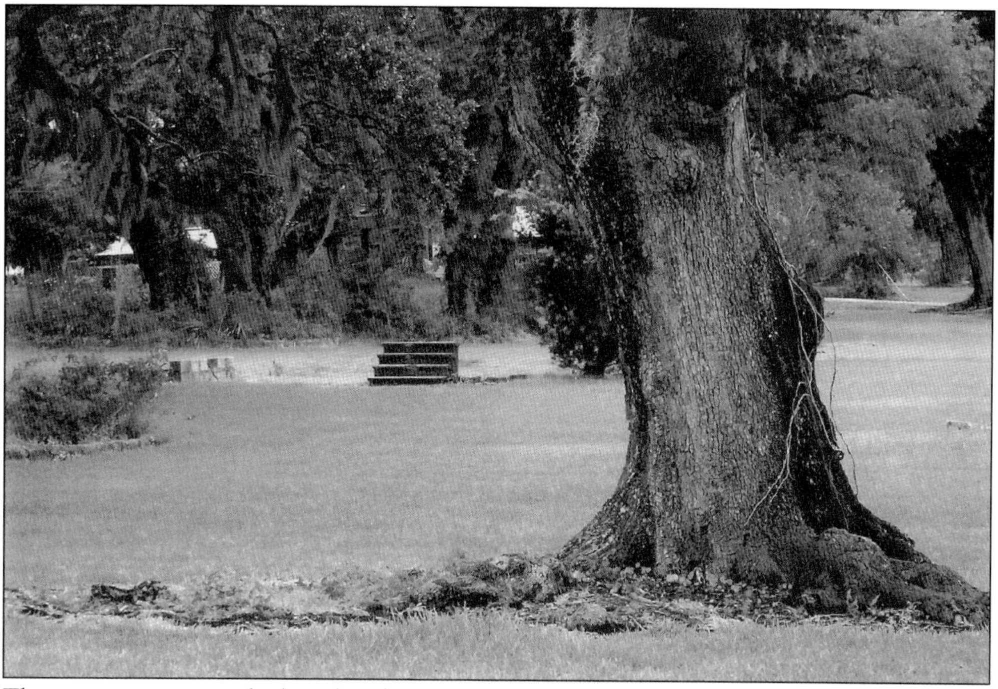

These concrete steps, which replaced wooden ones, are all that remain of the Santa Cruz home and trading post of antebellum days. It once served as a social center and postal kiosk. After World War I, it was only the family home until Hurricane Camille (1969). (Photograph by author.)

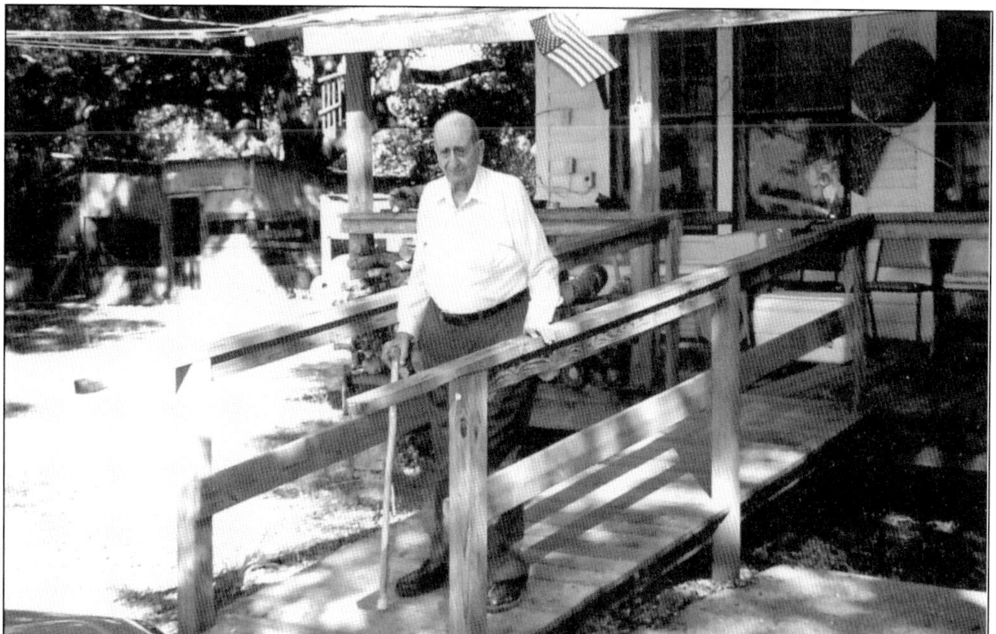

"Uncle Charlie" Simon was the last of the residents of Lickskillet before the small village divided into subdivisions in the late 20th century. The village was an offspring of the Henry A. Lienhard's timber operations, headquartered at Vennie on Cedar Lake, which shut down in 1926 under the L.N. Dantzler name. (Photograph by author.)

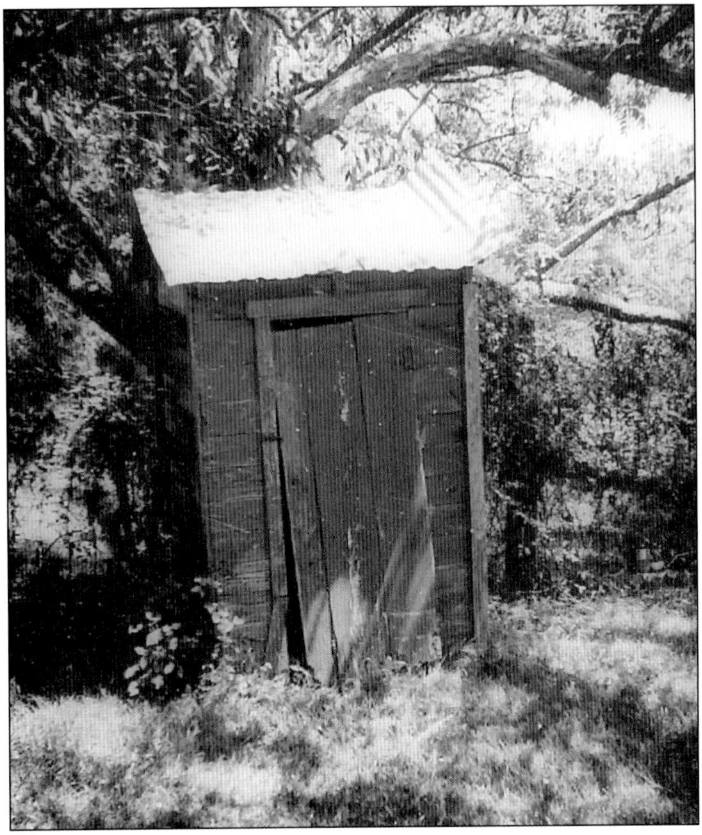

Every encampment, village and home had an outhouse behind houses, and it was not uncommon for two cabins to share one. The danger was having an outhouse too near a well. Still, not all wanted an indoor toilet; to many it was a disgusting thought. Indoor plumbing replaced these one- and two-hole backyard structures. (Photograph by author.)

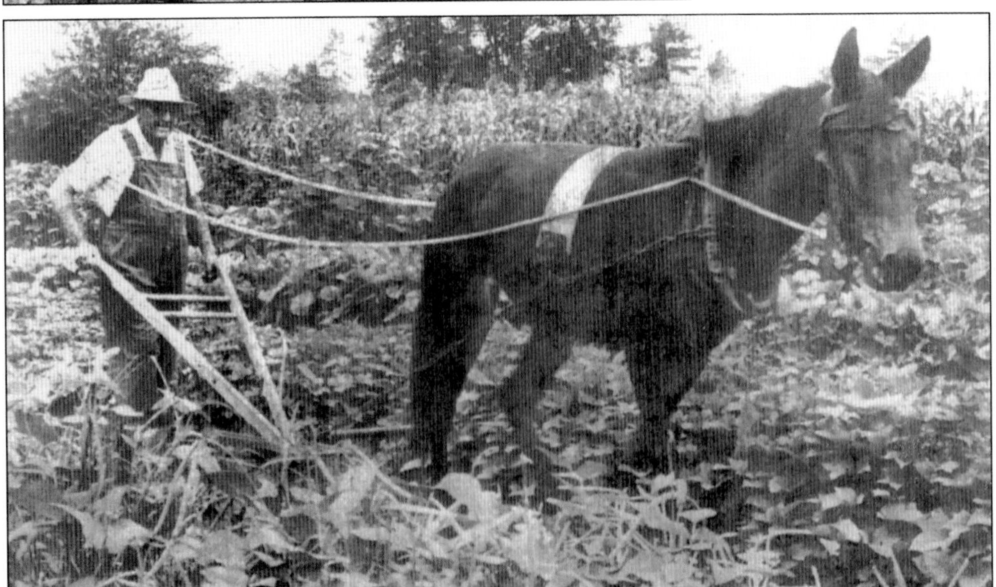

Johnny Bosarge, one of the last cowboys, loved farming as much as ranching. This ground was once a heavy forest of giant yellow pines, then open range. By the time of this plowing, farms and ranches were fenced. Cattle and sheep had but a few years left on the open range. (Courtesy Laura Thompson.)

Four

The Open Range

The loss of forest did not interrupt the gathering of wood used in making charcoal, a process with roots farther back than the discovery of America. Scraps left by stripping trees for logs provided fuel for the seafood factory boilers, and charcoal kilns that were everywhere on the coast. Turpentine stills remained, and younger trees produced sap just as well as the giant pines that had recently disappeared.

Although the giants were gone, and the lumber market in Europe could no longer count on southern Mississippi for its building boons, the paper industry quickly evolved in the absence of the giant lumber mills. The first generation of regrowth provided the perfect trees for the paper industry. Timber about 30 years old was perfect for the pulpwood needed. But there were other uses for the land not yet reproducing marketable trees.

Unfenced and left unused by owners who were actually selling their local assets to pay to move their mills and rails elsewhere, the hundreds of thousands of acres invited range riders and cowboys into the raw territory. Soon, herds of cattle and sheep were everywhere. All that the herds needed, water and grass, was free. The work was in branding, driving, and shearing.

As late as the 1940s, cattle were still rounded up in the outback by men on horseback and penned up in our communities. This writer watched many herds driven by cowboys popping whips and their dogs running with the herds on their ways to Nick Seymour's corals on the bay. Earlier, the herds were driven across the bay and loaded on cattle cars on the rails. Sheep were sheared in backyards in every neighborhood, and among the sheep and cattle families were the butchers and meat-market retailers; most grocery stores on the north side of the bay included meat markets and butchers. Most of the Seymour men were butchers. There were others.

In the 1920s and 1930s, hoof-and-mouth diseases plagued much of the United States' cattle and sheep regions. The north shore of the bay was no exception; the government placed "dipping vats" everywhere. There were no less than six in D'Iberville and two in St. Martin. One remains today on the old Charles Byrd sawmill property.

The loss of animals from infection cut into the profits, and wallets began shrinking. Routines had changed, and the cost of ranching curbed plans. A sick cow could lead to the execution of a herd; it happened more than once.

Open-range fencing by new owners and accidents on busy paved highways that had been slowly traveled dirt roads, created new problems. By the 1960s, the open range closed. New laws requiring pasteurization cut into the profits of dairymen. In the 1950s, the following families operated dairies: Kornman, Malpass, Bond, Seymour, Smith, Grantham, and Hengen.

The blessings were that people did not have to close windows and doors on hot, dry days, because of clouds of road dust raised by herds driven by cowboys wearing bandanas on their faces and dogs barking at hooves; and the day of chasing cows out of flowerbeds was finally over.

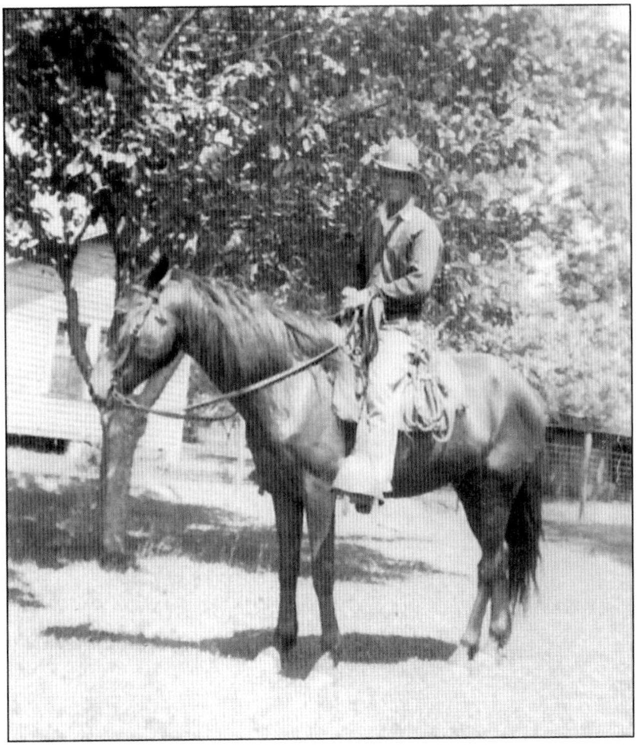

Joe Saucier and his horse put years on the open range rounding up cattle in the woods and cutover. Open-range attitudes began changing with the arrival of autos and highways, which meant serious accidents. Branding calves while separating cattle for market was common on the open range. (Courtesy Tay Greenwell.)

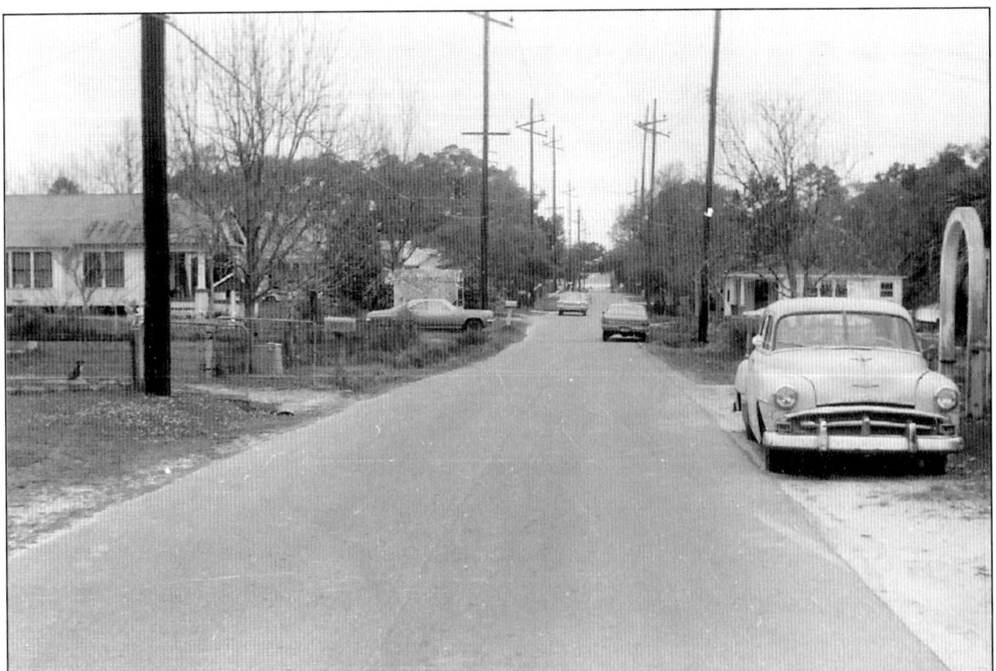

Looking south, this photograph shows Boney Avenue, the last cattle trail to the bay. To the left are the homes of Maurice Beaugez and Charles Styes. To the right is the home of Joe Watson. Cattlemen Joe Saucier and Nick Seymour were the last to drive cattle herds to the bay on "Boney Road." (Photograph by author.)

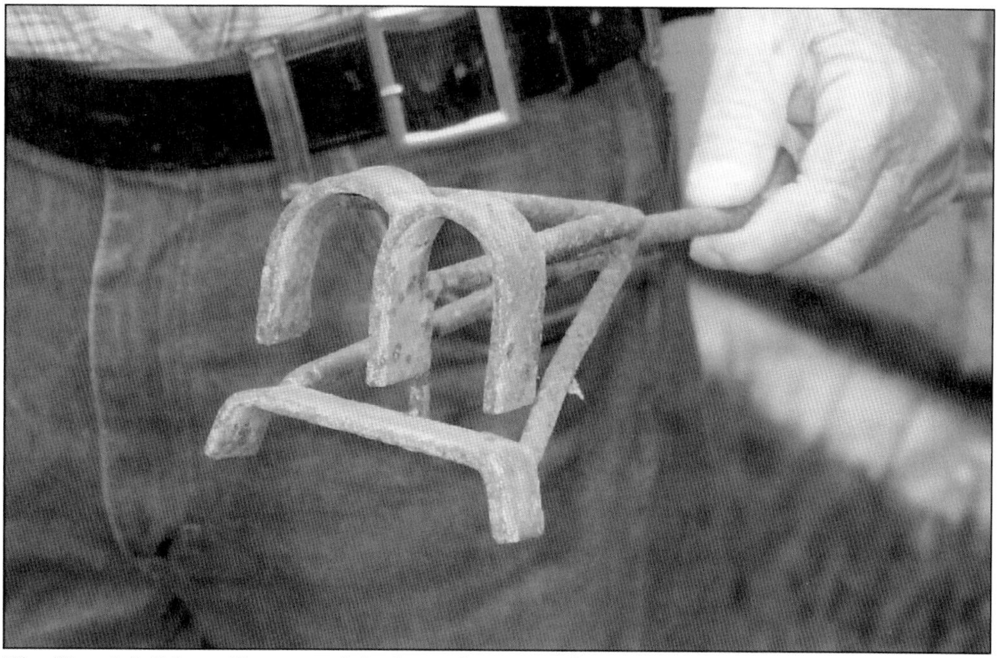

The "Bench M" brand has seared the hips of many cattle over the last 60 years. Its owner, Rufus Mallet, still uses the brand to mark cattle. His operation is consistent with the traditions of the open-range days, which included corrals, separating chutes, troughs, stables, and pastures. (Photograph by author.)

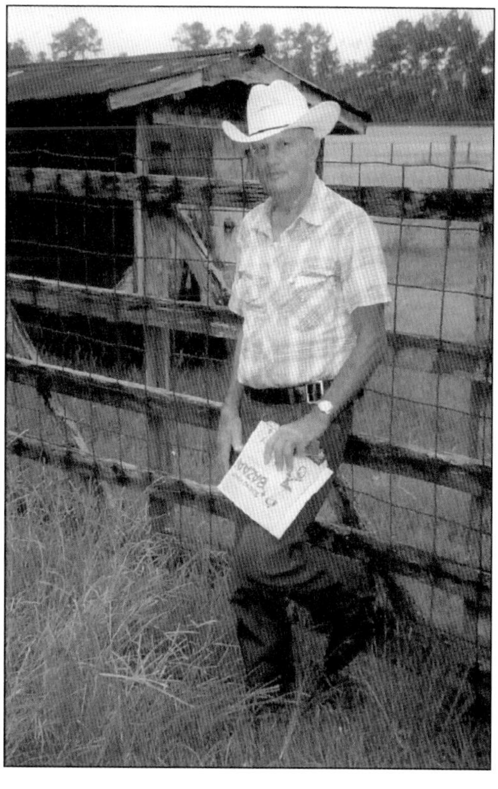

The last real cowboy is Rufus Mallet, a Navy veteran of World War II, seen here taking a break after hauling most of his small heard to market. Raised in the saddle, he built his own ranch during the open-range days on the coast. With the city growing around his spread, he holds on to his heritage. (Photograph by author.)

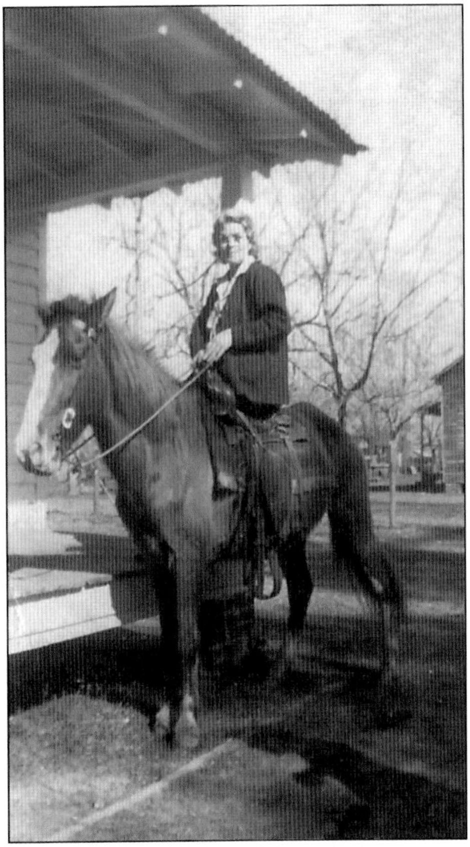

Gladys Boney spent her life on Boney Road, where cowboys and dogs raised clouds of dust while driving herds of cattle down the shell-dirt road through the neighborhood in the days of the open range. Her riding days ended due to an auto accident at a young age. (Courtesy Paul Fayard.)

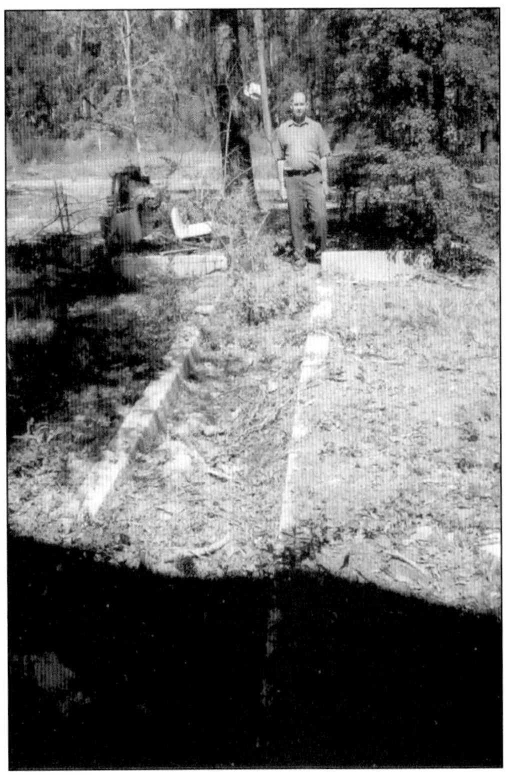

Paul Fayard is studying a buried "cattle and sheep chemical dipping vat" on the old Charles Byrd property. This vat, installed around 1928, was one of many during the scary days of the cattle hoof-and-mouth disease and anthrax epidemics. (Photograph of author.)

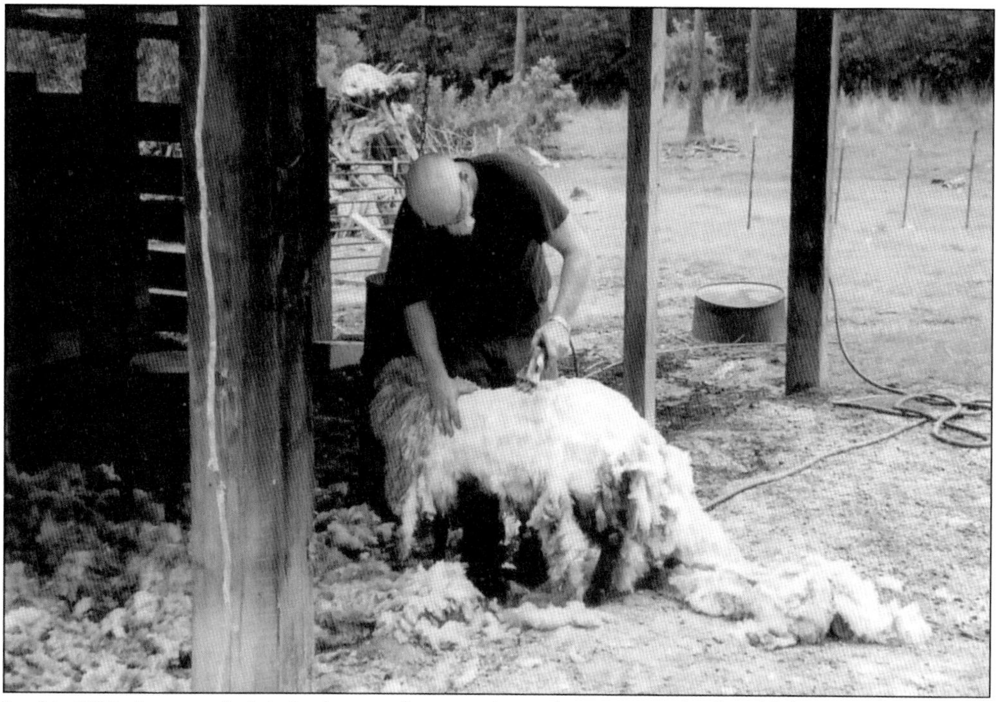

In this 1981 photograph, Mr. Ladnier is shearing sheep the new way. In the old days, manual clippers required frequent rests for the shearer's hands. During breaks, they sat beneath the trees with the dogs, enjoying coffee and sandwiches prepared by their ladies. (Photograph by author.)

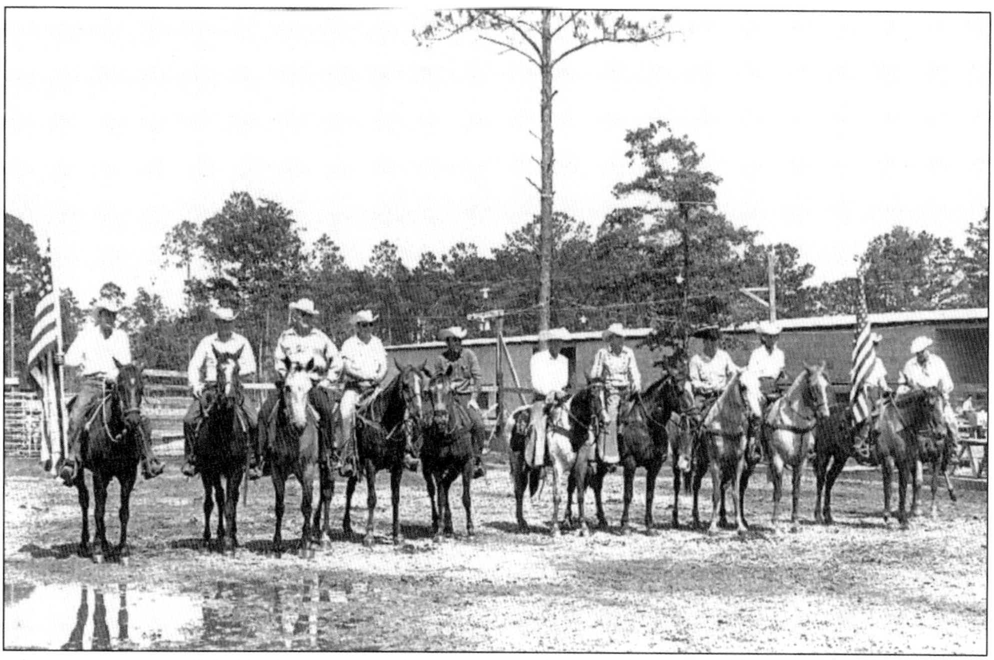

The cattlemen in this 1940s photograph are waiting for the show to start. Among them are past grand marshals and veteran parade riders. In the 20th century, all coast parades included cowboys and cowgirls; nothing excited children more. (Courtesy Laura Thompson.)

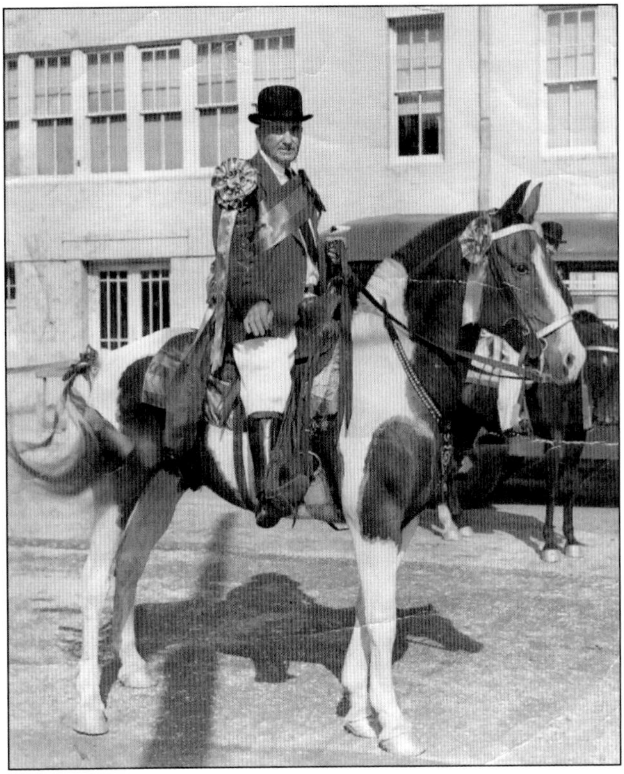

Cowboy and butcher Octave Borries, the grand marshal of the 1940s Firemen's Parade, is ready for the start. The most popular parades, especially this and Mardi Gras, were on Howard Avenue in Biloxi. Many participants were from the north side of the bay. (Courtesy Janet Derouen.)

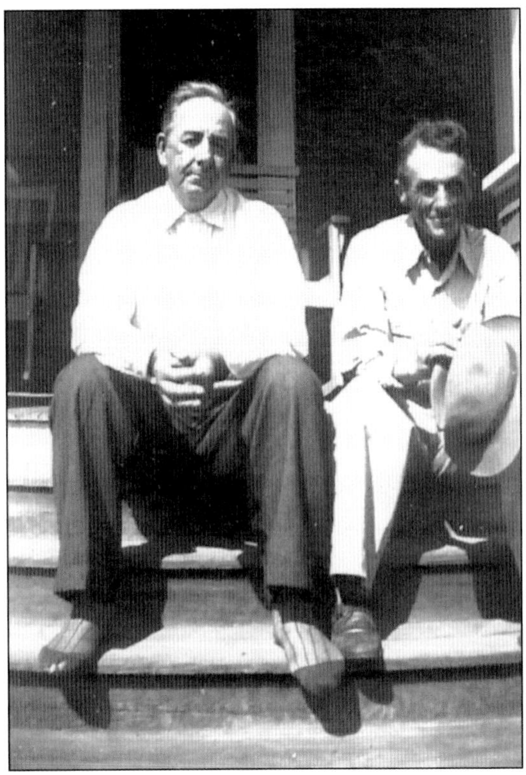

Cowboys Nick Seymour and Joe Saucier on break around 1955. Both spent their lives in the saddle, working the open range. They were in the last long-distance roundup and trail drive, which ran from Jones County to D'Iberville, then to the L&NRR. (Courtesy Stanley Santa Cruz.)

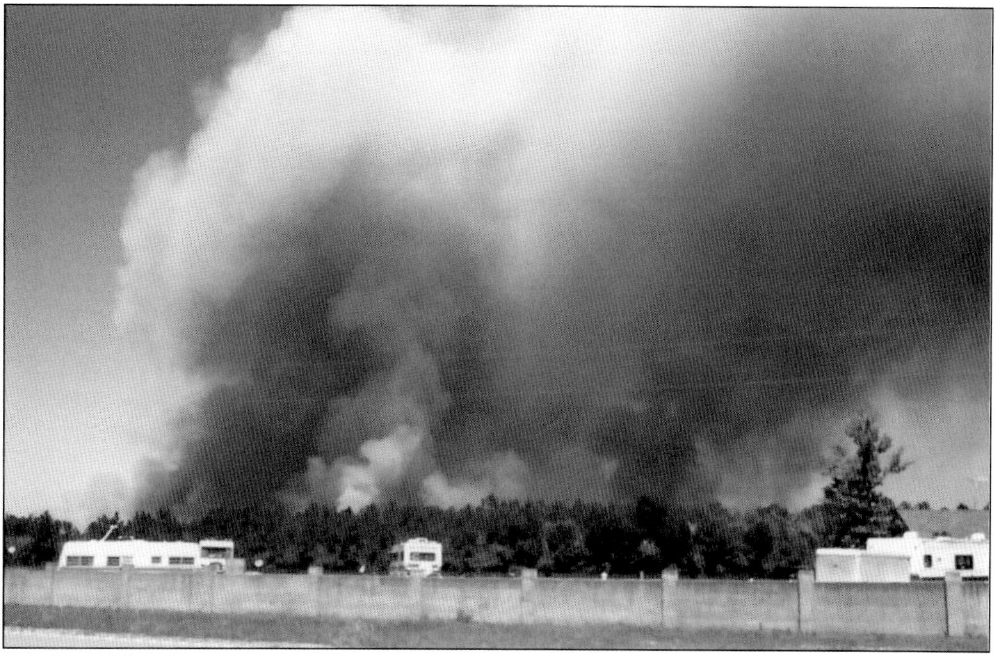

Cattle and sheep men have historically burned the forests and open range, without authorization, to create healthier protein grasses for the herds. Now, the burns are all performed where and when needed by forest rangers; other burning is illegal. (Photograph by author.)

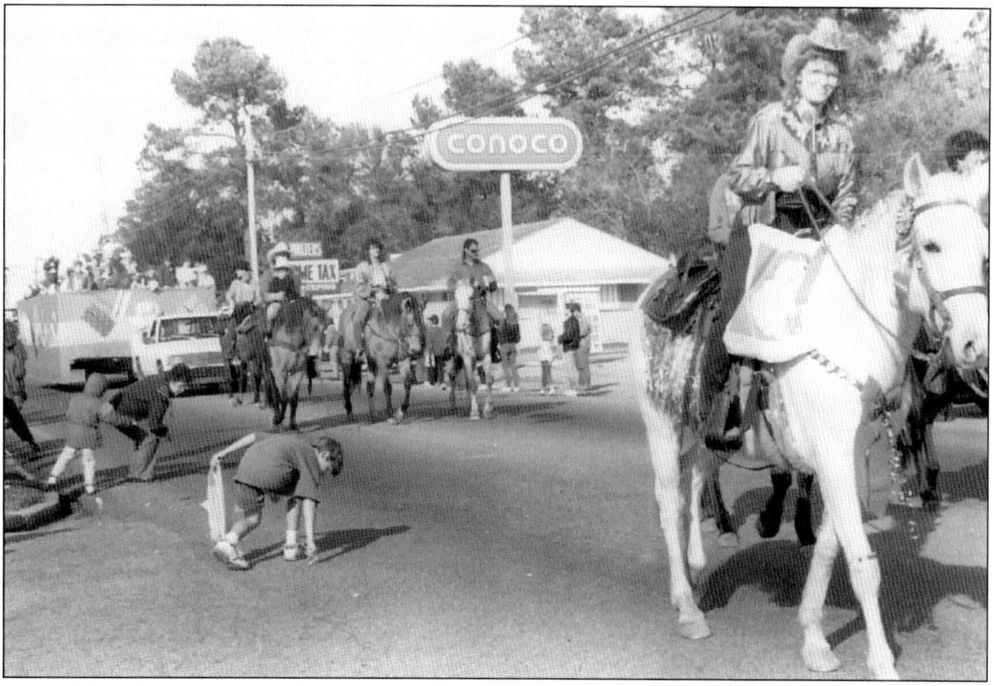

This 1993 Mardi Gras parade photograph was taken at the Central and Quave intersection, D'Iberville. As years passed, cowboys and cowgirls all but disappeared from parades. Cities are more conscious of the risks involved and the necessity of cleaning the streets after parades. (Courtesy *Bay Press*.)

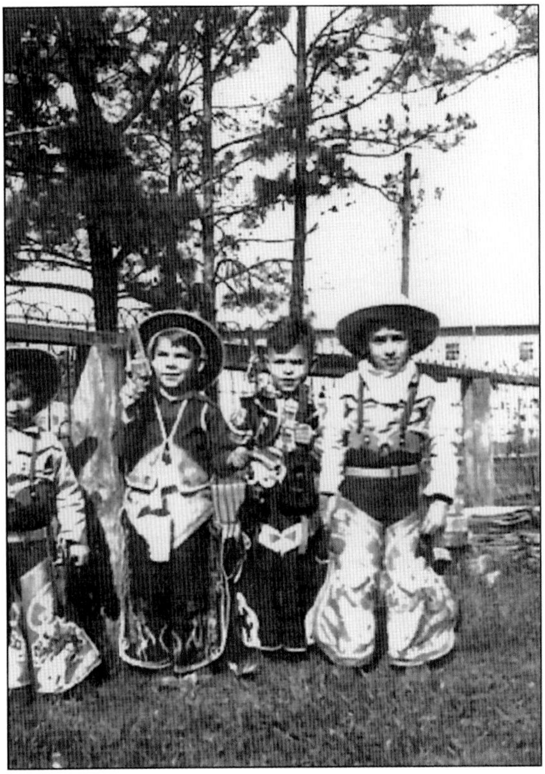

The Five Desperados of the 1940s are, from left to right, Danny Boy Moran, B.G. Fournier, Eddie Voyavich, and Henry Toncrey Jr. Nothing made a boy happier at Christmas than to find a cap-pistol and cowboy hat under the tree. (Courtesy Jackie Toncrey.)

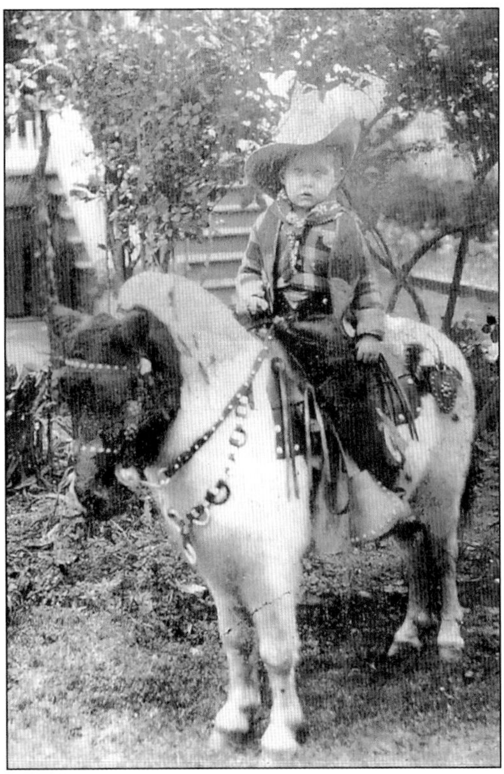

In this 1937 photograph, Arnie Gollott looks like a weathered cowhand. A half-century ago, photographers visited neighborhoods with ponies and western wardrobes for boys and girls, capturing on film children's imaginations. Every family had photographs of their young ones in saddles. (Courtesy Alice Mae Voght.)

Arnot and Selma Smith moved to D'Iberville in 1924 and operated Smith's Cash Grocery in Biloxi and a dairy on Cedar Lake Road, behind their home. They were very active in community affairs. Their son Roy volunteered to help organize the Warriors first football team. (Courtesy W.A. Smith.)

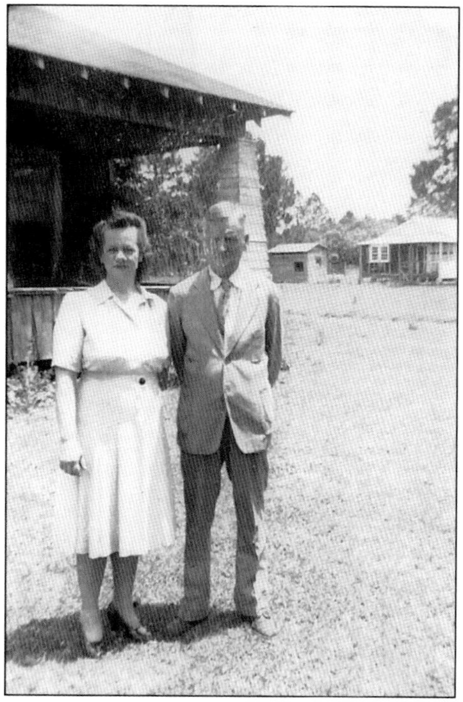

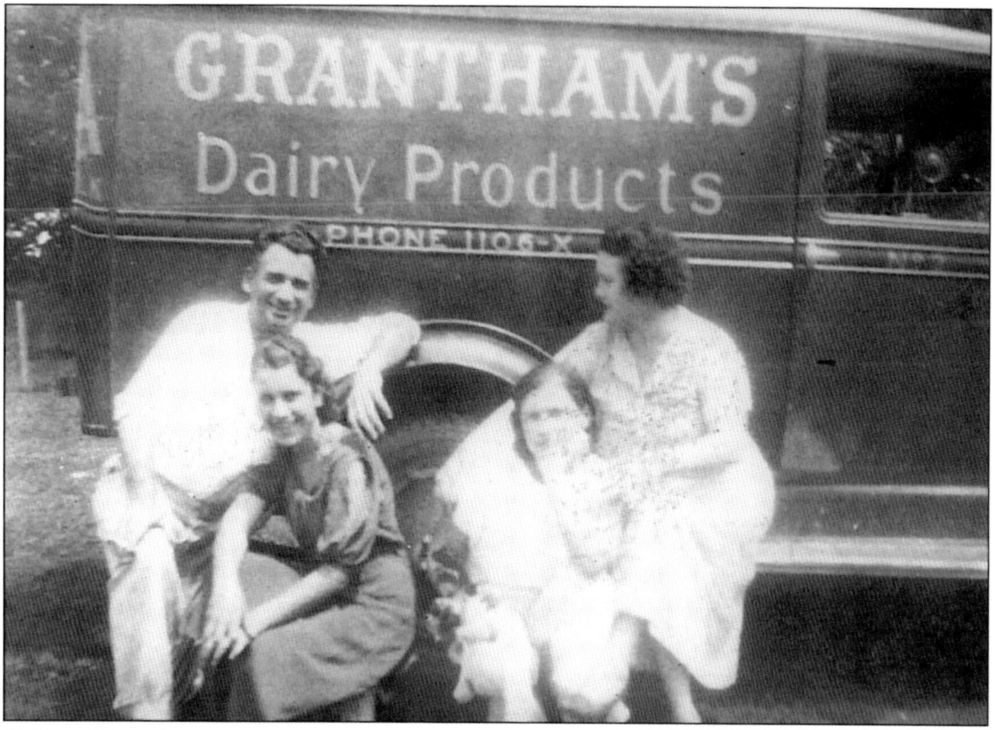

Holland Grantham, an active citizen, owned and operated one of the several commercial milk dairies in the community until after World War II. Many families milked cattle in their backyards, producing products for themselves and neighbors. He and members of his family pose by his delivery truck in this photograph. (Courtesy Hunter Grantham.)

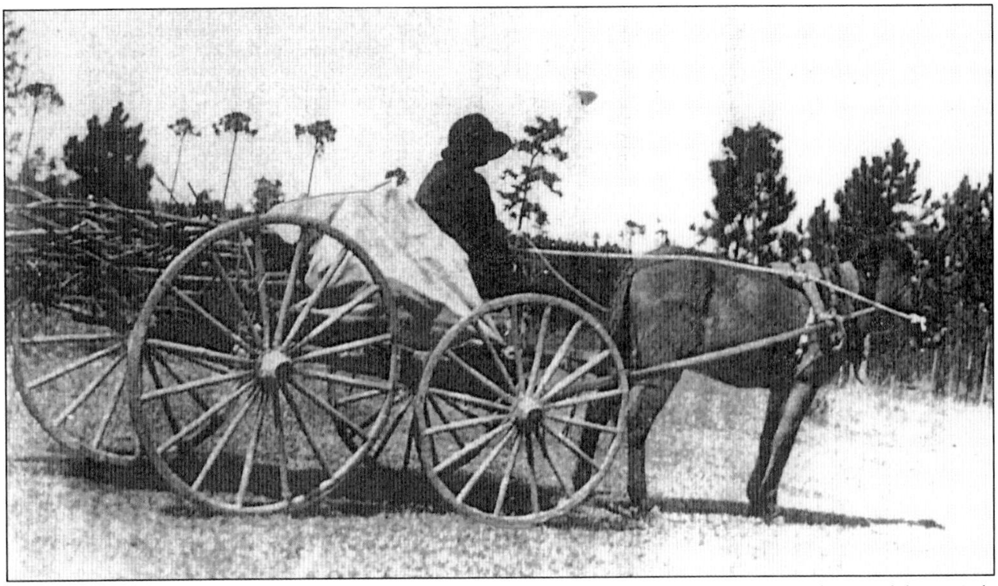

This was the late-19th and early-20th century method of transportation among the wealthy. With the arrival of the auto in the early 20th century, the horse and buggy disappeared and paved roads were on the agenda. (Courtesy Earl Wetzel.)

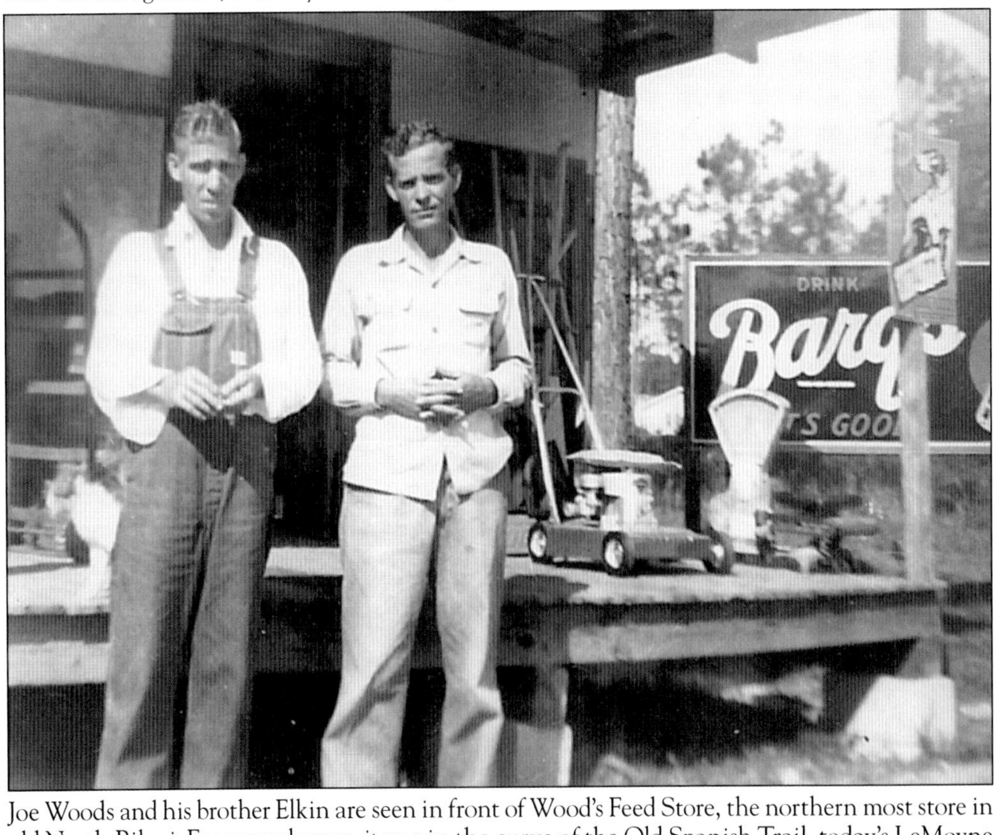

Joe Woods and his brother Elkin are seen in front of Wood's Feed Store, the northern most store in old North Biloxi. For several years, it was in the curve of the Old Spanish Trail, today's LeMoyne Blvd. Here, folks could purchase fuel, feed, food, and fishhooks. (Courtesy Jeff Woods.)

Five

FROM THE WATERFRONT

The story of our coast is a story of the sea. The seafood industry blossomed following the arrival of the New Orleans & Mobile Railroad (CSX today) in 1870–1871. Women who had lived through the Civil War and left widowed were usually reduced to scavenging the wilds to help feed their families. The factories helped. In the growing numbers of factories, they stood in lines before dawn, hopeful of finding vacancies at the picking tables, which migrants from the Chesapeake, Europe, and Louisiana also needed.

The industry was not unlike a gold rush. Many families came during seasons and returned to their respective homes out of season. Eventually, many remained. Before the first bridge spanned Back Bay in 1901, women and girls from the north side, who worked at the factories, were awakened by factory whistles on the south side, prepared for the workday, and crossed the bay in the predawn darkness, hoping to find a place at the picking tables in a factory, which was never guaranteed. Even after the bridge opened, many rowed skiffs across in the darkness. The men and boys worked on the boats or in the boiler rooms and on the docks, loading and unloading boats and boxcars. Most men were on the shrimp and oyster boats.

After the bridges were built (1901 and 1926), trucks made the rounds. With their brown lunch bags, the ladies and girls climbed into the canvas-backed small trucks among others, laughing and talking on the ride to the factory. For the lucky ones, a 10–12 hour day of standing before a tall table of boiled shrimp or crabs for a few dollars or a handful of "shrimp nickels" to put bread and coffee on the table was in store. In the early 1900s, three seafood factories operated on the north shore: Radio, Imperial, and Foster. Before World War II, there was C.F. Gollott & Son, Ramon Fournier & Son, and Harris. There were Gollott & Sons, Doty Fournier, and North Bay Seafood.

Oyster shucking shops were everywhere along the waterfront. There are none today.

The early boat-builders on the north shore were Sanchez, Foretich, Quave, Fountain, Groue, Moran, and Santa Cruz. The next generation included Cannette, Fayard, Harvey, and Brashier. Others built their own small boats. Today, Bill Holland of D'Iberville has the only boatyard on the north shore. Buddy Jumonville is doing a great job on smaller boats. Boats under construction in a family yard are not rare sites today.

During and after World War II, the community stores (small one-room structures, often inside the residence) were Mat Moran's at Five Point; George Moran's, Clementine Fournier's, Pearl Fournier's, Little Joe Cannette's, and Armond Fayard's (Salvador Lepre's after war) on Race Track Road; Dora Powell's on Reynoir Road; Letort's, Bullock's, Saucier's, and Joe Woods' on Old Spanish Trail (LeMoyne today); Lamey's on Brodie Road; others on Big Ridge, Cedar Lake, and Popps Ferry. There were others farther out. Few sold gasoline; most sold kerosene. Autos and electricity had arrived. Wagons and oil lamps were stored for hurricanes. All homes had radios. Television wasn't even a word.

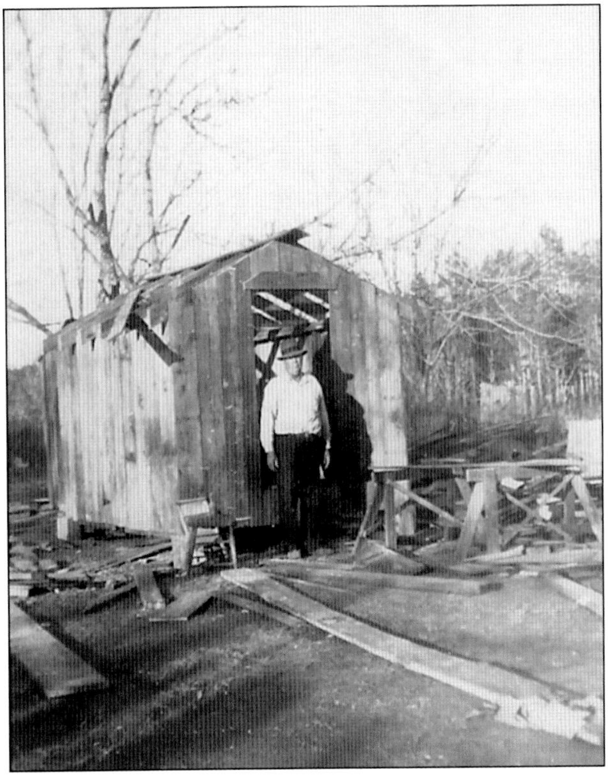

Paul Beaugez, carpenter and fisherman, is building an oyster shed behind his new home on Race Track Road, Point St. Martin, in 1942. Many living far from the bay had small sheds behind their houses used primarily for shucking oysters and washing clothes on a scrub board. (Courtesy Tay Greenwell.)

Back Bay was an oysterman's haven before the bay was closed to them in the mid-20th century. Oysters were collected by dredging, tonging, and gathering by hand from the reefs and shorelines. Oyster shops (the larger ones called factories) lined the bay. This oysterman is unidentified. (Courtesy Biloxi Library Archives, HCL.)

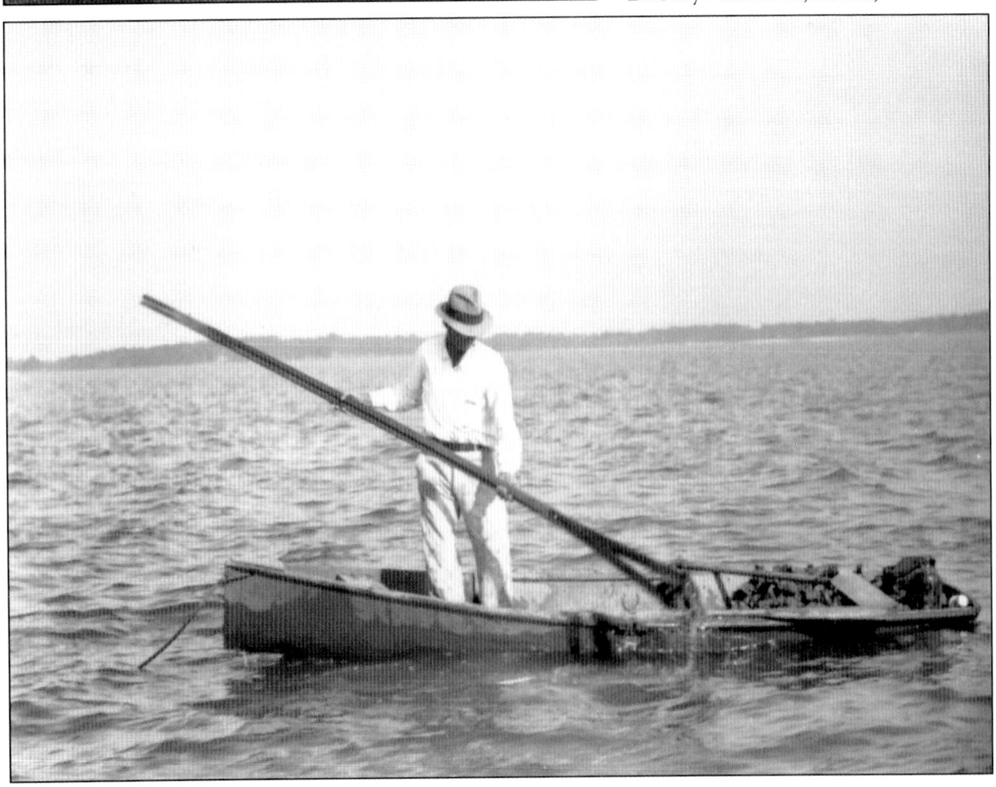

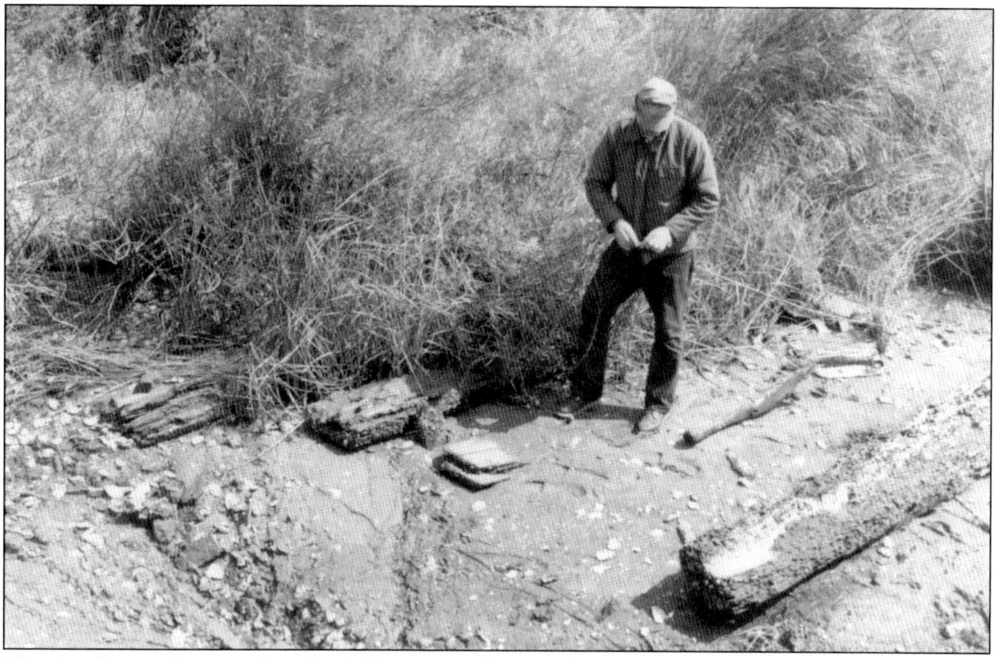

The first known boatyard on Back Bay was at Emanuel Sanchez's homestead in the 1830s. John Foretich operated the yard from 1844 into the mid-1850s, when his health failed. Sanchez worked it again then sold to Raymond Quave in 1889. Bill Holland's boatyard is now on the site. He is seen here examining the old yard's ruins at low tide. (Photograph by author.)

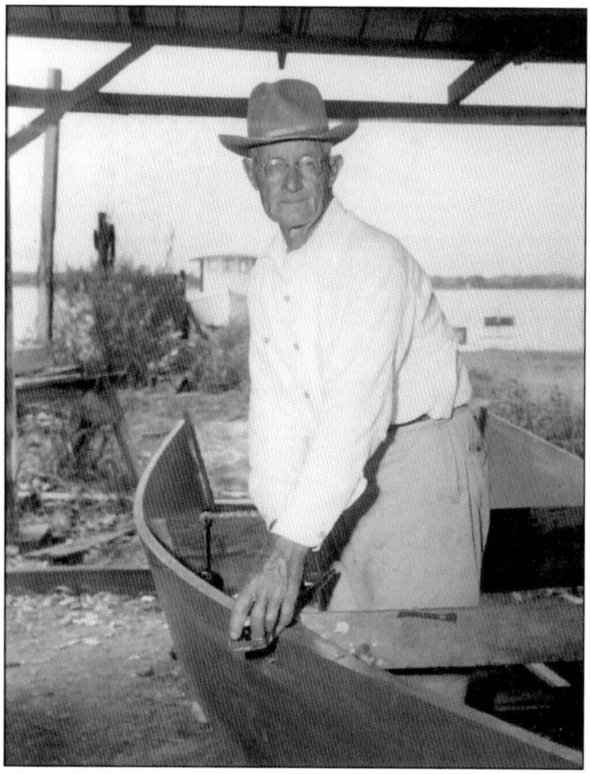

Martin Fountain Jr., son of a master boat-builder, is constructing a skiff on Back Bay in the 1940s. On Fountain Beach in 1893, his father was building the first of 10 schooners for Jean Trochessett when a hurricane destroyed the boatyard and schooner. The family moved to the south side of the bay and resumed building the fleet. (Courtesy Wayne Creel.)

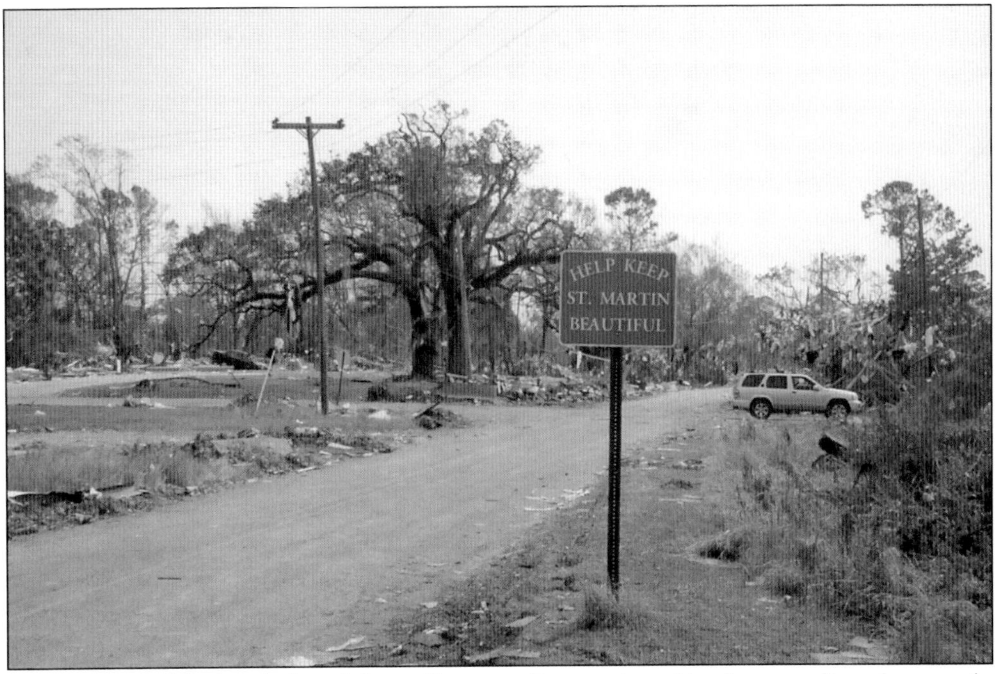

This is the neighborhood where Martin Fountain Sr., mentioned in the preceding photograph, began building schooners. This area was swept away by other hurricanes—the last was Katrina. Note the St. Martin sign at the intersection of Race Track and Beach Bayou Avenue, shown here after Katrina swept 38 homes from the latter. (Photograph by author.)

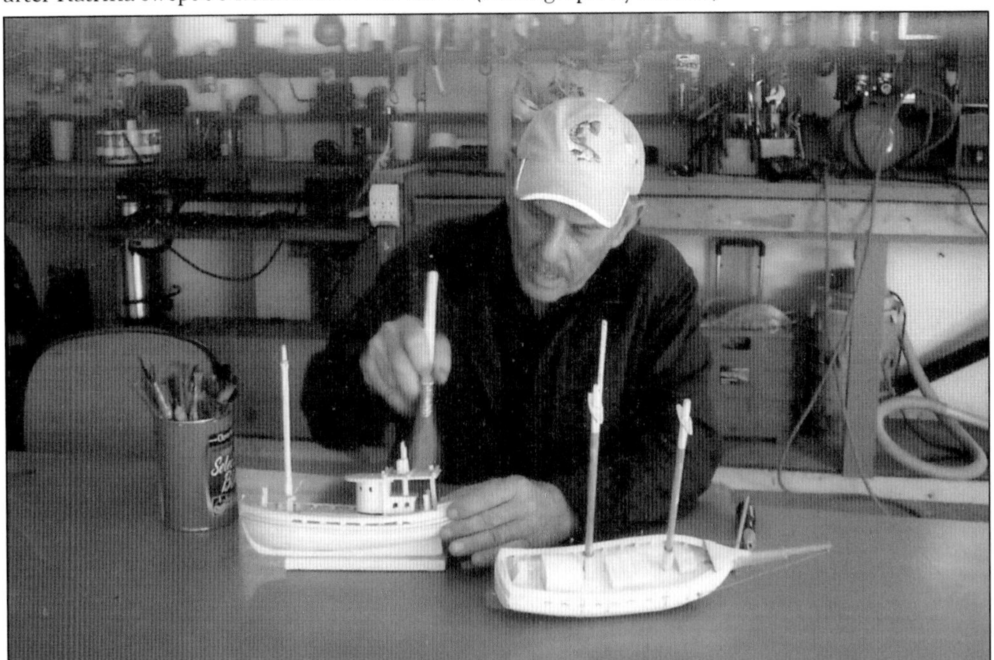

August Derouen Jr., a noted local artist, captures the history of boatbuilding on Back Bay as he experienced it through his years among the master boat-builders of his family in Point St. Martin. His home is an art gallery of model schooners, wildlife, and other art. (Photograph by author.)

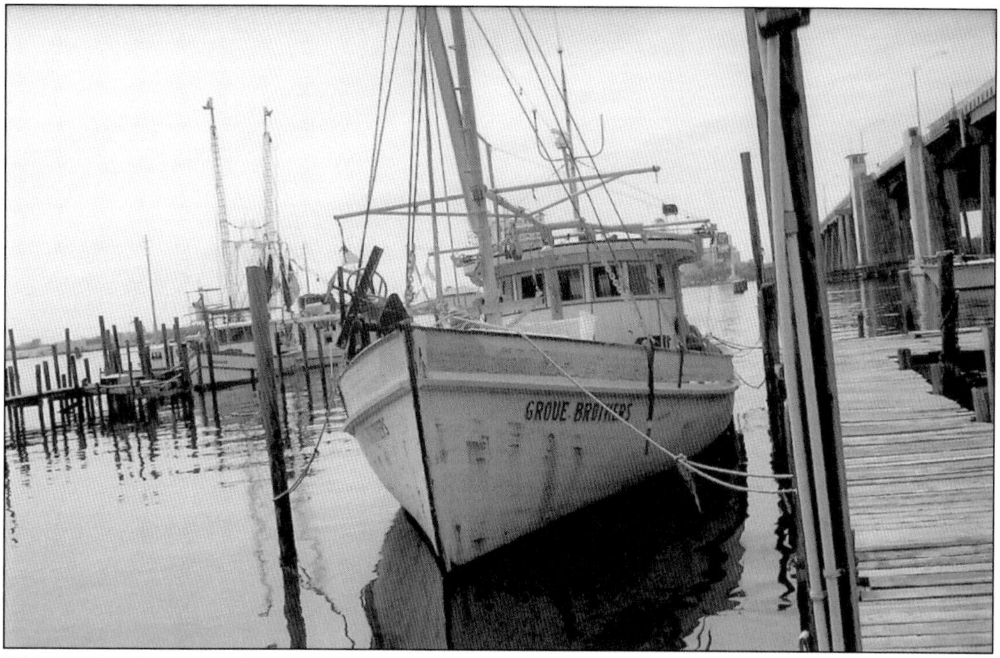

The trawler *Groue Brothers* was built by master boat-builder Davis Fayard in 1947, at his yard next to the historic Casimir Harvey home and boatyard on Bay Shore Drive. At age 67, it was moored at the D'Iberville Marina on the bay in 2010. (Photograph by author.)

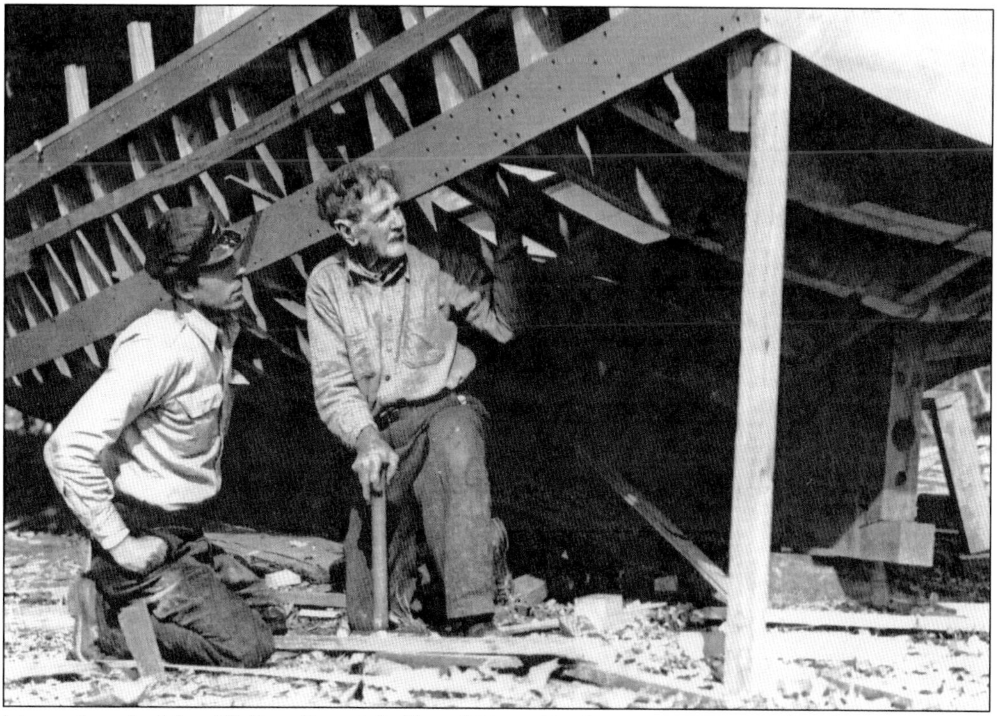

Master boat-builders Wallace Fayard (left) and Ishom Brashier are inspecting the ribs of a shrimper at Ishom's boatyard under Chapman's Hill in the 1950s. Over a century, wooden boats were built infrequently on this tiny beach. (Courtesy Paul Fayard.)

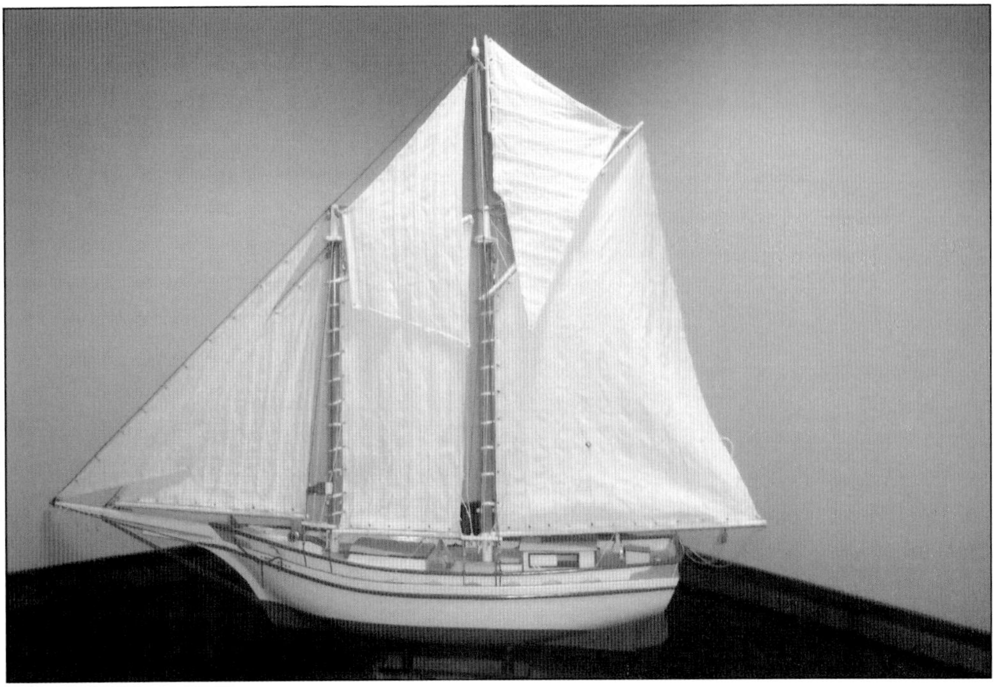

Mack Hall, a D'Iberville barber, is also a model boat artist. Like Auggy Derouen, Wayne Creel, and Russell Barnes, his attention to accuracy is precise and detailed. At the time of this photograph, the model was displayed at D'Iberville City Hall. (Photograph by author.)

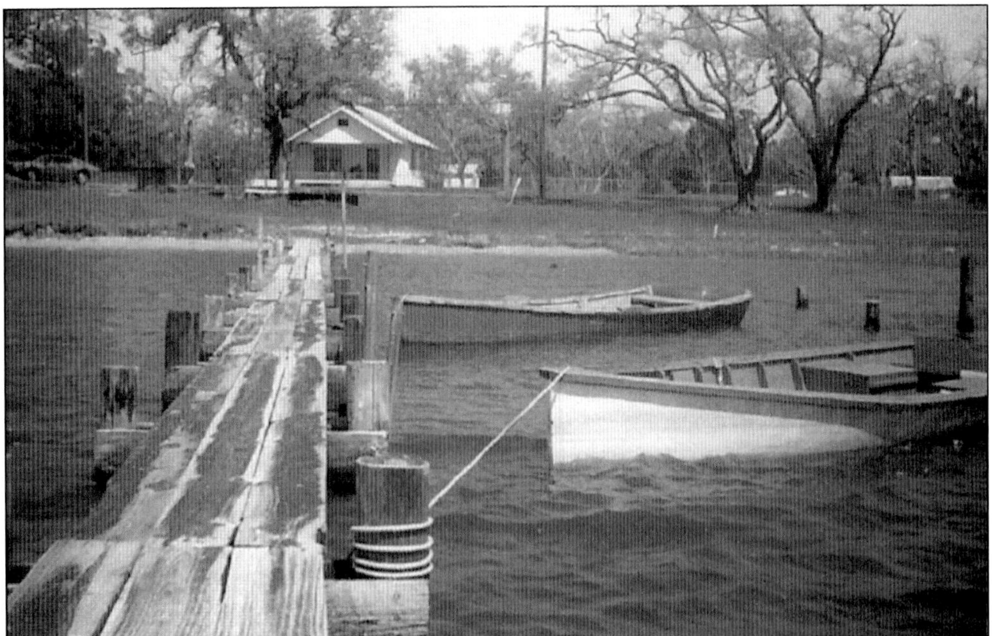

Shown here is Arthur Boney's wharf. A century ago, Joe Boney's pier was in this place and an oyster shop was just off the pier on shore. The Harvey Ferry Landing and home was 30 yards west. Every property on the shore had a pier or wharf, and many had a small oyster-shucking shop on or near the foot of the pier. His home is in the background. (Photograph by author.)

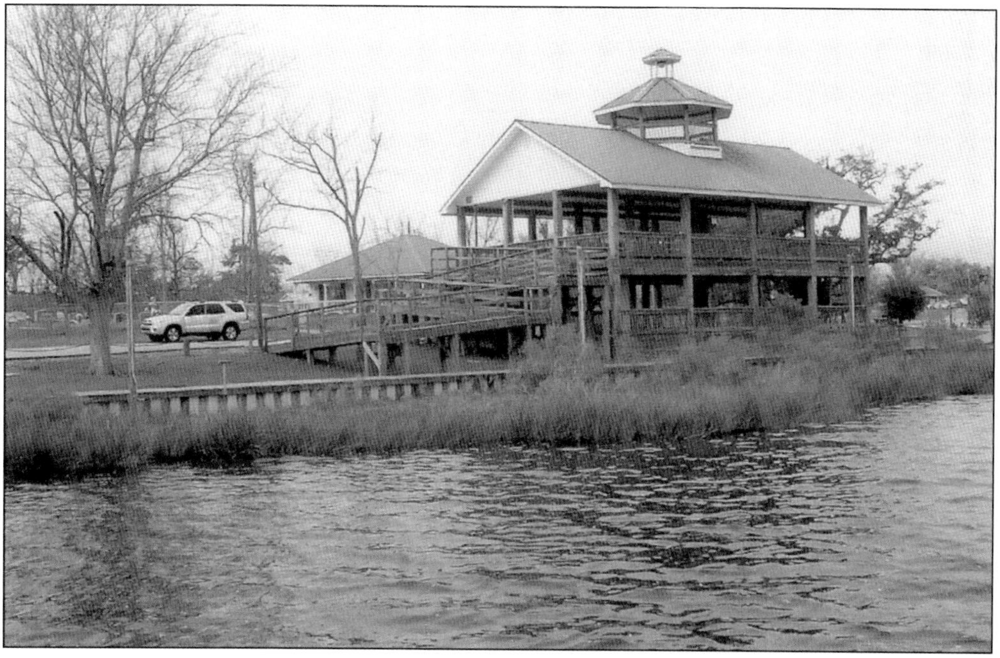

Shown here is the city of D'Iberville's Fountain Beach Pavilion. Beneath it are the scant remains of a century old boatyard, first operated by Willie Fountain and his sons, and later by World War II combat veteran George Kelly. The terrace in the background is the site of the old homestead and cemetery. (Photograph by author.)

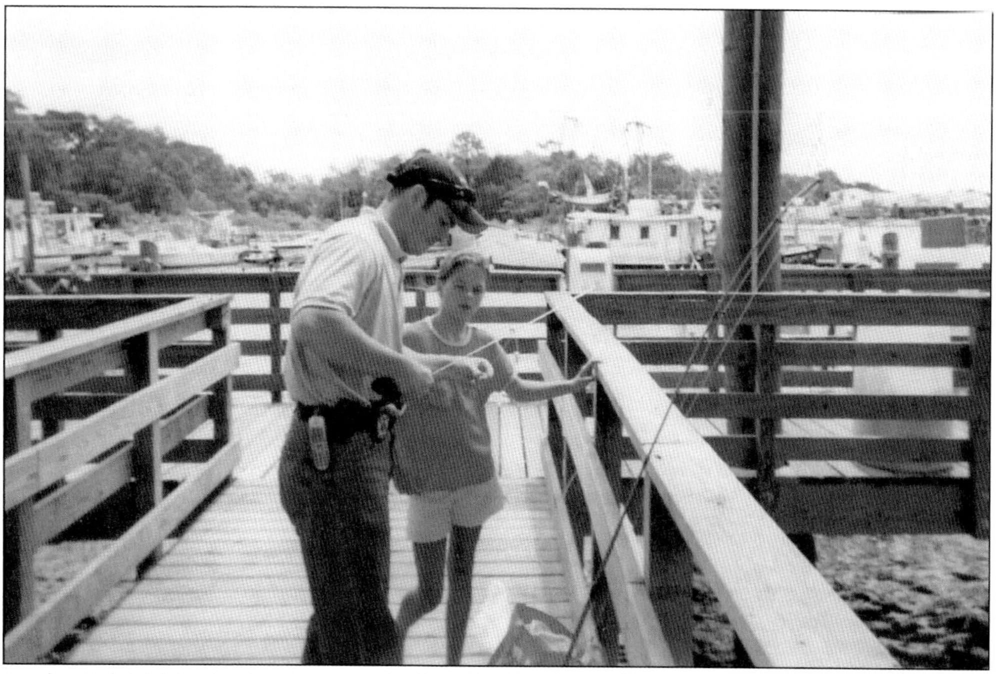

At the Kids Fishing Rodeo beneath the I-110 Bridge, Jay Williams is instructing an unidentified participant. This bridge is the third one across Back Bay and is named after Lee Seymour Jr. of the local chamber of commerce. He chaired their bridge committee. (Photograph by author.)

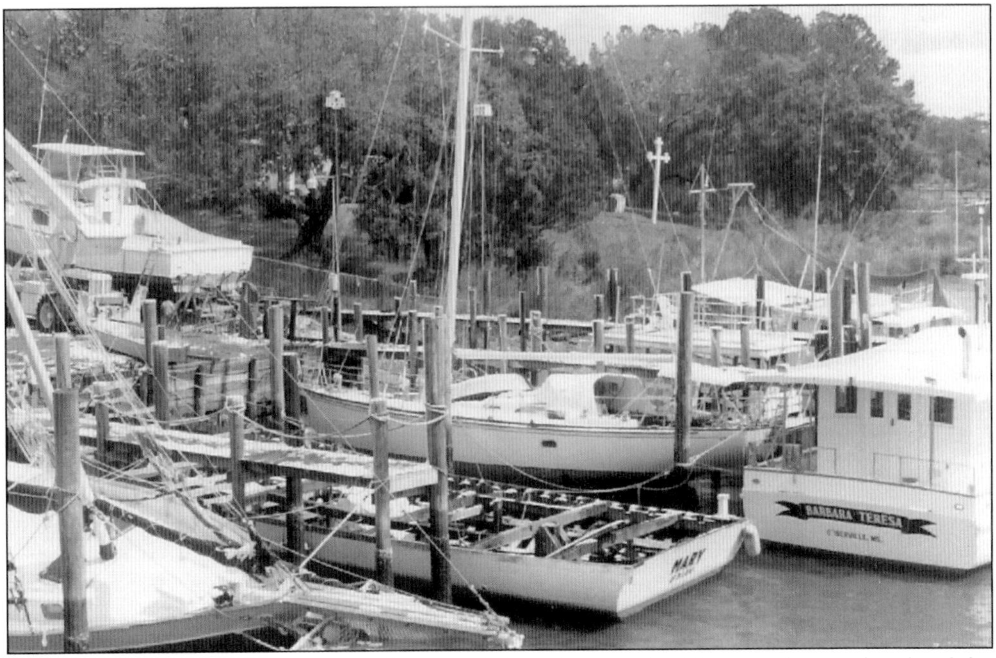

Bill Holland's boat yard today is on the site of the oldest boatbuilding on the north side of the bay. The first builders were Emanuel Sanchez (1840s), John Foretich (1840s–1850s), and Ramon Quave (1870s–1880s). Having learned from Davis Fayard and the Fountain brothers, he has a national reputation. This is also the site of the first Blessing of the Fleet (1927), two years before the 1929 public celebrations. Note the cross in the background. (Photograph by author.)

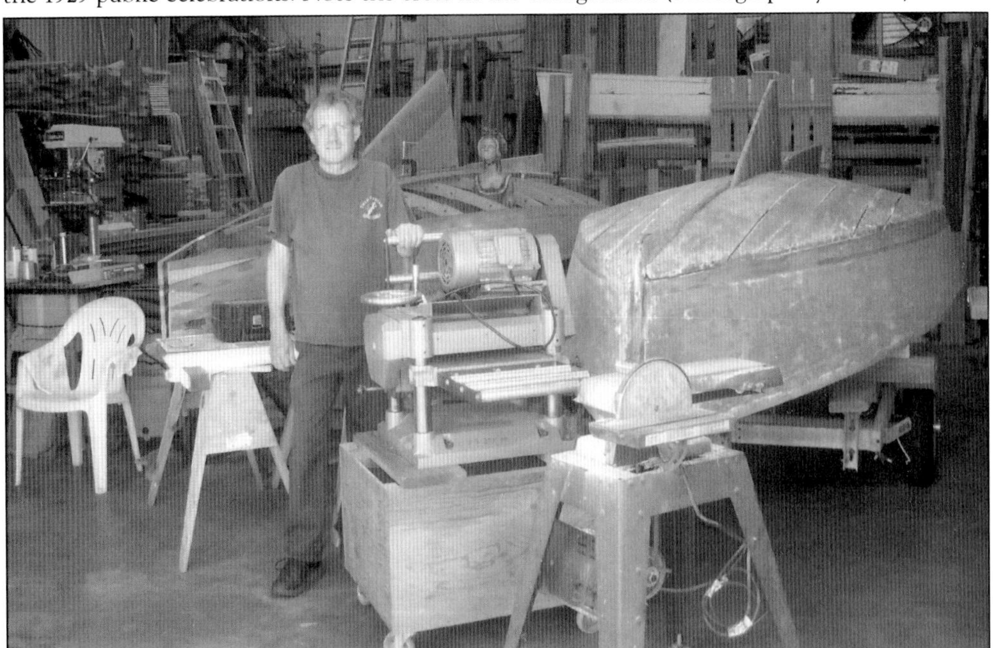

Mike Bray assists Buddy Jumonville in restoring antique sailboats. To his left is the catboat *Fat Cat*, built by Capt. Joe Scholtes decades ago. Uniquely Scholtes, it was crafted with narrowed strips of wood rather than planks. (Photograph by author.)

Brothers-in-law Maurice Beaugez and Davis Fayard are constructing a Texas rig in this photograph. For more than half a century, they teamed in boatbuilding from Biloxi to Galveston. Maurice was from a fishing family; Davis was from a family of boat-builders. (Courtesy Paul Fayard.)

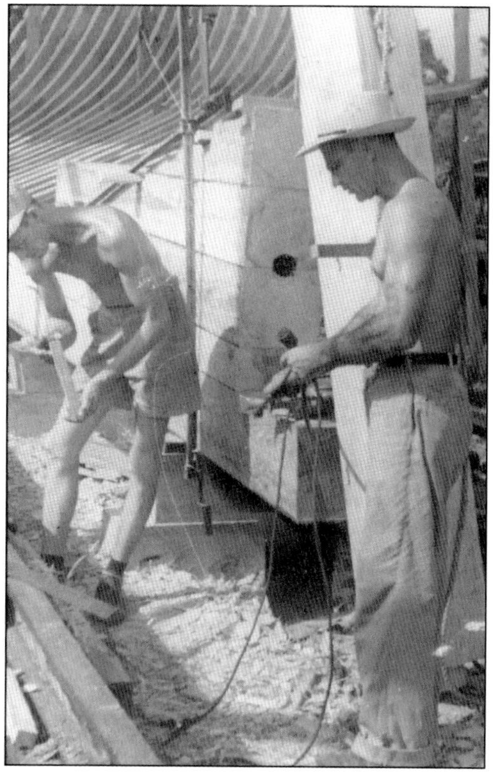

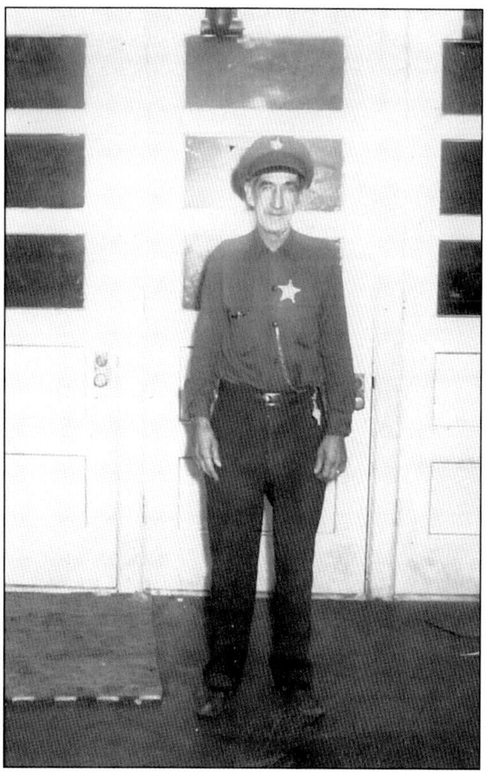

Albert Diddlemeyer, a seafood factory boilermaker and mechanic from the Chesapeake, worked local factories. After retiring from C.F. Gollott & Son Seafood, he volunteered to help discipline student activities and control traffic at D'Iberville School. (Photograph by author.)

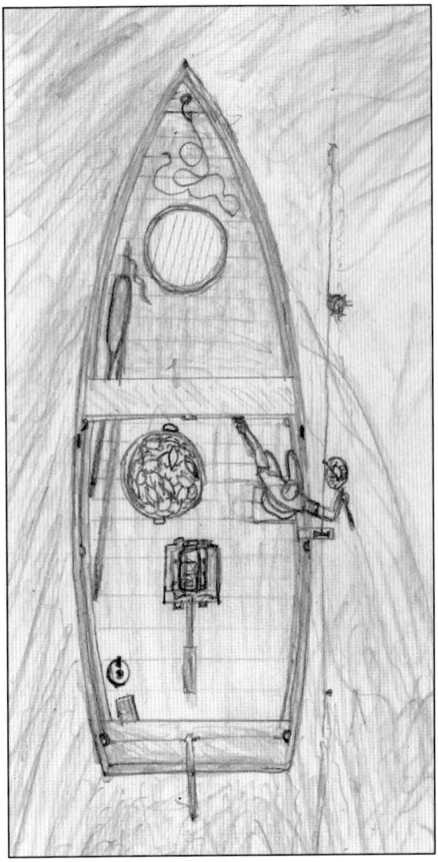

This is a sketch of a skiff used for crabbing in Back Bay in the mid-1950s. Baits of tripe or cows cheeks and ears were tied about five feet apart on a quarter-mile stretch of line between flagged poles. Crabs were scooped from the line as it passed over a roller. They were dropped in the barrel and delivered live to the factories. (Sketch by author.)

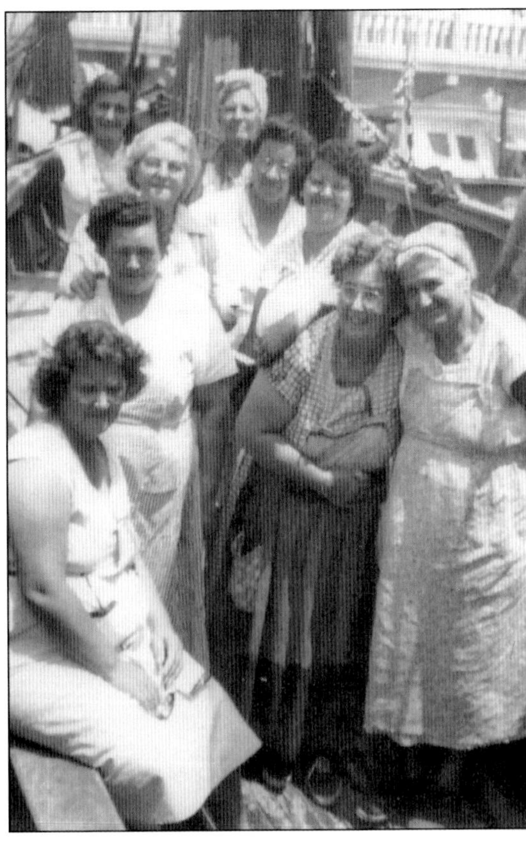

Crabmeat pickers on break at C.F. Gollott & Son Seafood in the 1950s are seen here. Hairnets, aprons, soft-sole shoes, and fingerstalls were absolutes as knives and crab shells were tough on hands. Each picker carried a bagged lunch and alum for their hands. Work began long before dawn. (Courtesy Paul Fayard.)

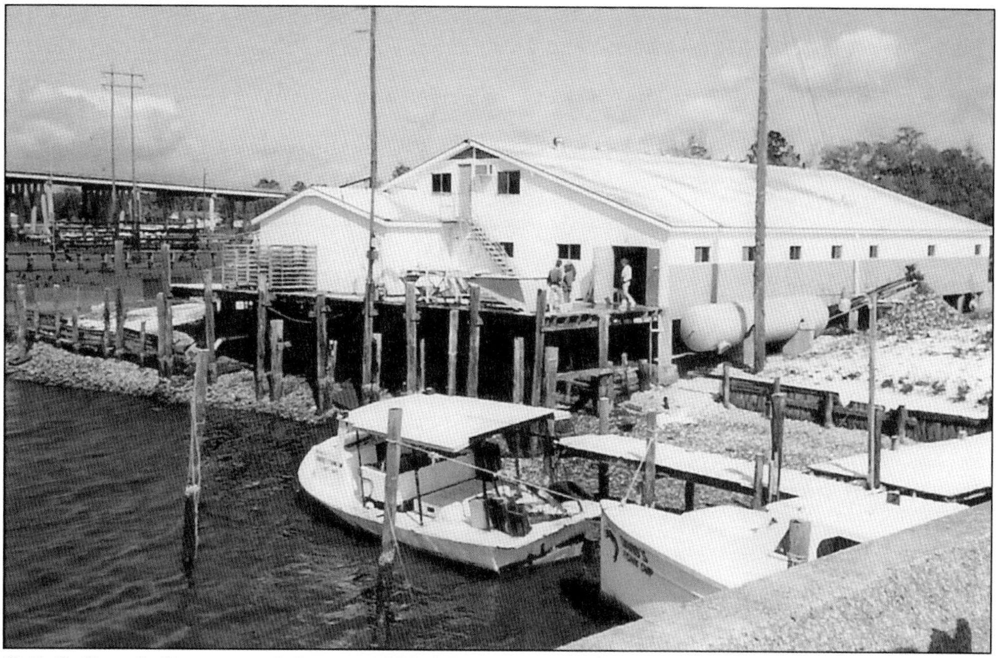

C.F. Gollott & Son opened shop in 1937. After numerous bouts with hurricanes, it was destroyed in Camille and reconstructed the following year. This photograph is of the factory and double-rig trawlers in 2013, eight years after another hurricane, Katrina in 2005, destroyed it. (Photograph by author.)

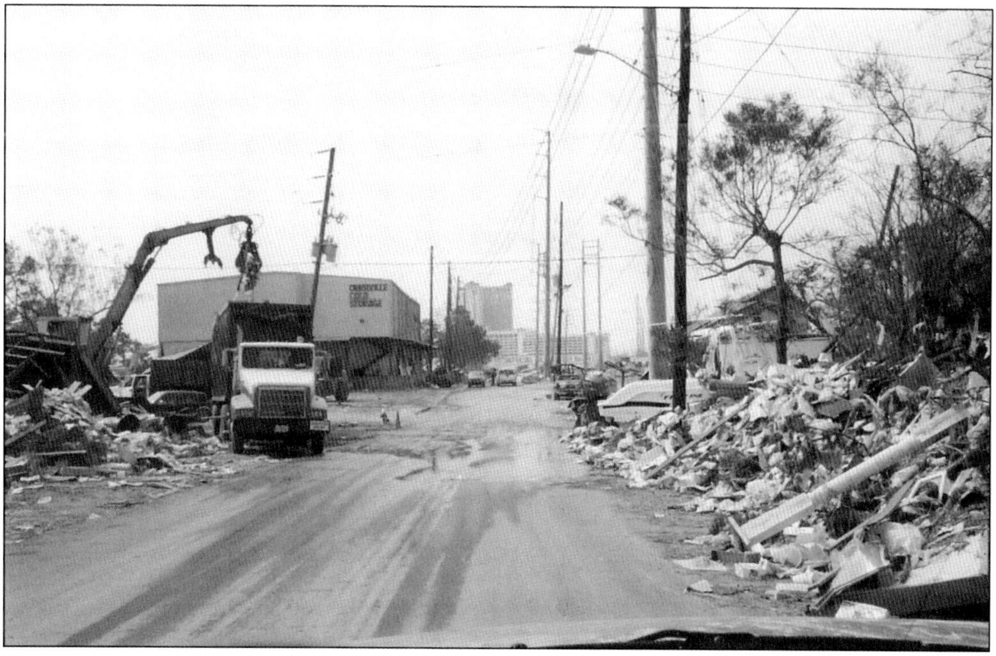

This image is looking south at Central Avenue after Katrina destroyed relics of the original town. The demise of that old town began in the 1960s, was hurried by Camille in 1969, and was completed by the 1975 fire, but the business center had been moving northward as the town grew. A scenic walkway now traces the old business strip. (Photograph by author.)

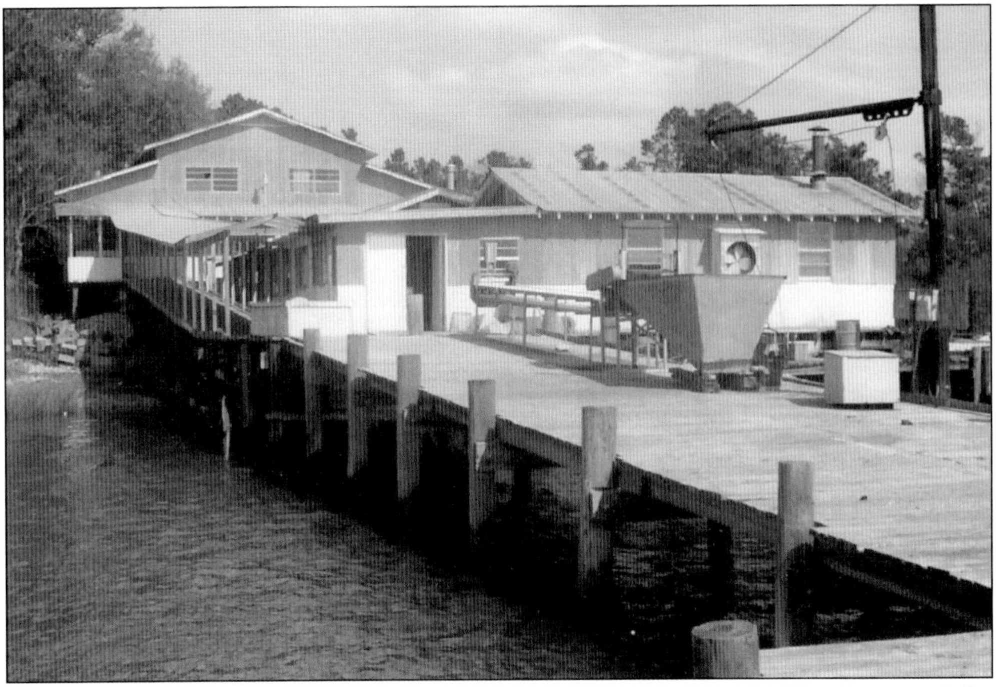

Ramon Fournier opened R. Fournier & Sons Seafood Co. in 1928. His son, Doty, continued the operation and employed his own sons. The factory was destroyed in Karina. Doty Jr. now operates a small seafood business at another location. (Courtesy Carolyn Fournier Anderson.)

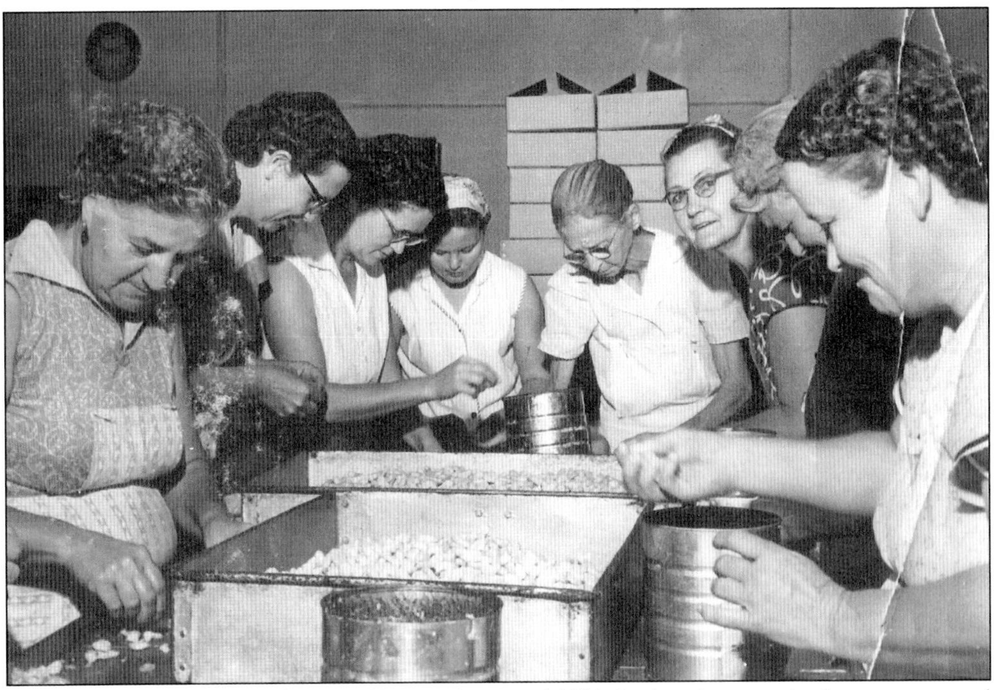

These ladies are picking crabmeat at Fournier's around 1950. In this photograph, they are squeezed together, posing for the camera. In reality, each had her own space. During oyster season, men opened oysters in an adjoining shucking shop on west side. (Courtesy Lee Cannette.)

Six

SEARCHING FAMILY ALBUMS

Nothing has been more difficult in the communities around the Bay of Biloxi than the challenge of finding photographs of our heritage, ancestors, or even our own children—thanks primarily to hurricanes.

Not a generation on our coast, going back into prehistory, was spared from nature's wrath. The earlier people, native and migrant, from every cline and time, settling on the coast learned the results of hurricanes: destruction of home, assets, and family members—and often entire families and neighborhoods. Putting together a photo album of our heritage is quite difficult.

In this chapter, you may wonder why the images of our loved ones and their loved ones are so few. Everyone would like to gaze upon the face of a dear friend or relative that the young generation could never envision: how they dressed, lived, worked, and danced, and "What did they look like, Mama?" are not easily described. We might answer, "Honey, I can't say for sure but your grandmother told me when I was a child. . . ."

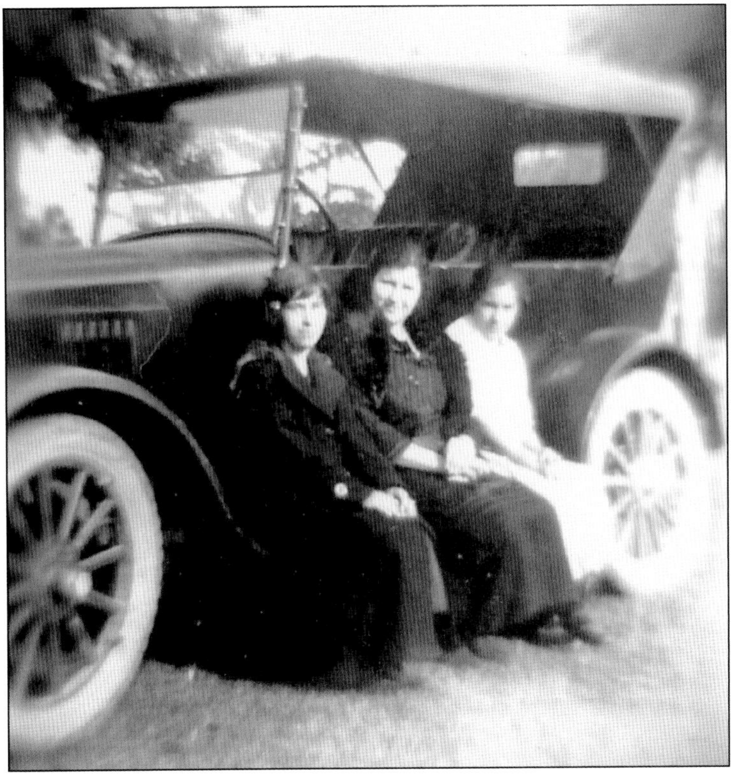

Autos were few north of the bay before World War I; one per neighborhood might have been the average. In this early 1940s photograph, (from left to right) Juanita Fountain, Myrtis Smith, and Lurelle Bullock are enjoying the luxury of a drive through the country. (Courtesy Paul Fayard.)

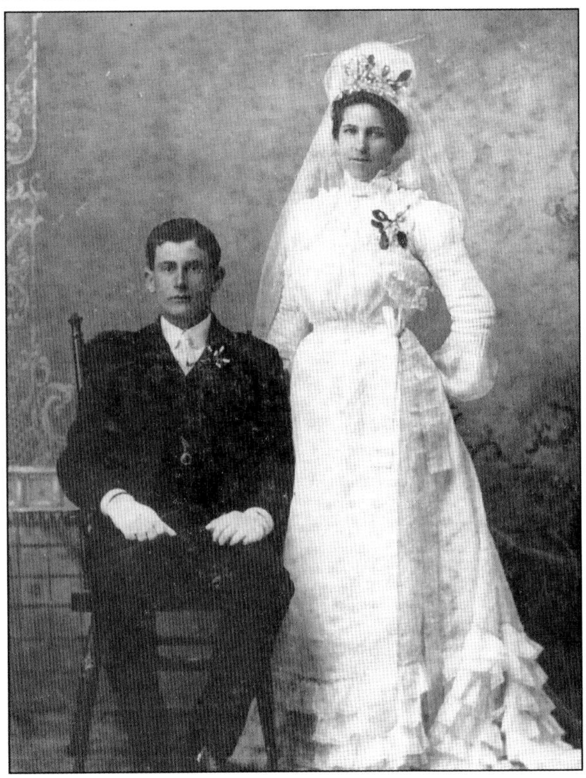

Alphonse Groue and Louisa Fountain pose after exchanging wedding vows. Most men of the area were involved with cattle, timber, and seafood; however, Alphonse chose a career with the L&N Railroad. His weekends were spent with his family in St. Martin. (Courtesy Cathy Lawrence.)

Mat Moran (standing) and two friends at the bridge-tender's tollbooth on the old wooden bridge across Back Bay, about seven years before the new concrete bridge was opened in 1927. Mat held various commercial and residential properties in D'Iberville. (Courtesy Jackie Toncrey.)

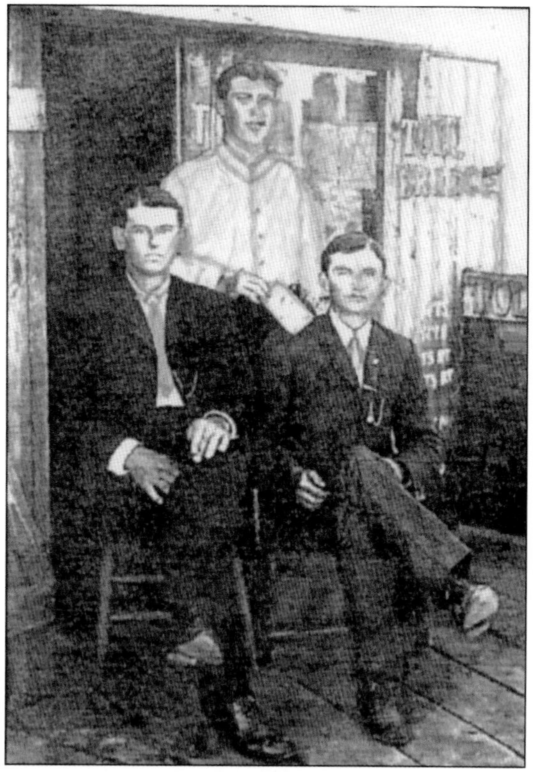

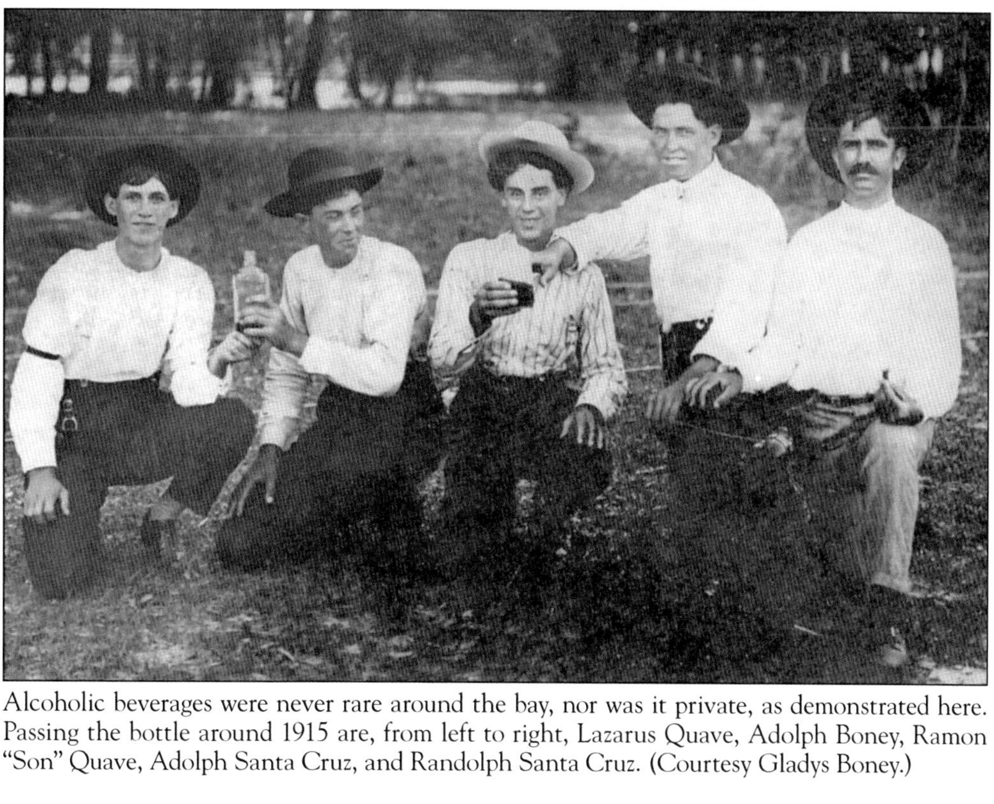

Alcoholic beverages were never rare around the bay, nor was it private, as demonstrated here. Passing the bottle around 1915 are, from left to right, Lazarus Quave, Adolph Boney, Ramon "Son" Quave, Adolph Santa Cruz, and Randolph Santa Cruz. (Courtesy Gladys Boney.)

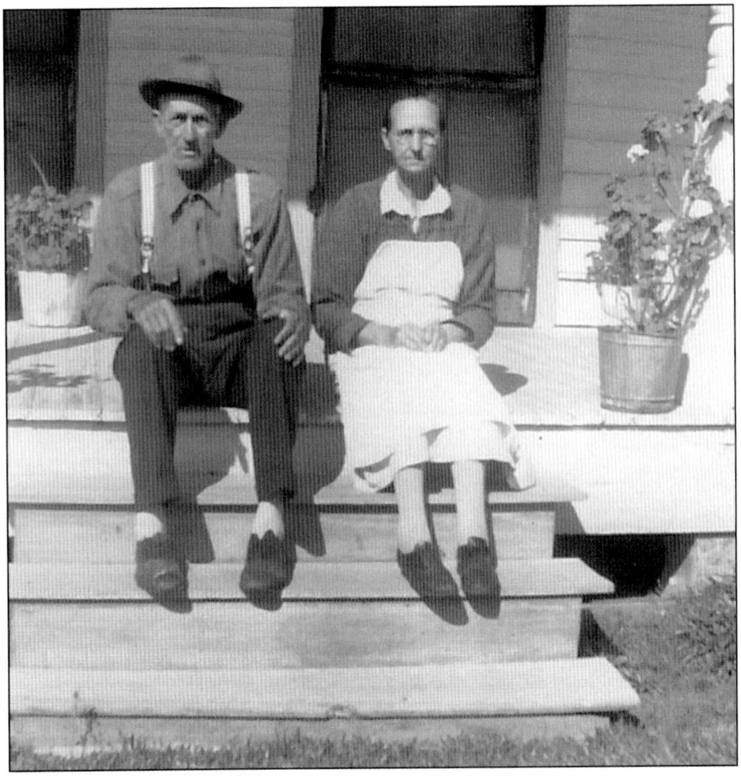

John Fountain and his wife, Olivia, are seen here in the early 1940s. He owned and operated the trawler *Marie Inez* but was more than a fisherman. He managed a farm and herds of cattle and sheep before the open range closed. In his 80s, he traveled by bicycle and loved to dance. (Courtesy Ken Fountain.)

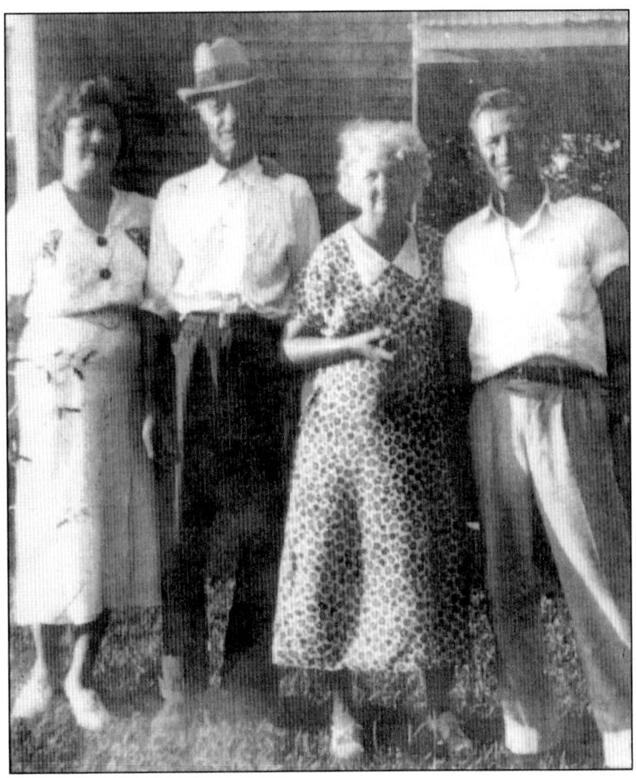

Shown here are Ruby, Willie, Tamelia, and George Fountain. Willie worked with Martin Fountain, Sr. in boatbuilding. When Martin moved to Biloxi, Willie remained at the boatyard on Fountain Beach. The last to build boats on the site was George Kelly in the 1950s. (Courtesy Deanna Comer.)

Many local men joined the armed forces in World War I, and most returned. Henry Fayard, pictured here, was one of the fortunate. He and Henry Boney, another veteran of the trenches, often shared tales of that war, but not with the public. (Courtesy Paul Fayard.)

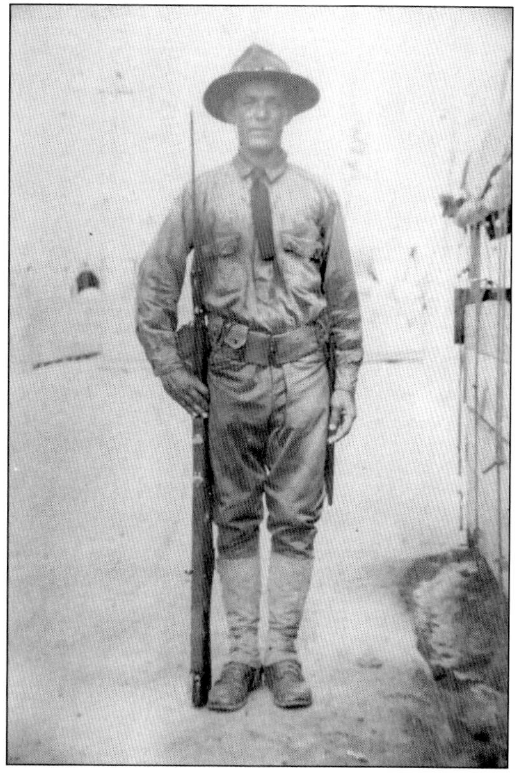

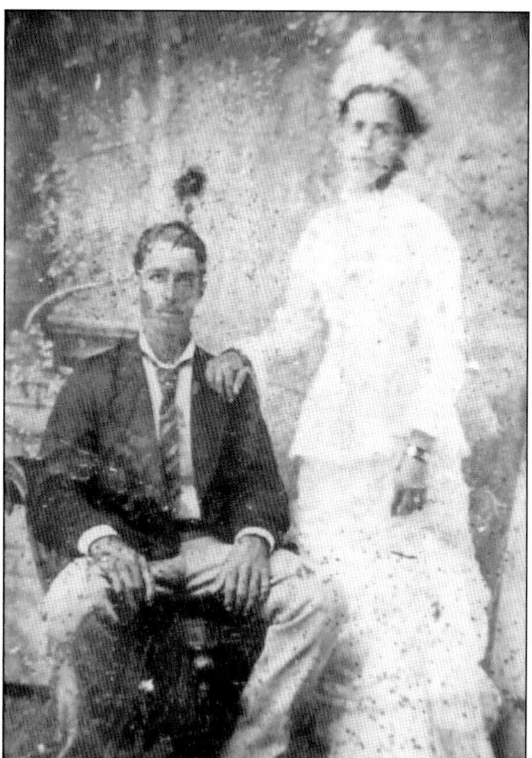

Joseph Boney and Rose Hartense (Seymour) pose after exchanging wedding vows in the 1880s. They acquired the "Boney strip," which center became Interstate 110 from the bay to the Big Ridge. Before the highway, their children inherited the strip. (Courtesy Paul Fayard.)

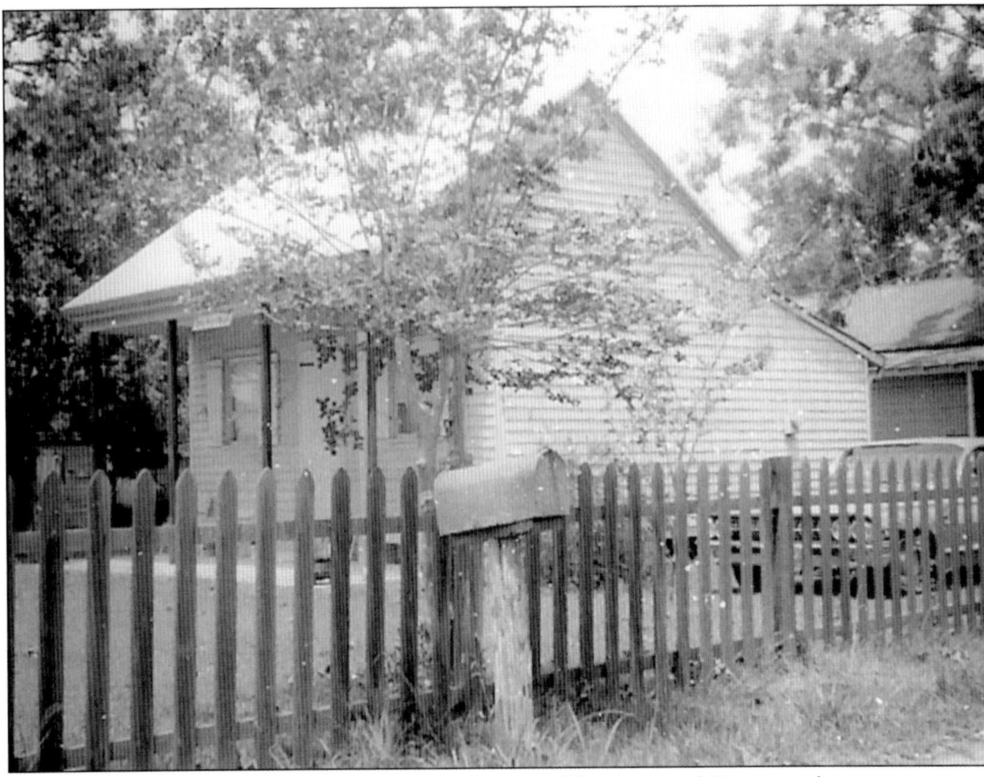

The Armond Cannette home on Reynoir (Brittany today) is pictured in 1958. Wife Emily was forever a pioneer woman: ankle-length dresses, bonnet, tobacco pipe, gardener, etc. He was a farmer and fisherman. The interior walls were plastered with pictures cut from magazines. (Photograph by author.)

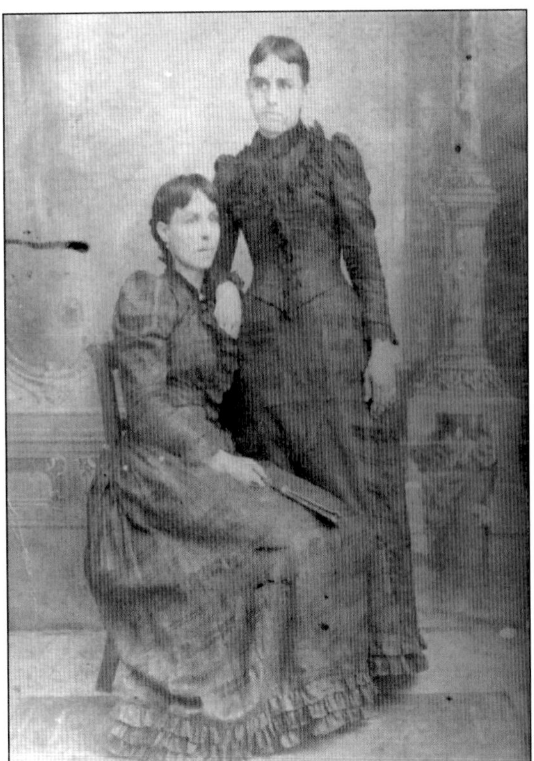

Ida Seymour (sitting) and Cecille Seymour Lepre are shown here in the late 1800s. Note the hair and dress styles of the period; sleeveless and shortened dresses were not yet proper. (Courtesy Paul Fayard.)

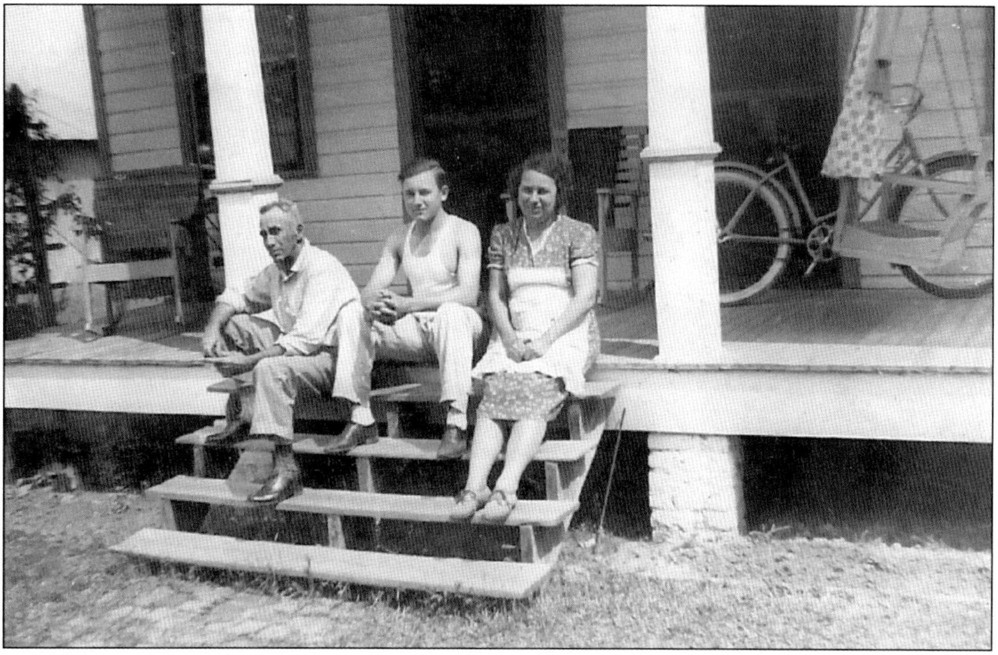

Napoleon, Buster, and Daisy Groue are descendants of Jean B. and Louisa (LaFontaine) L'Adner. Jean B. received a land grant (1793) in St. Martin from the Spanish government, which was confirmed by the United States in 1812. When his daughter married Louis Groue, he gave them a strip of the land near Langley Point. (Courtesy Betty Duggan.)

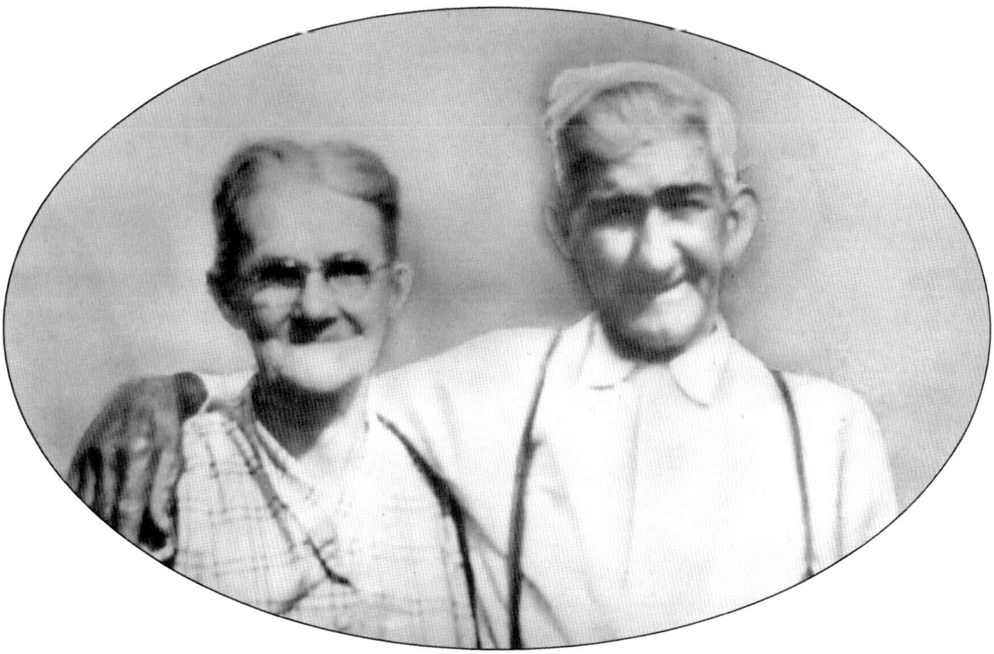

This photograph of Maggie (Quave) and Delmas "Bebe" Diaz was taken before World War II. He was recruited by a minor league baseball team as a pitcher, but with Maggie waiting for him in D'Iberville, he gave up the career and returned to her, never leaving again. (Courtesy Alice Mae Vogt.)

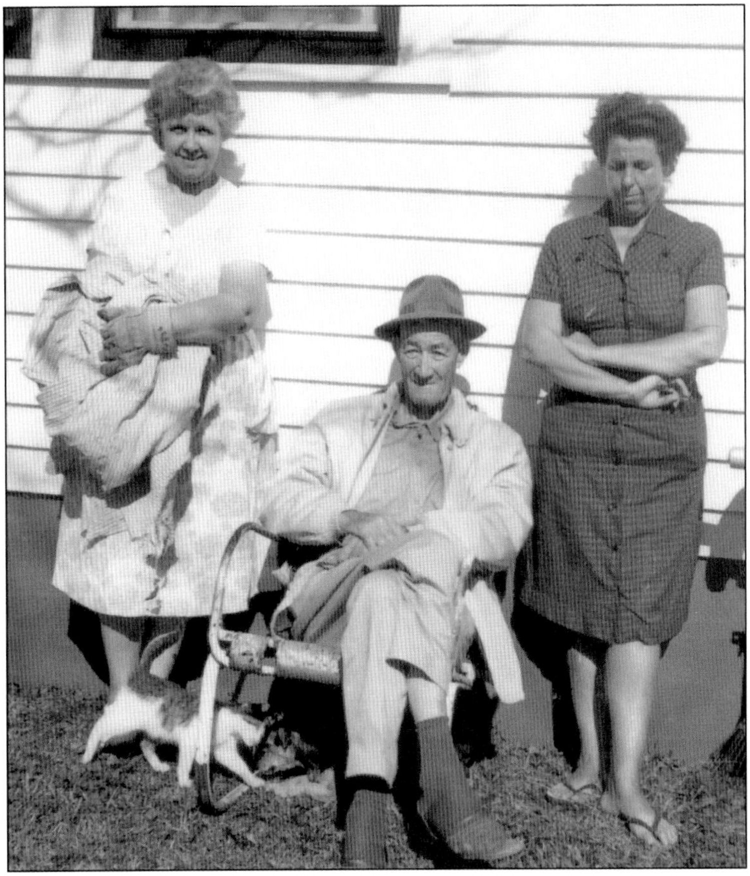

Henry King is with his daughters, Nellie Styes (left) and Irma "Tut" Beaugez (right), at his home on Boney Road in the 1950s. He married Cora Husley and worked at Dantzler's mill and the L&N Railroad. Later in life, he was best known for his artful carpentry work. (Photograph by author.)

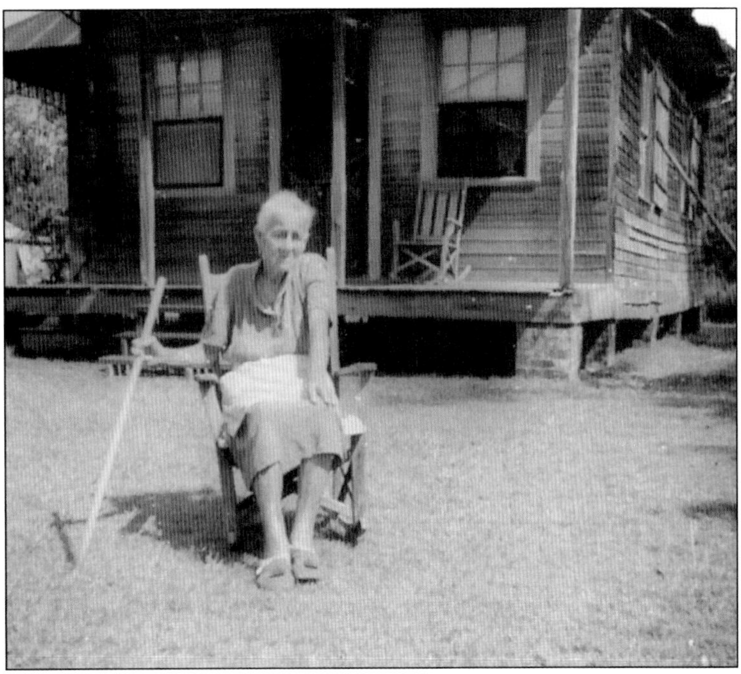

Leonide (Groue), wife of Rudolph Fayard, was "Aunt Loon" to everyone. She was one of the Groue's third generation here to claim her grandfathers Louis Groue and Francois LaFontaine were associated with pirates Patrick Scott and Jean Lafitte. (1968 photograph by author.)

Spanish Patriarch Jacques Batia and his wife, Marie Jeanne (LaFontaine), are seen around 1873. He owned two schooners used in transporting lumber and charcoal from the bay to New Orleans. (Courtesy Snooks Batia.)

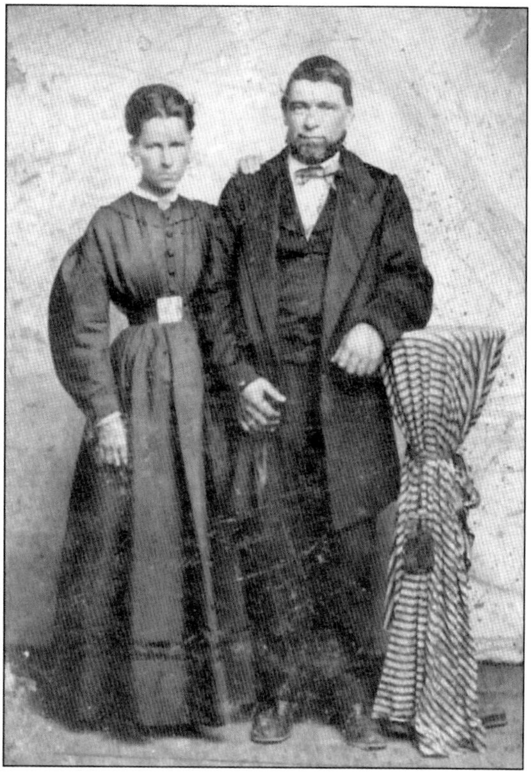

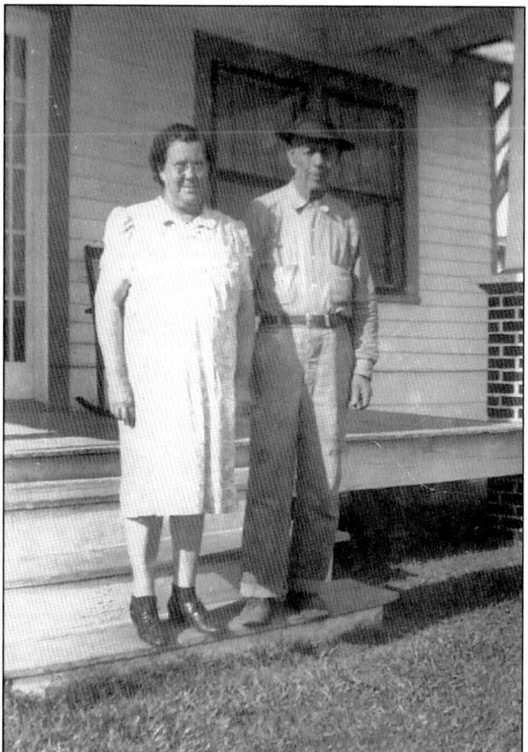

John and Cornelia (Fountain) Beaugez are shown in this c. 1950s photograph. Until his death, he traveled by bicycle and never missed a chance to dance. Like his four brothers, he spent his life as a fisherman and carpenter. She worked the local seafood factories as a picker. (Courtesy Lou Moore.)

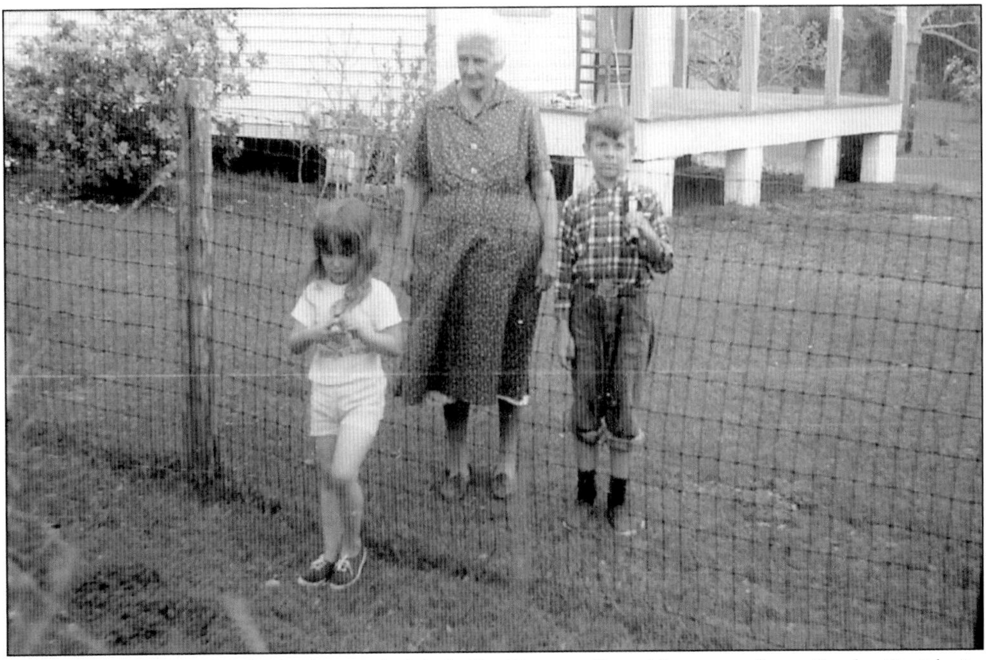

Millie Seymour (wife of John) is with Michelle Greenwell and her grandson, Rocky Smith, in 1967. They had a pecan orchard, persimmon trees, gardens, chicken yards, hog pens and dairy cows. In the woods, he jacked up his Model A, removed a wheel, and connected a belt to turn a portable saw blade. It worked! (Courtesy the author.)

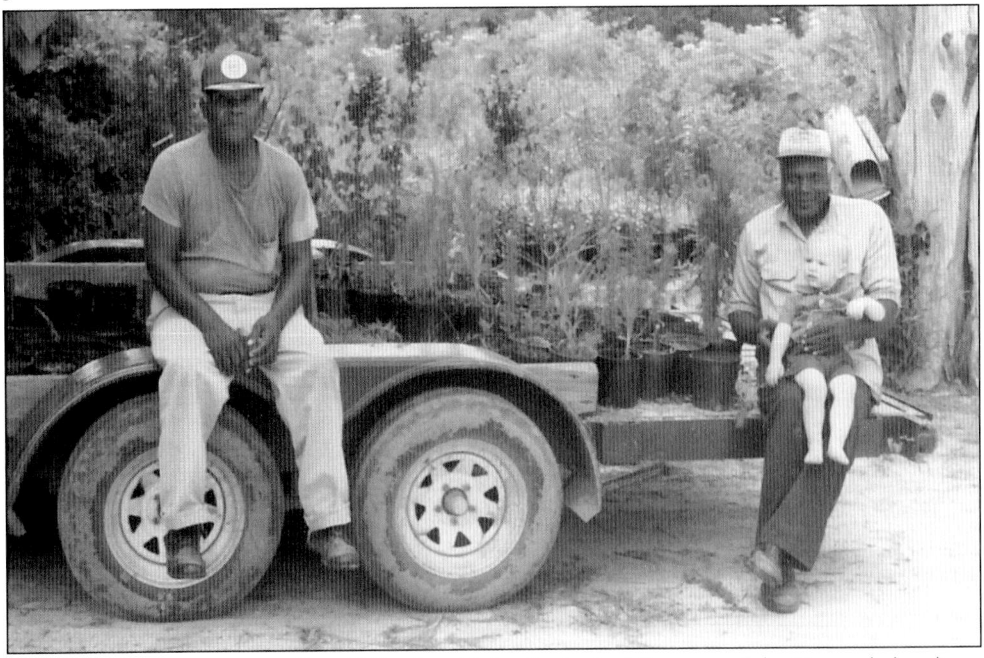

World War II Army veteran Ben Hillard and John Poole (holding one of the Kennedy boys) are on break. For years of faithful service with Brodie's Biloxi Nursery, both were given homes on the nursery, where they raised families. When James and Bob Brodie died, so did the nursery. (Photograph by author.)

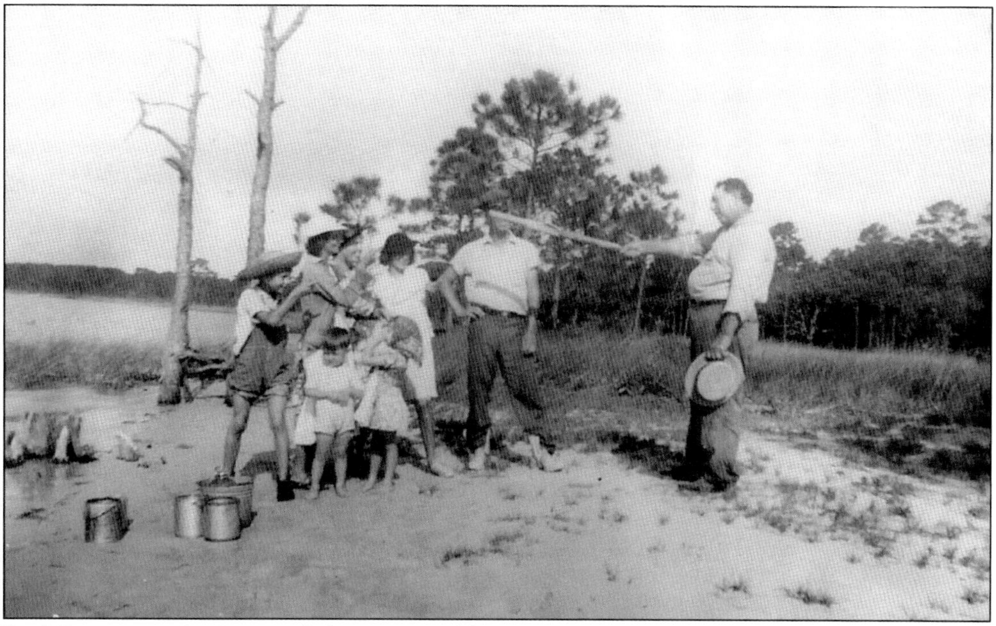

Paul Beaugez, a St. Martin fisherman and boat captain (including the *Dauntless* and *Mary Margaret*), is with his wife, children, and grandchildren at Reno Point on a berry-picking outing. The most popular wines in their time were from wild berries, usually fermented beneath a bed or in a closet. (Courtesy Tay Greenwell.)

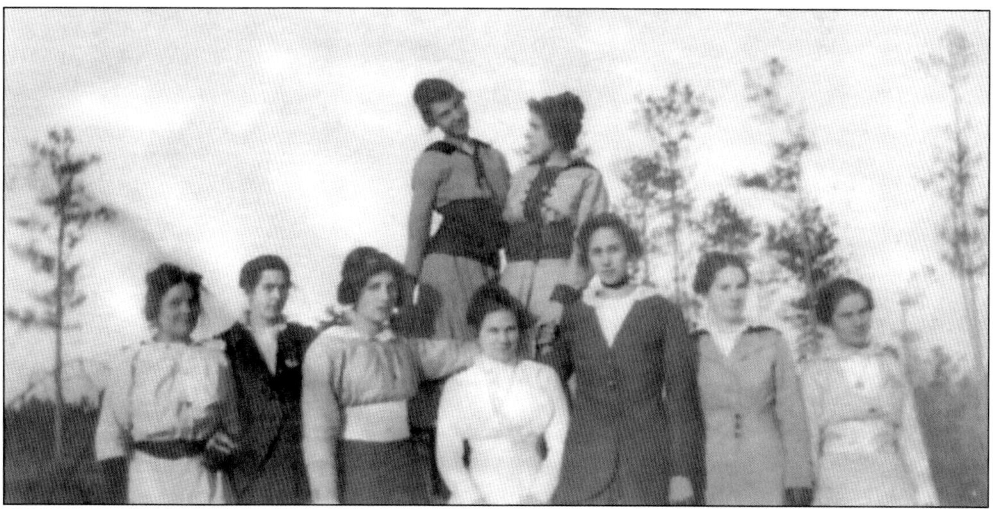

At a popular picnic site at Holly's Bluff on the Tchoutacabuffe around 1905 are, from left to right, (first row) Ada Langley, Agnes Boney, Barbara Seymour, Sophie Quave, Aline Seymour, Stella Quave, and Mamie Quave; (second row) Blanche Seal and Gladys Boney. (Courtesy Paul Fayard.)

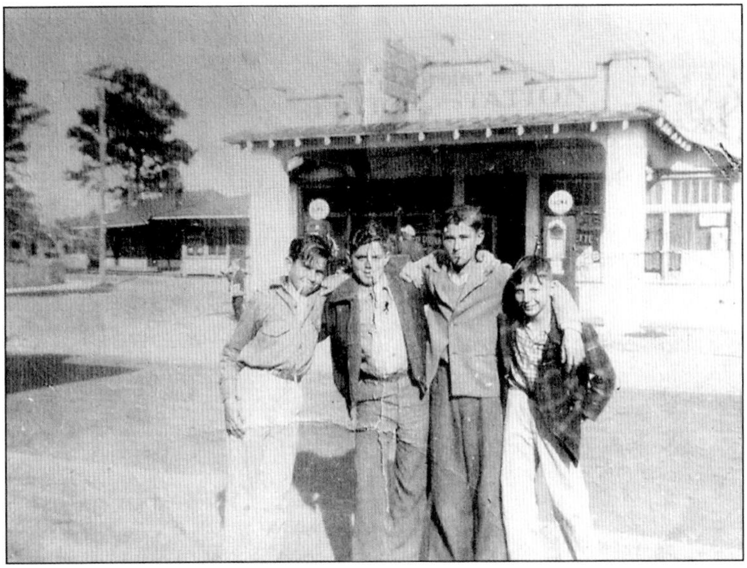

Billy Trochesset, Arnie Gollott, J.C. Boney, and Buck Bosarge are ganging up for a photograph in the Five Point intersection in the late 1940s. Lee's Five Point Service Station is in the background; the Moran's store and home, on the left, is where the first local silent movie was shown, before 1920. (Courtesy J.W. Fletcher.)

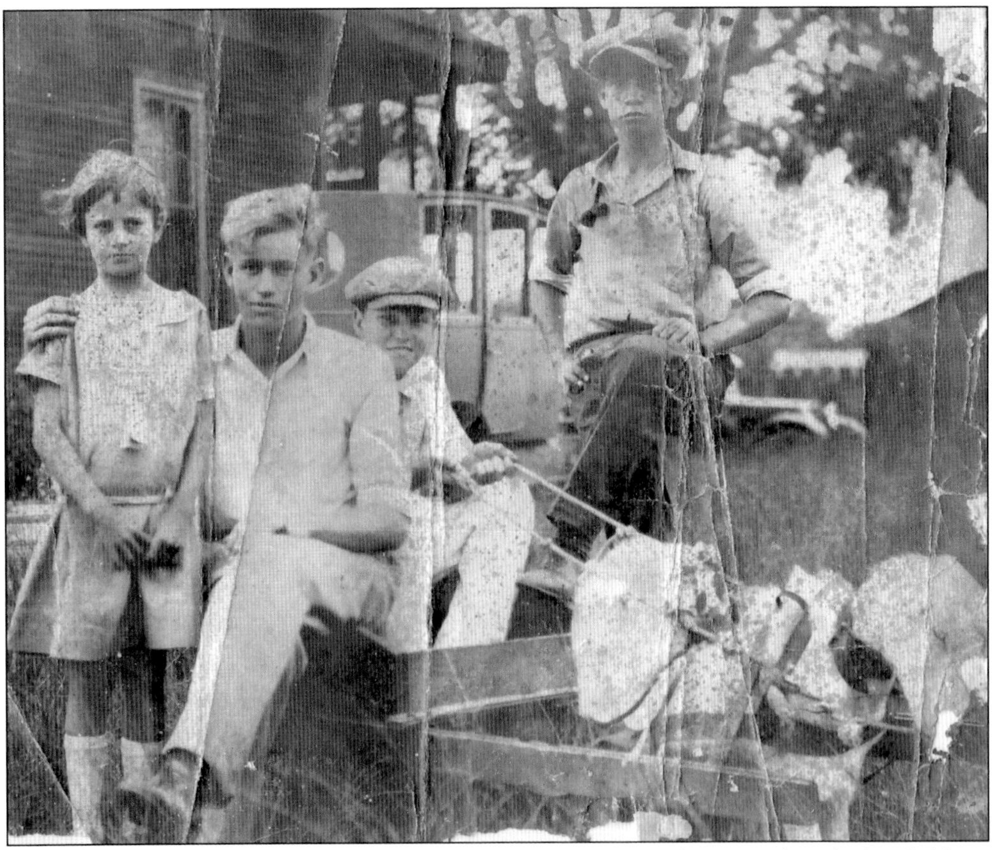

This photograph, in the Lickskillet neighbhorhood about 1900, does not identify the children. However, they are believed to be of the Husley and Krohn families. Even though the names are unknown, this scene with the goat-drawn wagon is worth sharing. (Courtesy Linda King Hasley.)

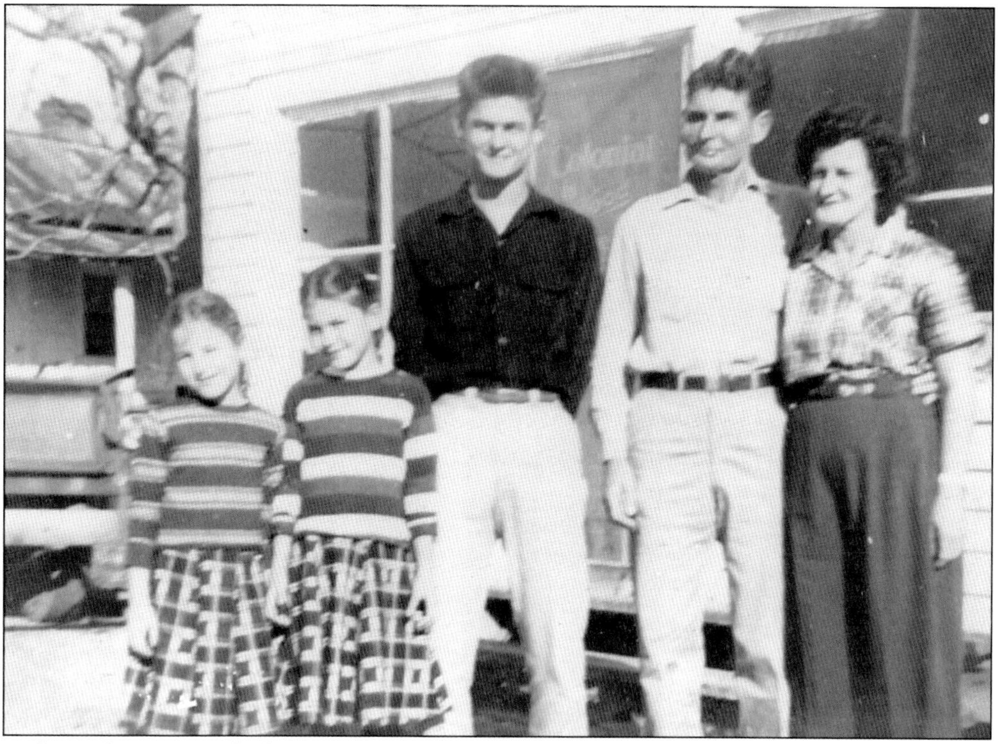

Willis and Dora Powell, shown with their children, Elaine, Yvonne, and Joseph, in 1953, owned and operated Dora's Grocery at the intersection of School House (today Quave Road) and Reynoir (today Brittany Avenue). Note the bread sign. (Courtesy Yvonne Battaya.)

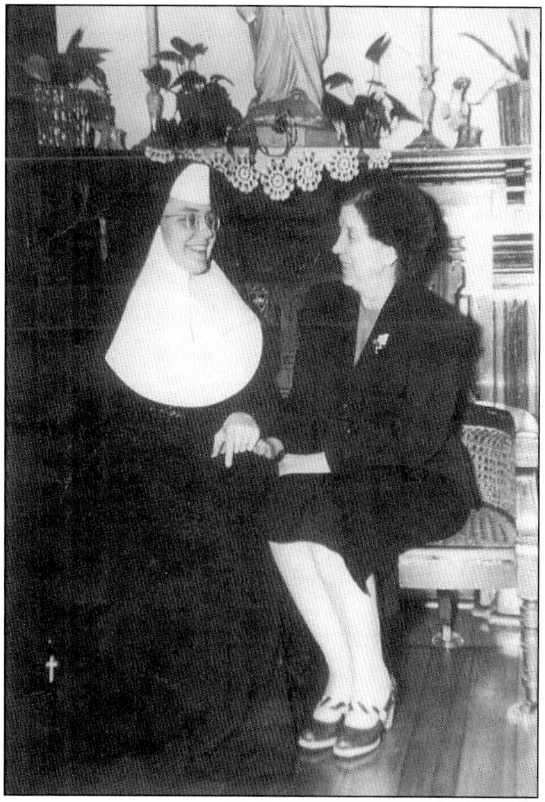

Sister Mary Owens taught at St. Theresa Parochial School in the 1950s. She and May Ibele often shared moments discussing school events. Sister Owens and Dale Greenwell (a ninth grader at DHS) organized the first track & field events at St. Theresa and the first football team north of the bay. (Courtesy Paul Fayard.)

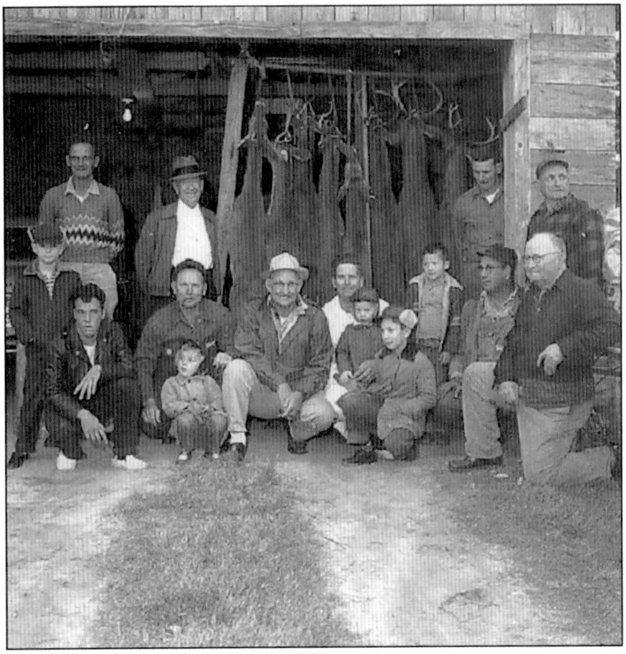

After this hunt in the 1950s, the deer are hanging at Elvin "Slick" Bosarge's shed. Shown here from left to right are (first row) Jimmy Ladnier, unidentified, Frank Graham, Melvin Ramsey, R.J. Parker, Carl Parker, Robert Earl Parker, unidentified, Chester Cates, and Willie Quave; (second row) Avery Scarbrough, unidentified, Byron Ramsey, and Elmer Richards. (Courtesy Maxine Ramsey.)

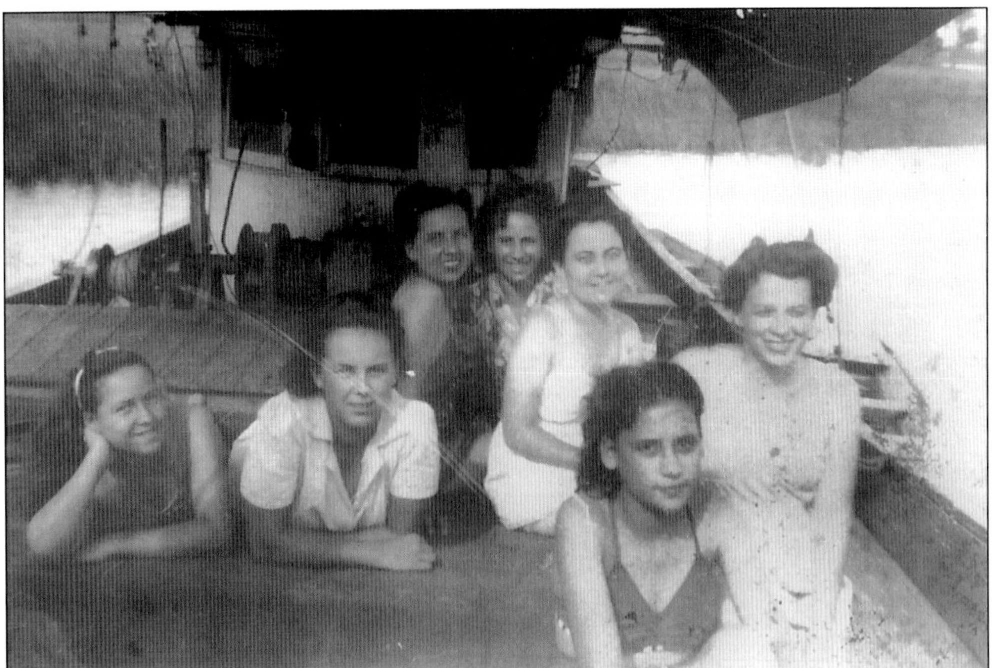

Boat outings have always been a popular form of socializing in the Biloxi Bay area. Finding passengers for a cruise was never a problem. Aboard the *Groue Brothers* in this 1940s photograph, are, from left to right, Catherine, Gloria, Doris, Beatrice, Bernice, Betty, and Mildred. (Courtesy Catherine Lawrence.)

Seven

Tour of Duty

There is more to life than just work. Traditions that developed on the north side of the bay required people to work long hours and work hard to keep up with, or perhaps a little ahead of, the basics in life. Sundays meant church, gumbo or chicken dinner, ball games on pastures, and sailing races on the bay. When time permitted, folks gathered at any excuse.

The first radio on the north side was on Fournier Road (Avenue today), pieced together by Fred Fournier in 1922. Phonographs had been around awhile and a single-song record cost a day's income for many, but people had music and dances in stores, theaters, lawns, and private homes on special and non-special occasions. The first known public dances were at Santa Cruz's store and in private yards. The music was usually from guitar, harmonica, and violin—or just one of the three, and there were bands playing jazz, country, blues, and gospel.

Through the 1930s to 1960s, Peter "Fiddlin' Pete" Lepre and his musical group entertained crowds of all sizes, in public places or in homes, and on any occasion, especially holidays.

As populations grew and schools developed, so did entertainment. Eventually, there were community houses and schools with auditoriums. Musical bands entertained the young and the old, who often came from afar, especially for ticketed dances or just performances, such as the minstrels and womanless weddings, where the bride was a man dressed for the part.

By the 1920s, silent movies were experienced by quiet audiences in dance halls, storerooms, or on lawns where electricity was available. The piano player had to watch the screen carefully, so as to adjust the rhythm with the silent action. The first silent film was shown on the outside wall of Peter Quave's store. The next was at Alphonse Seymour's café on Little Island adjoining the 1901 wooden bridge. The next, by Alphonse, was at Matt Moran's store at Five Point. In 1937, the first "talkie" played at the Dixie, a dance hall lined with benches. It was later converted to a theater with rows of seats. It was renamed the Star Theater. C.F. Gollott leased the theater until it closed when the town moved northward. There were no more movies on the north side until the 18-screen Grand Cinema opened north of I-10 at the turn of the century.

In the early 1900s, minstrels became popular. Whites acted all parts. These were comical presentations. Dewey Lawrence, Octave Borries, and Bud Patronas loved to blacken their faces.

Sports also evolved as schools and student bodies grew. School rivalries were inevitable. Basketball and baseball were at first the most popular. Football arrived in the 1950s. School buses, which replaced horses and wagons the generation before, made team trips possible. Meanwhile, the world was at war!

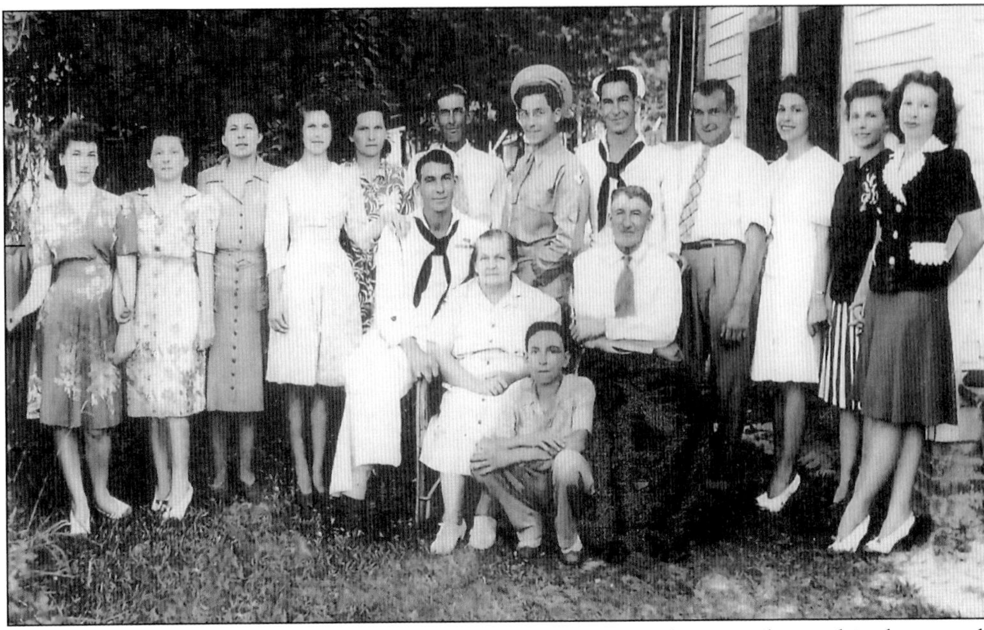

During World War II, while four of the seven sons in service were home on leave, this photograph of the Phillip and Edith Trochessett family included Jerry in front of mom and dad; Jack at his mother's right; and, from left to right in rear, Carman, Dolores, Irene, two unidentified, Oswald, George, Will, Seymour, Melvina, Ruby, and Beatrice. (Courtesy Mrs. Mark Caillavet.)

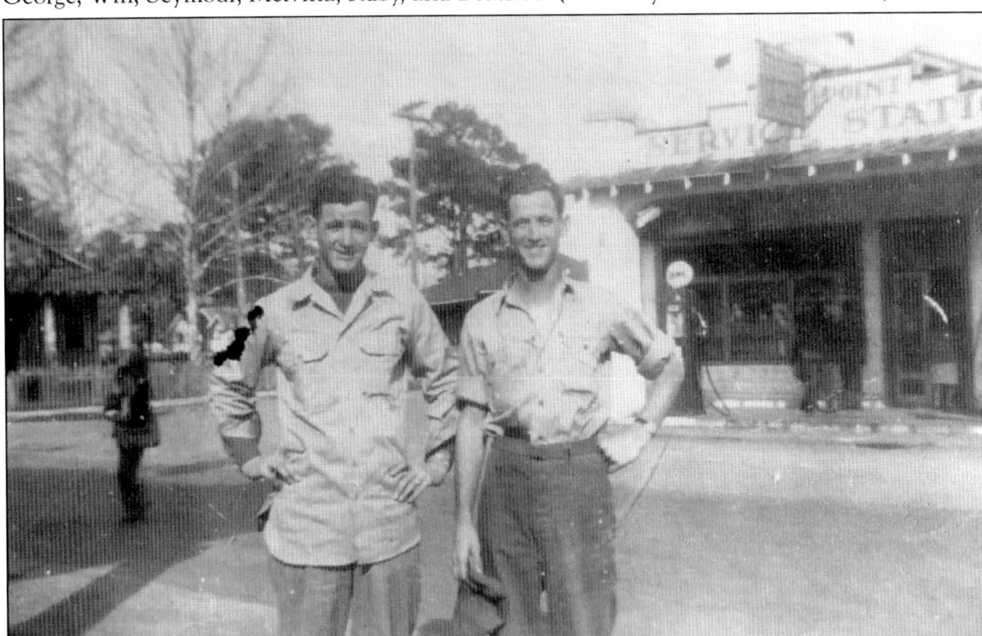

Les Barnett (left) and his brother, Hilton, share military leave. The Five Point Service Station and Mat Moran's home and store are in the background. Young men and women from D'Iberville and St. Martin joined the different branches of service in World War II. Many wives worked in the factories to help their families survive. (Courtesy J.W. Fletcher.)

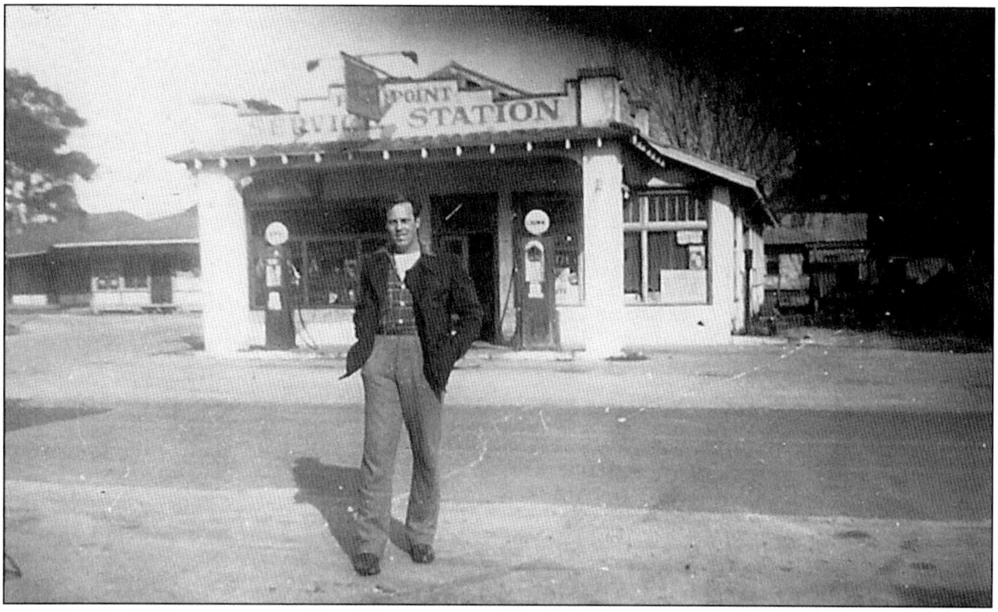

World War II Navy veteran Floyd Fountain is home on leave. Later, he served with the local National Guard in occupied Germany. Behind him is Five Point Service Station, opened in 1921 and owned and operated by Lee Seymour. In the 1950s, Carey Quave owned the station. A small postal kiosk was added at the north wall and managed by Alice Fletcher. (Courtesy J.W. Fletcher.)

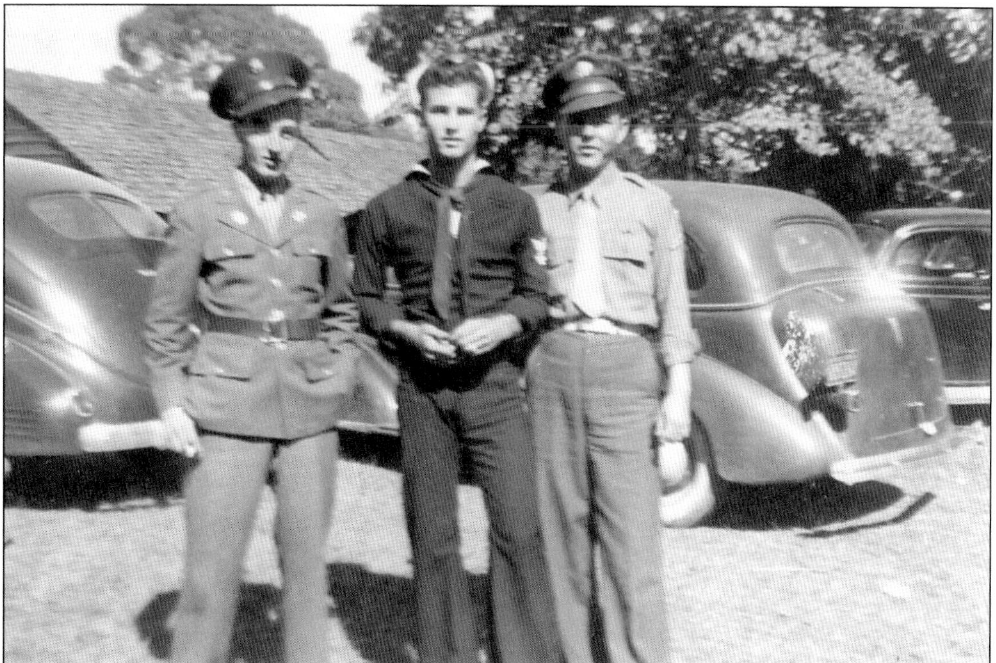

This group's last gathering before leaving for World War II included, from left to right, R.C. McMillian, Durell Quave, and Lamar Bond. All three returned. R.C.'s brother, Warren, lost his life in southern France. (Courtesy J.W. Fletcher.)

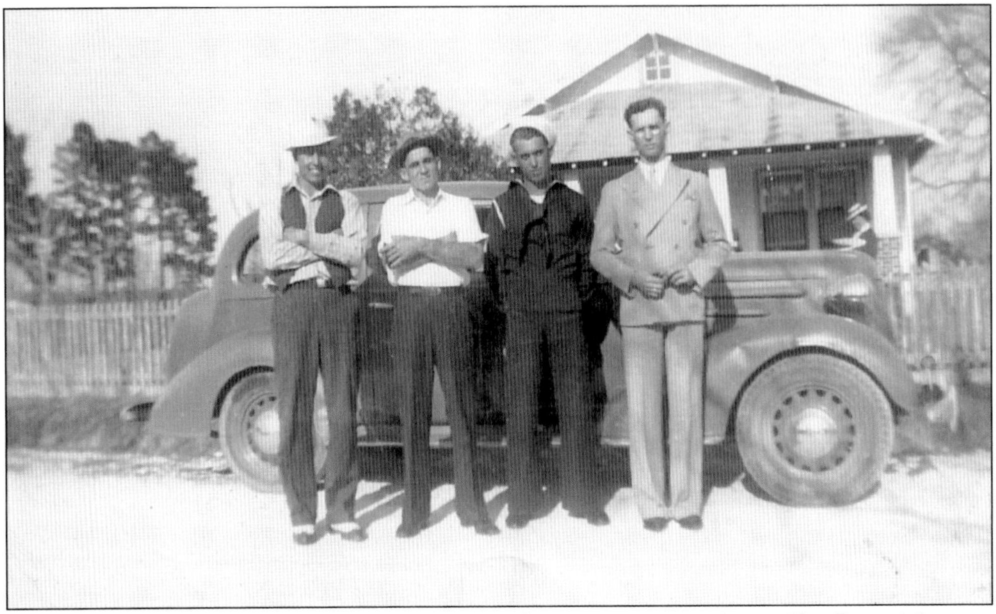

Warren Boney, Davis Fayard, and Maurice and Walter Beaugez are in front of Joe Boney's home a month before Pearl Harbor. Warren went to the Pacific and Walter to Normandy. Maurice stayed stateside because of poor eyesight. Davis, with four children, remained behind to build ships at Westergard and Higgins for the Navy. (Courtesy Tay Greenwell.)

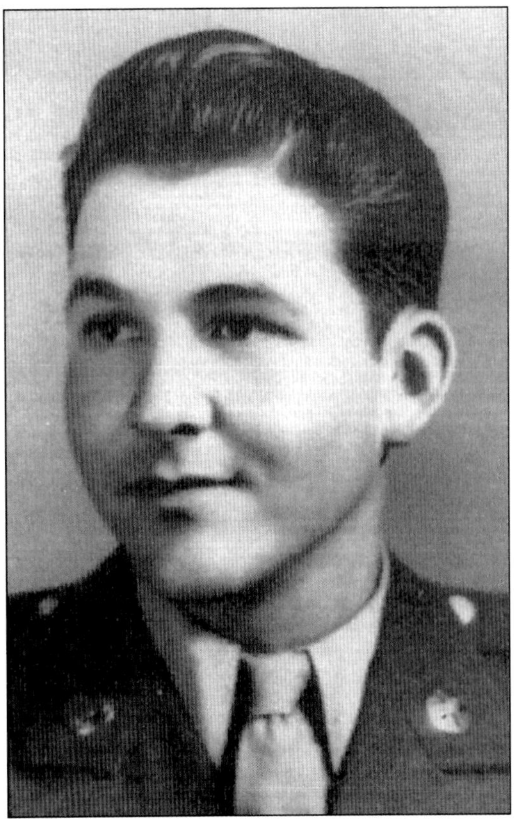

US Army veteran of World War II Vernon Santa Cruz was involved in the invasion of Okinawa in April 1945. During the invasion, splinters from gunfire stabbed his face, then a mortar round took out a knee. On a stretcher lifting him, he hung over the side during a kamikaze raid. He married Shirley Seymour when he returned home. The family engaged in local businesses. (Courtesy Shirley Santa Cruz.)

Navy commander Floyd "Bee" Hungerford (on left, with gunner) is shown after 26th World War II mission. He piloted dive-bombers from the decks of the *Saratoga* and *Yorktown*. His last bomb run was on Japan's flagship *Nagota* in Tokyo Bay in August 1945. (Courtesy Floyd Hungerford.)

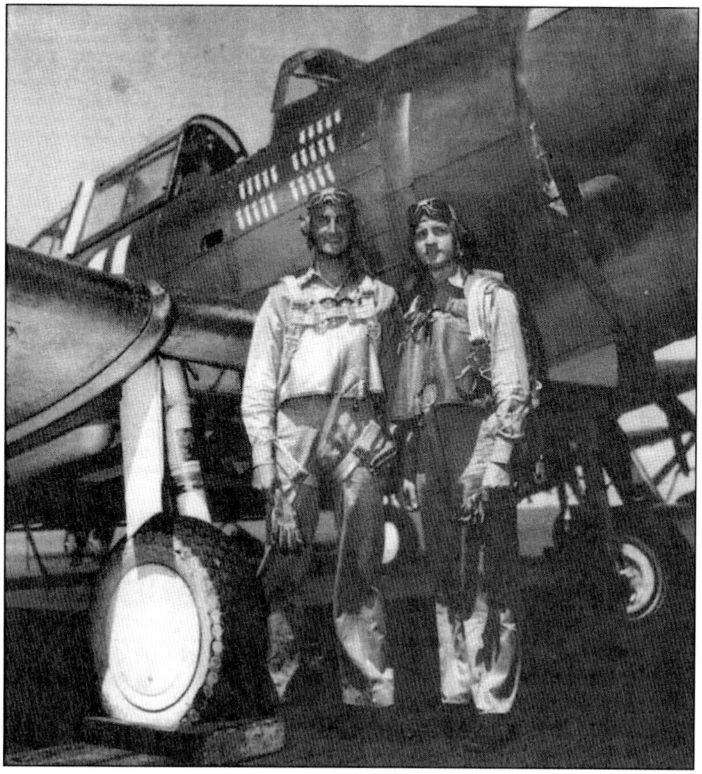

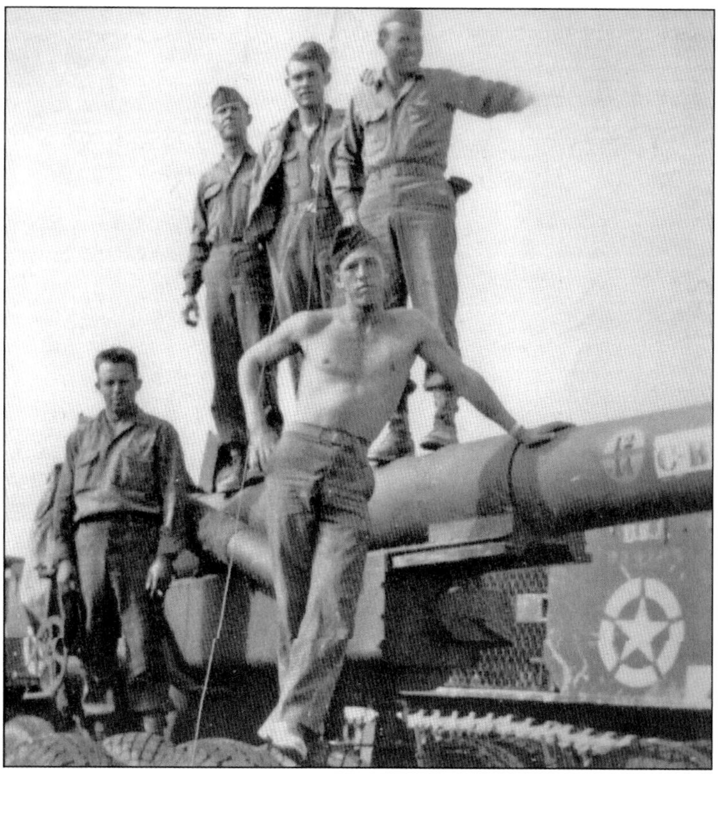

Near Monte Casino, Italy, in 1944, this 932nd Field Artillery Battery (formerly of the 114th Field Artillery, Mississippi National Guard) is fighting its way to Rome. These men from the bay area are Sgt. F.H. Letort, Hershell Robinson, Joseph Martinolich, Julius Seymour, and Opia Wilson. They were in combat 417 days without relief. (Courtesy F.H. Letort.)

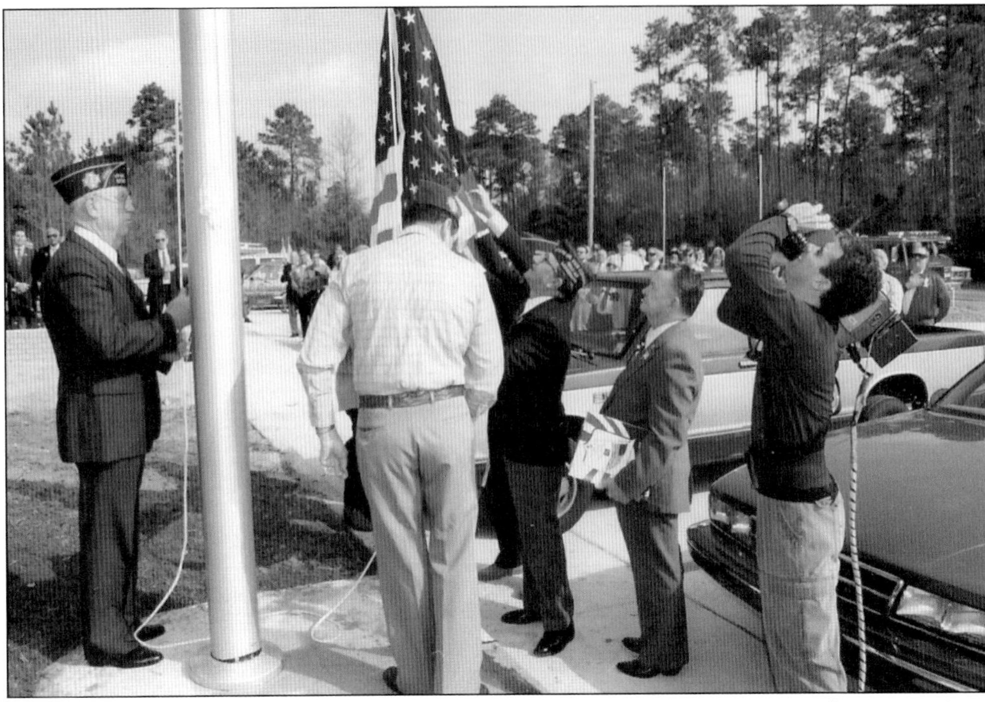

VFW officers Joe Roberts, Lorenzo Akins, and Wallace "Doc" Blanchard, as well as Mayor Jerry Lawrence, are opening the annual Veterans' Day ceremonies in 1995 at War Memorial Park near the tank and chopper. The solemn event memorializes men and women of all wars who suffered and died to keep Americans free. (Courtesy the City of D'Iberville.)

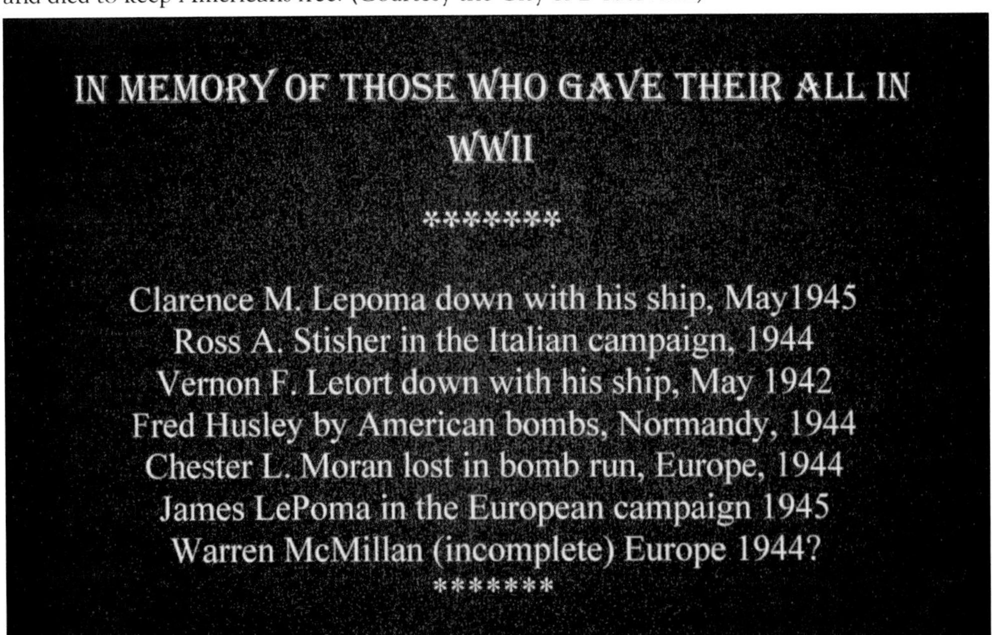

Shown here are known local boys who lost their lives in World War II. As information is gathered, this list might be enlarged. It does not include the many who lost limbs and blood on foreign soils—young men and women who returned with different views and minds. (Illustration by author.)

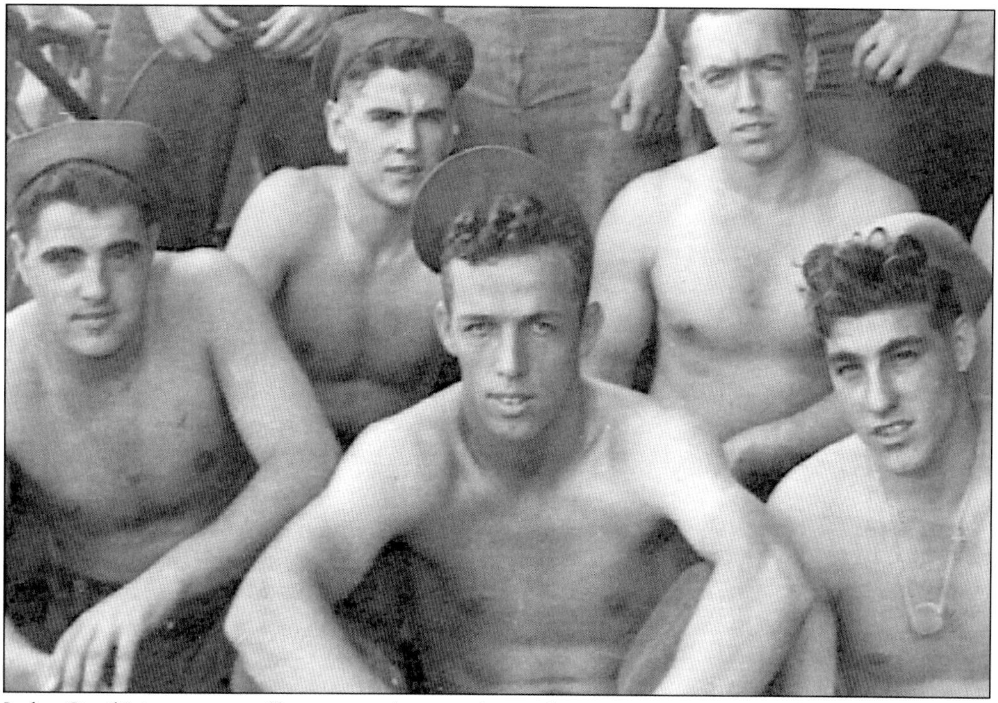

Judge Cecil Montgomery (front center) is seen here when a gunner's mate in the US Navy on the USS battleship *Colorado* before the invasion of Okinawa. In one of the 10 battles, a kamikaze plane hit the ship, killing 42 off Tinian. He served 20 years with United Gas Co. and 12 on the bench. He was a staunch opponent to Biloxi annexing land north of the bay. (Courtesy Cecil Montgomery.)

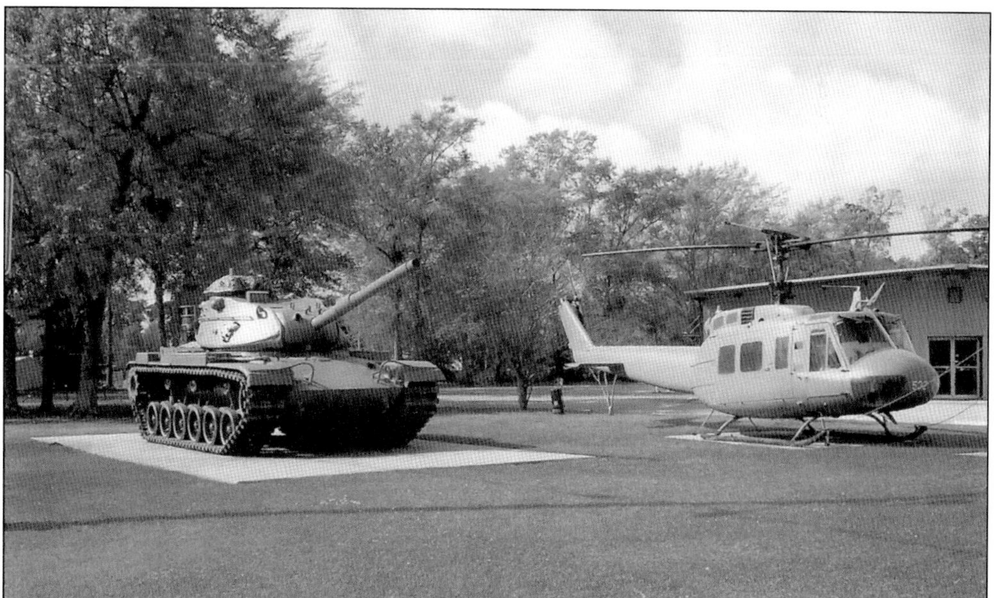

D'Iberville War Memorial's tank and chopper are stationed near the memorial flagpoles. These vehicles are veterans of war. There are many local vets who pause in deep thought when these two crafts are in view. They are one block south of D'Iberville City Hall. (Photograph by author.)

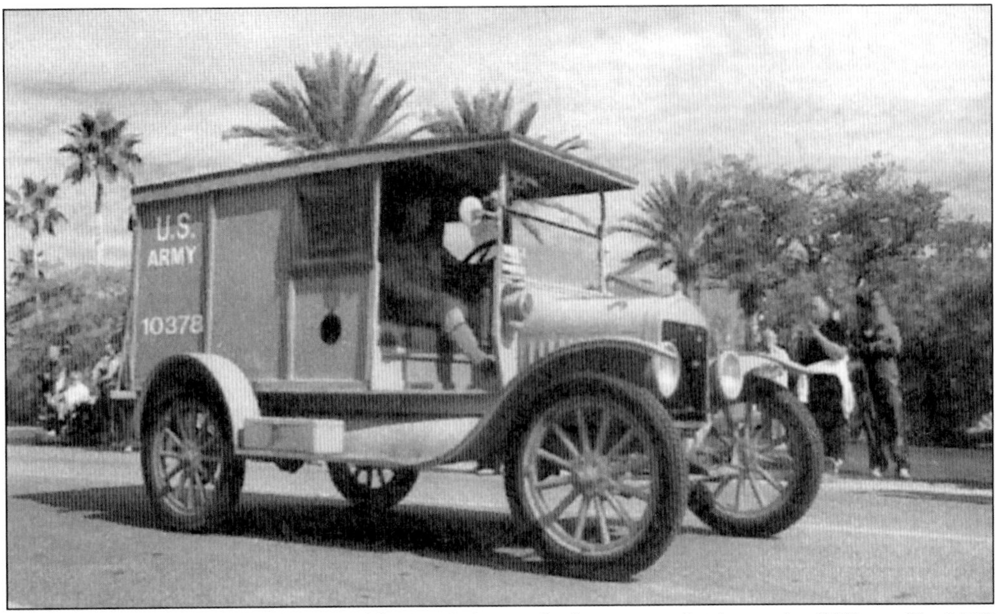

Veteran Jerry Dildy is in his World War I Army Ordinance vehicle in the D'Iberville 2012 Veterans Day Parade. Steve Thian, a disabled World War II submariner of the Pacific campaign, rode with him the year before, but passed away just before this event. The Gulf Coast Parade Association, organizers of this annual event, is rated among the best in the United States. (Courtesy Mike Mullins.)

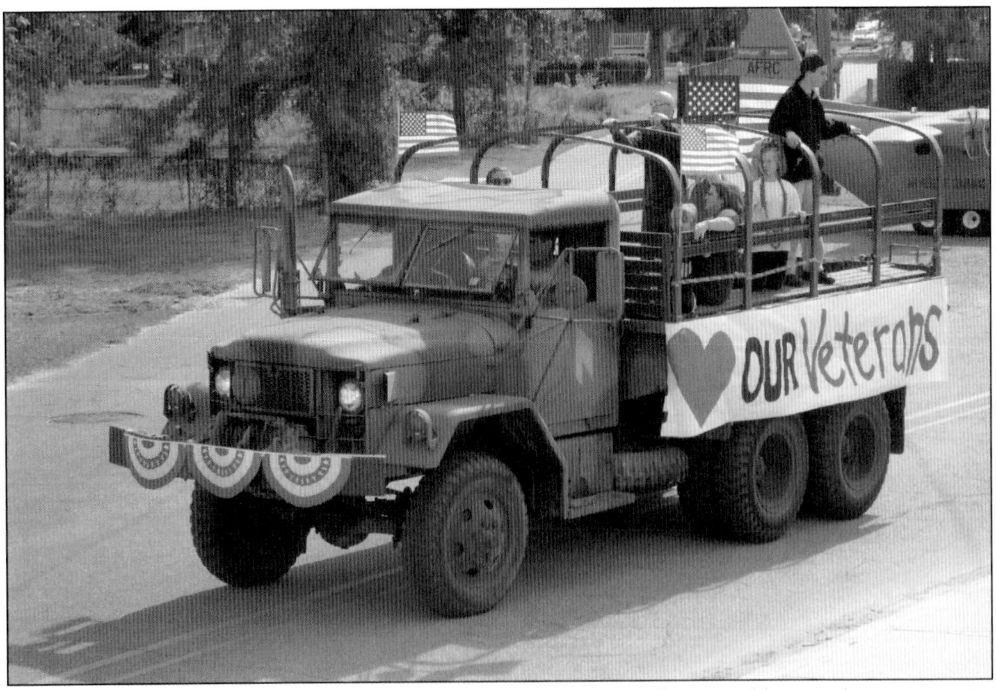

A "Deuce-and-a-half" Army truck, World War II vintage, moved more soldiers and equipment in wars than any vehicle yet. Often loaded with prisoners or victims of war, in this 2010 Veterans Parade it is loaded with vets of different wars. (Courtesy Mike Mullins.)

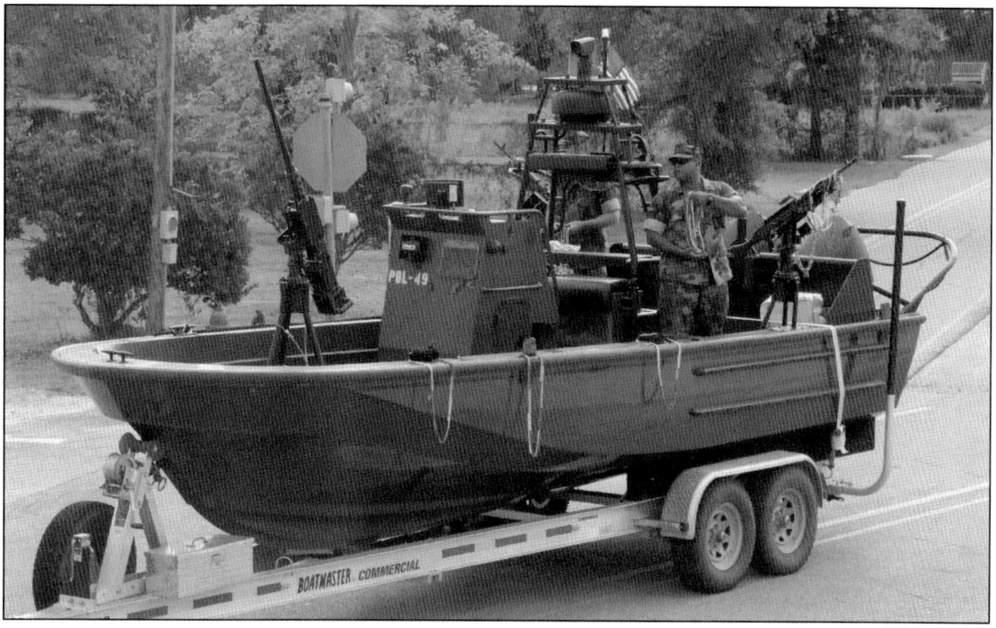

This US military special operations boat serves as surveillance, recon, and special team transportation craft used in clandestine operations. It is pictured here as a special attraction in the 2012 Gulf Coast Veterans Parade in D'Iberville. (Photograph by Mike Mullins.)

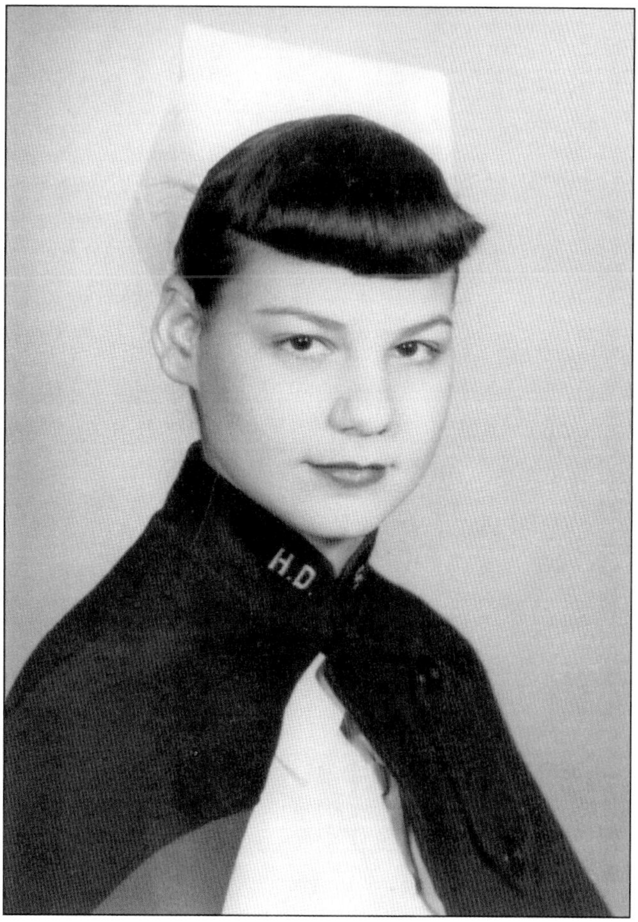

An Air Force nurse, Lt. Col. Annette Marie Beaugez of St. Martin is seen here as a graduate of nursing school. She served three tours in Vietnam. Her experiences in war and the effects she suffered from them changed her forever. (Courtesy Cheri Rowan.)

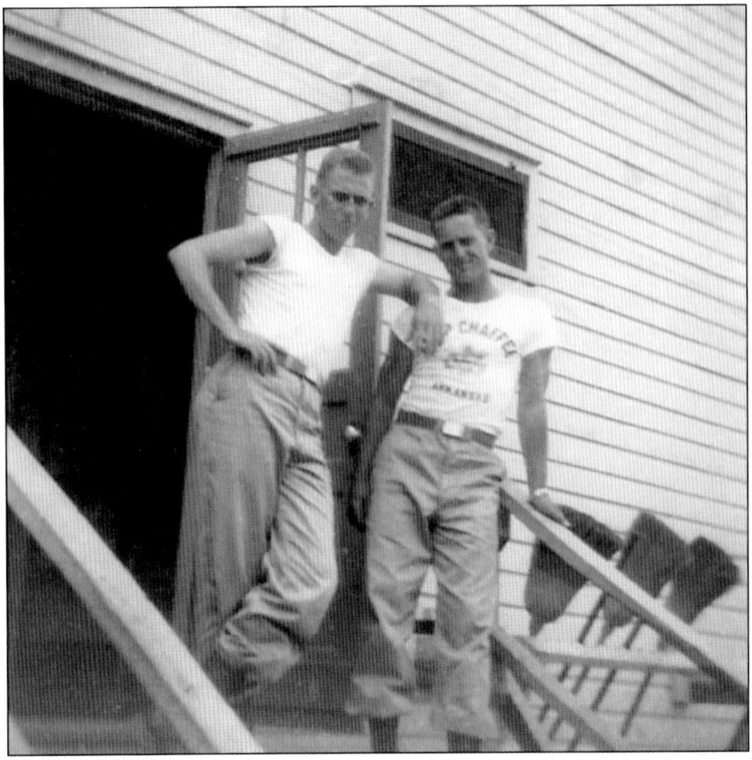

Eugene "Sonny" Hart and Dale Greenwell are at Army Basic in Camp Chaffee, Arkansas, in 1955. Not in the photograph but with them were Mike Fayard, Rolland Diaz, and Ira G. (Buck) Bosarge. Sonny, Mike, Rolland, and Dale later served in Vietnam; Buck served in Germany. (Photograph by author.)

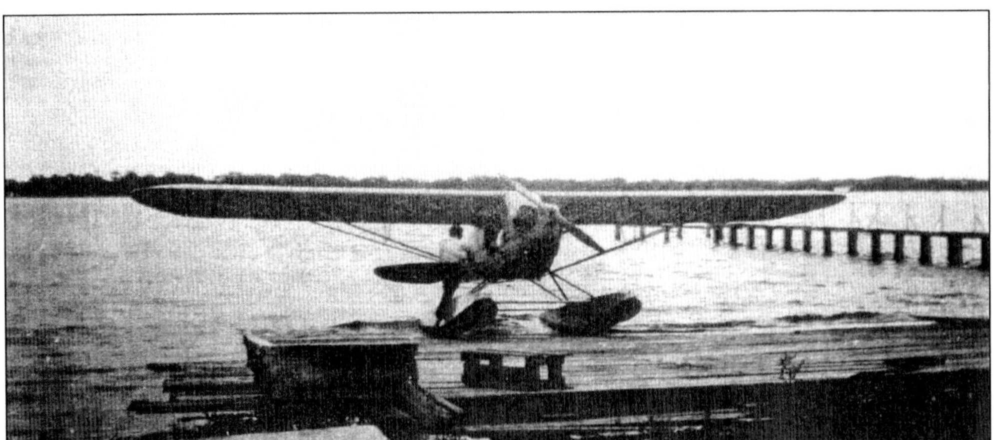

Pictured is one of three seaplanes owned by Ben Johnson's flying school on Fountain Beach in 1946. They were destroyed by the 1947 hurricane. Ben played an important role in designing B-29s that dropped atomic bombs on Japan. (Courtesy Ken Fountain.)

Eight

Faces in the Crowd

The three settlements along the north side of the bay did not have the same opportunities to evolve into mercantile centers that are necessary to create towns. In the beginning, everything for the stores arrived by boat or wagons from family farms or wholesalers. There was always at least a small company store at a large mill or a brickyard on water's edge. Point St. Martin was far from the bay channel, with an island blocking a direct route to Biloxi, making it neither easy nor quick.

The timber industry was doing well, and seafood shacks north of the bay had become seafood factories. Family sawmills and dairy farms were doing well. Vennie's mill and railroad were doing well. The conditions discussed in the fourth chapter had not yet evolved: turpentine and charcoal. Barges loaded with lumber routinely passed along the channel heading out of the bay for Ship Island, while empty ones were heading up the bay towards the river mills.

By coincidence, at the 19th century's end and when the 20th century was in the cradle, the village called Seymour (today's D'Iberville) watched a bridge under construction that was going to change their world forever. Pilings were driven into the bay from the ferry landing on the north side to the Old Portage Road landing on the south side. In 1901, a crowd gathered to listen to bands and political speeches on both sides as champagne celebrated the first vehicle crossing—followed by a very long parade of people from both sides of the bay. At last, waiting for ferries, while hoping they would show despite the wind and weather, had come to past. Before the end of the 19th century, the only bed & breakfast on the north side had closed. With the D'Iberville (toll) bridge, travelers had no problem getting to the fine hotels in Biloxi.

The only business area beyond the increasingly popular Ramsey Road (Central today) was the village of Vennie. The new roads being created for the new method of travel—motor vehicles—used the old wagon roads west towards Cedar Lake, Coalville, and Saucier; north to Ramsey Springs; and eastward to Ocean Springs. With the new bridge, the world had suddenly shrunk. Within a dozen years, motor vehicles were hauling wool, charcoal, turpentine, bricks, and seafood to markets, and Ramsey Road became the first business center in D'Iberville. It began at the convergence of the roads above at a place now called Five Point(s). From that intersection to the bridge grew the town.

When the wooden bridge was 25 years old, it was replaced by the new concrete one immediately adjacent to it. There were no tolls; traffic was unrestricted. The modern world of vehicles had arrived. The roadways leading to Five Point were now paved, where two service stations were fueling cars and cleaning windshields. The little line schools were replaced with 10-grade consolidated schools. The business area could be identified. Harvey and Santa Cruz stores and landings were no longer competing, and people wanted to go to "the Corner."

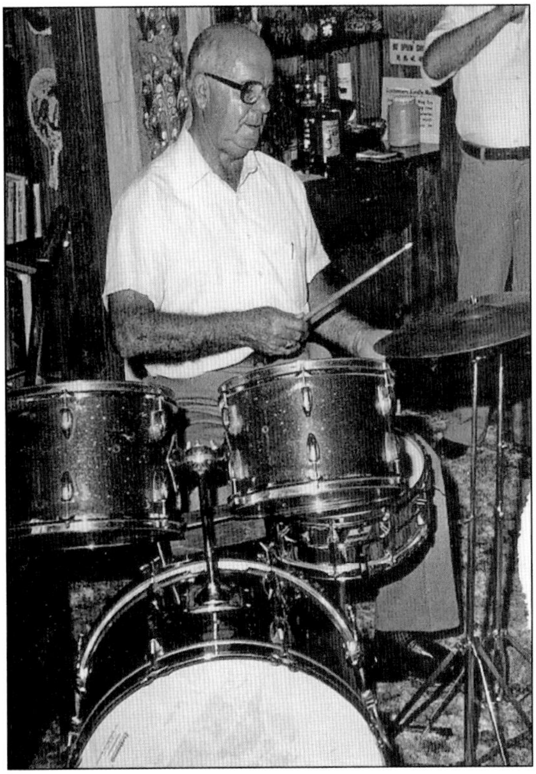

C.F. Gollott, owner and operator of C.F. Gollott & Son Seafood Co., had a band that performed at dances, carnival balls, and staged shows, especially womanless weddings, minstrels, and carnival balls. During the 1950s, he leased (from Madeline Quave) and managed the Star, D'Iberville's first movie theater. (Courtesy Alice Mae Voght.)

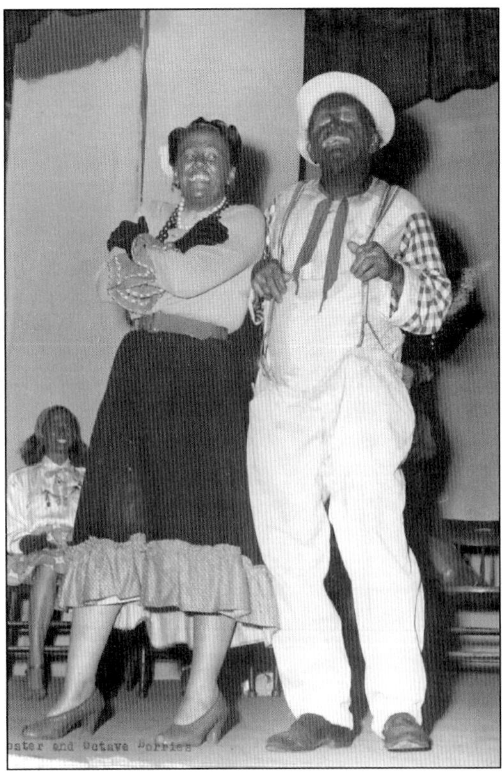

Mary Foster and Octave Borries are center stage in this photograph of a minstrel show. Before movies, minstrel shows were very popular, and they continued with packed houses into the 1950s. Regulars with the group were Bud Patronas, Johnny Tiblier (bass fiddle), C.F. Gollott (drums), and Ruth Collins (piano). (Courtesy Catherine Lawrence.)

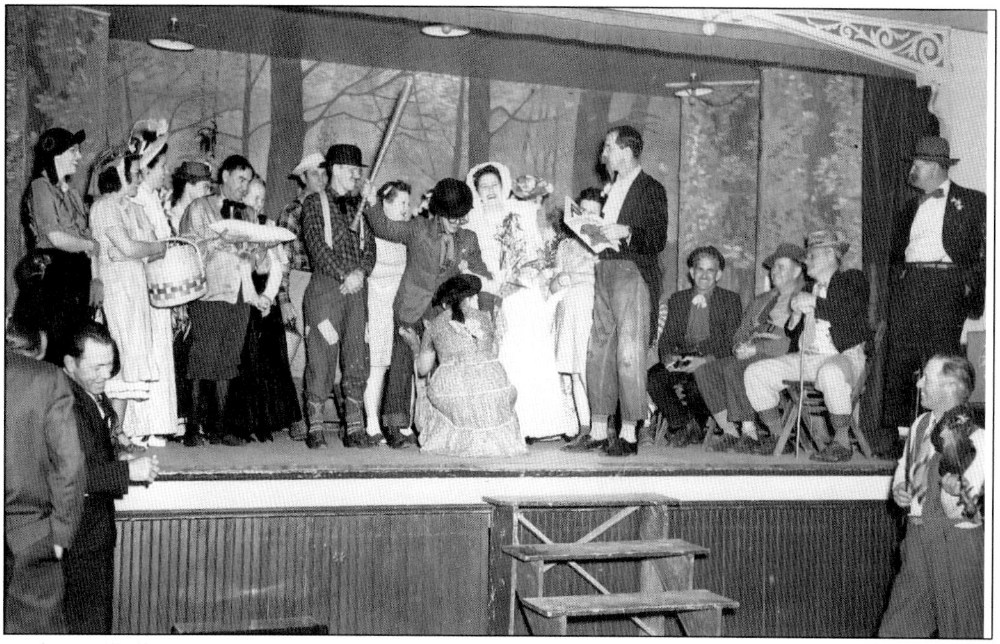

In this Hillbilly Shotgun Wedding, Borries and Lawrence are center stage. The group performed in school auditoriums and community houses across the coast, but more so in Biloxi and D'Iberville. All had other real jobs: Lawrence was on the board of supervisors for many years, and Gollott had C.F. Gollott & Son Seafood. (Courtesy Catherine Lawrence.)

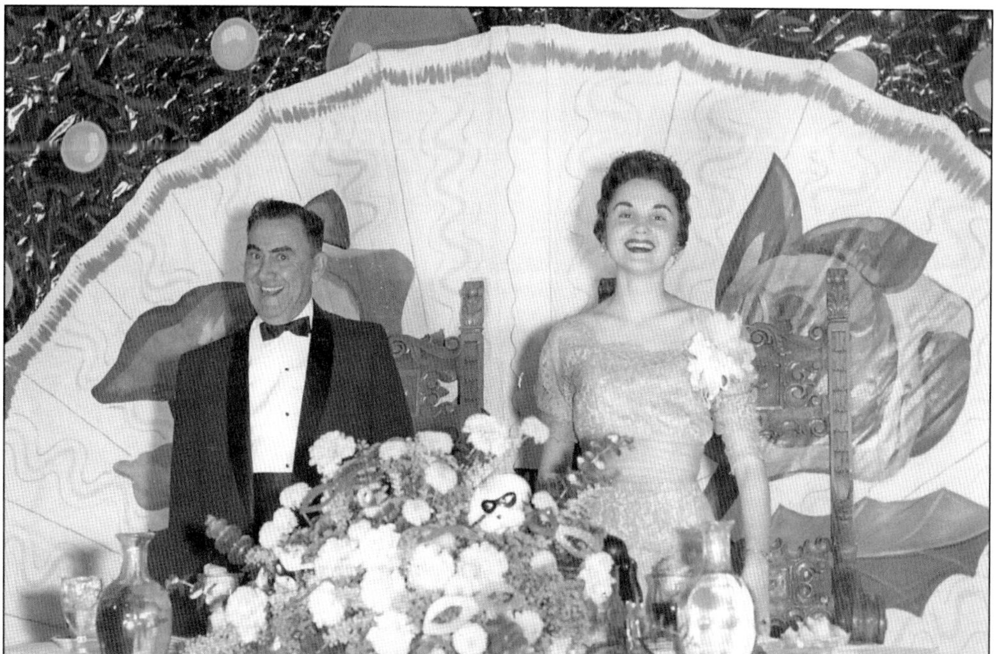

King Dewey Lawrence and Queen Johnetta Walker rule at this 1940s Gulf Coast Mardi Gras Parade and Carnival Ball. Dewey, a popular community leader, served on the county board of supervisors for decades. His son Jerry served as the first mayor of D'Iberville. (Courtesy Catherine Lawrence.)

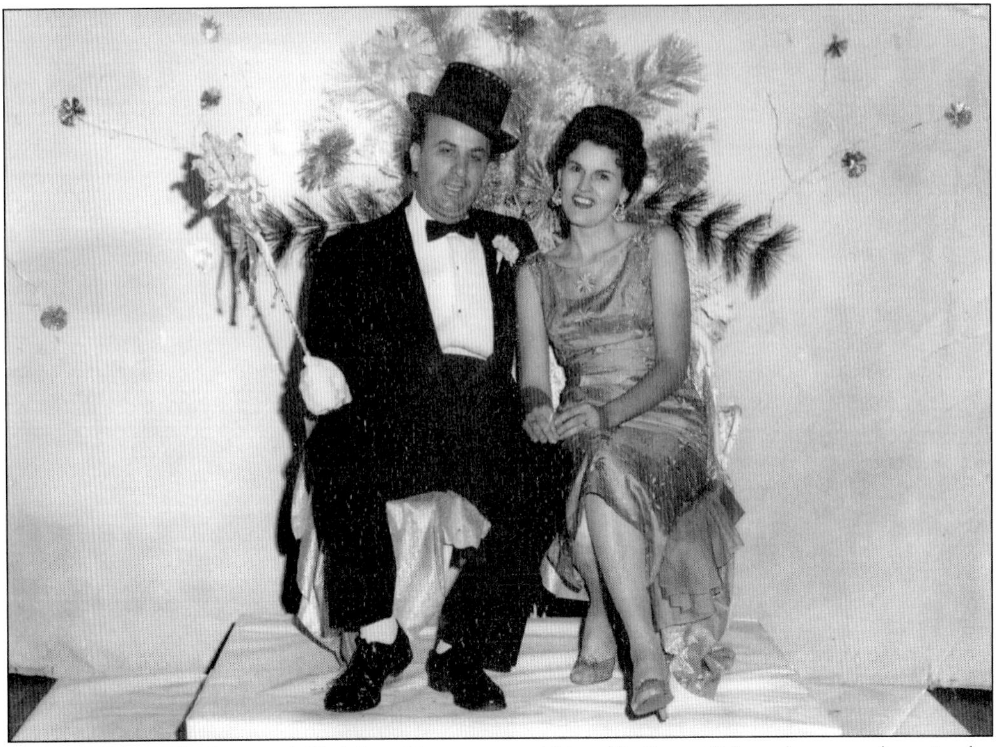

King of D'Iberville Carnival Club Lee Cannette and his wife, Patsy (Moran), are see here in the 1950s. Queen Mary Lawrence is not in this photograph. The ball was at the original community house (today's Rodriguez and Church intersection). (Courtesy Lee Cannette Sr.)

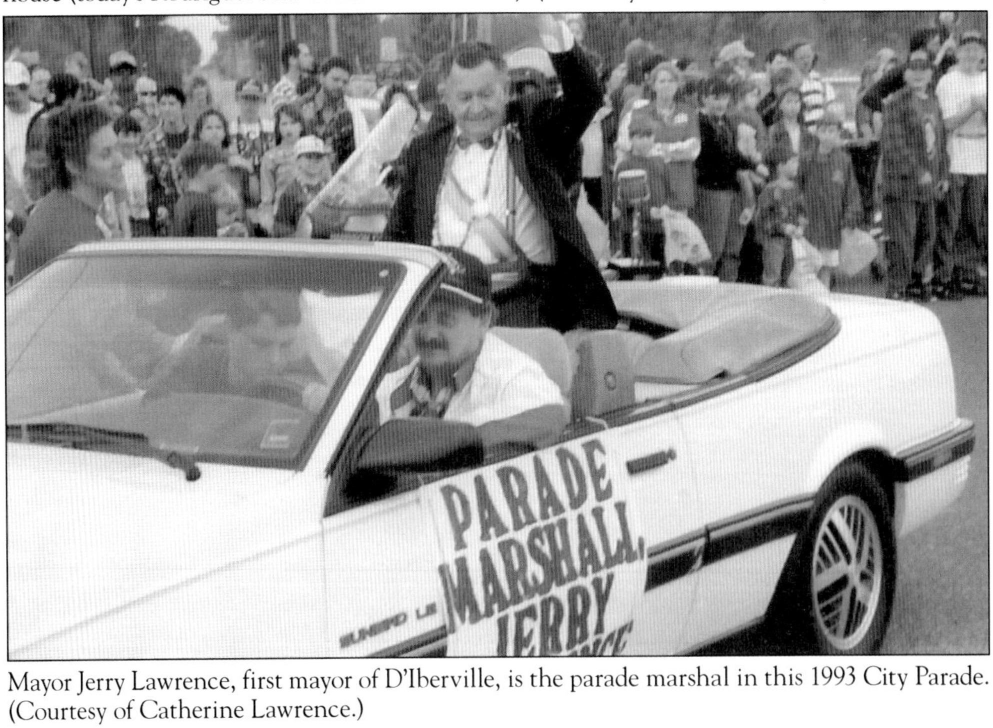

Mayor Jerry Lawrence, first mayor of D'Iberville, is the parade marshal in this 1993 City Parade. (Courtesy of Catherine Lawrence.)

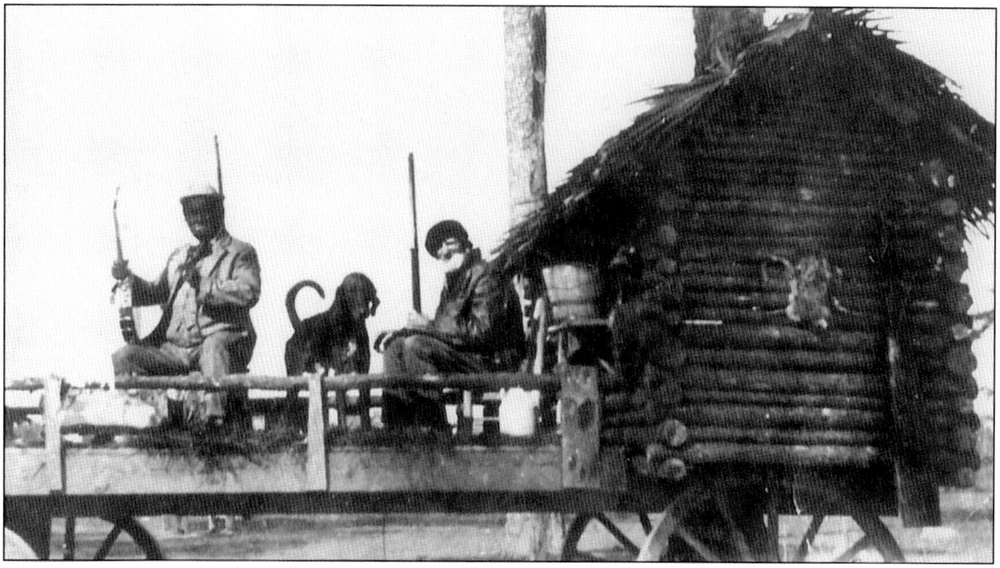

This horse-drawn wagon, decked with an old cabin, was another vehicle in the 1926 bridge dedication parade. This parade was the first to connect Biloxi and North Biloxi (as D'Iberville was called at the time). On that day, the Old Spanish Trail between the Pacific and Atlantic was completed. (Courtesy Ted Aycock.)

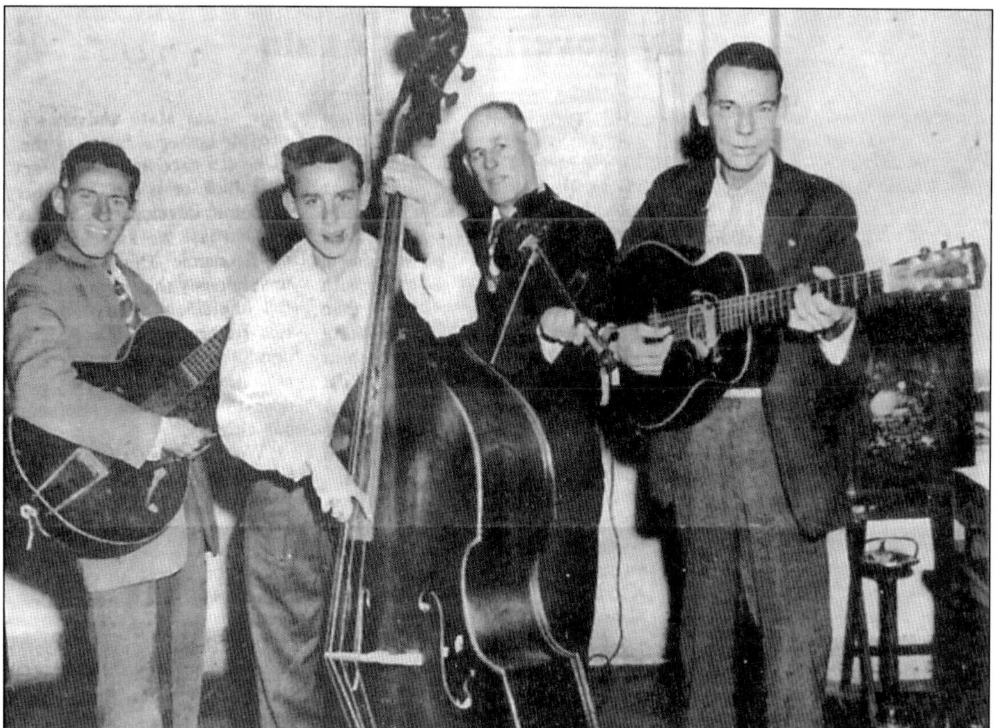

Peter "Fiddling Pete" Lepre Sr. was a popular musician in the bay area as early as the Great Depression. He and guitarist Jack Batia made traditional rounds to many homes during Christmas and other holidays. In this photograph are, from left to right, Robert Tiblier, Pete Jr., Pete Sr., and Edward "Bream" Batia. (Courtesy Peter Lepre Jr.)

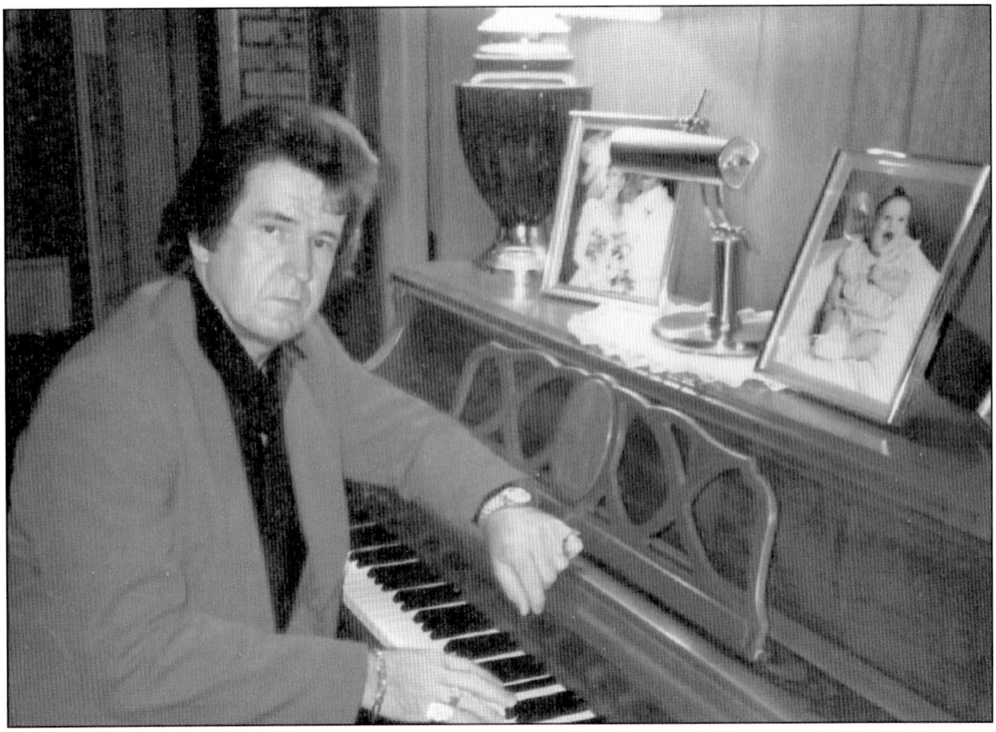

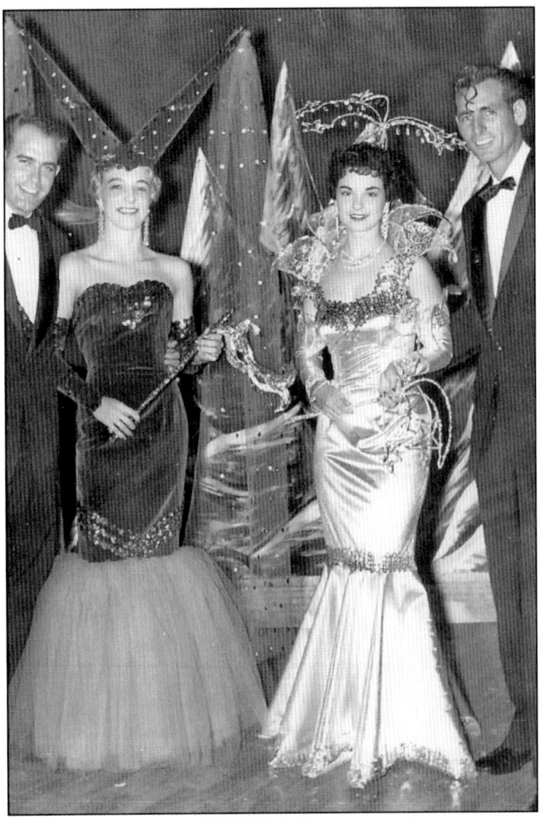

Rhythm and Blues was Jackie Holley's life. He grew up on his mom's piano without instruction. His lessons began by copying Fats Domino and Jerry Lee Lewis. He succeeded by age 14 and was getting paid to be in a trio-band at 15. After that, he spent years in Vegas and other circuits with many of the greats. He wrote songs and cut six records. (Courtesy Jack Holley.)

Queen Alice Mae Gollott reigns over a 1950s Bonne Vivante's Carnival Ball. With her are, from left to right, Edval Hughes, Pat Napier, and Clarence Cospalich. The group's membership is coast-wide and since the 1950s has been a favorite and glamorous association. (Courtesy Alice Mae Voght.)

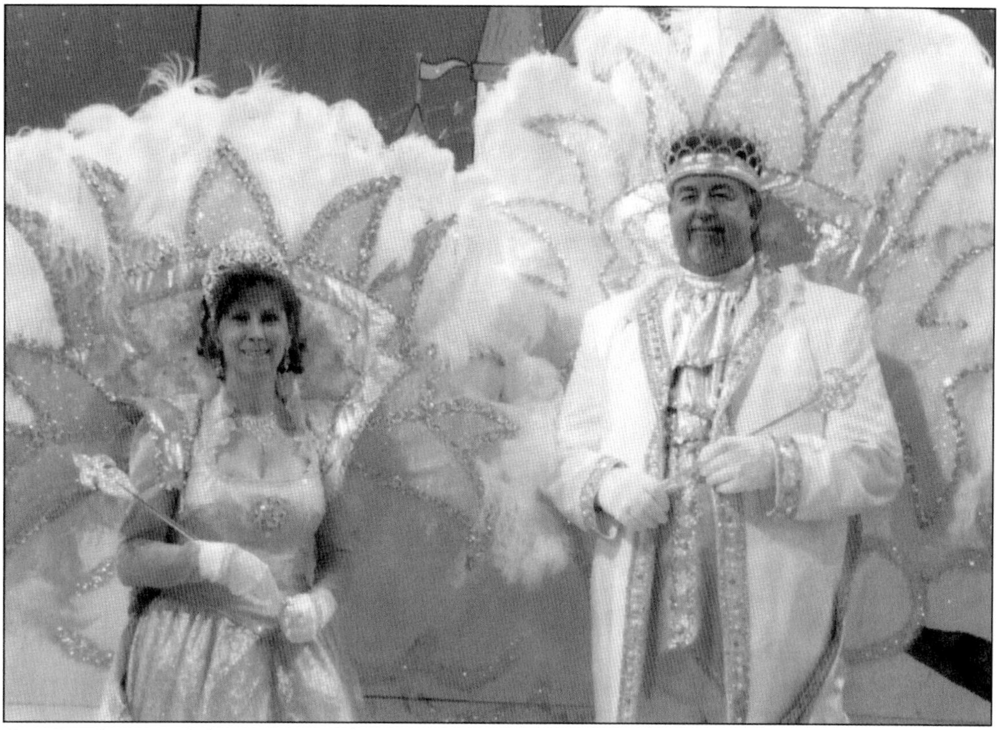

On the throne of the 2008 North Bay Mardi Gras Association are King Joe Ollier and (wife) Queen Deonne at Joppa Shrine Hall. Before Katrina, the carnival balls were at the old wooden community house (later replaced by one of concrete blocks) next to the old school and ballpark. (Courtesy the City of D'Iberville.)

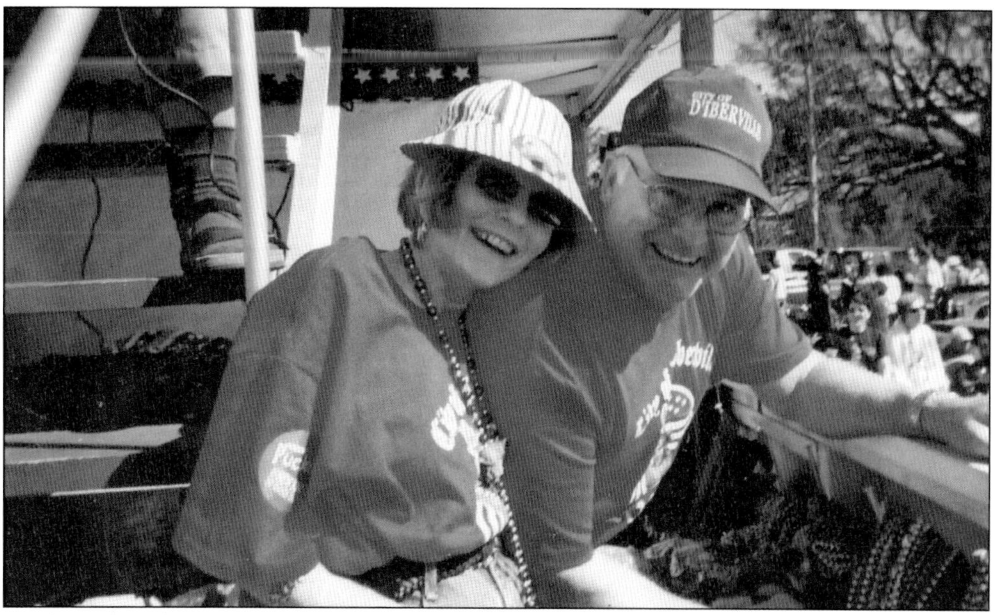

Cindy and Walter Freeman are pictured on a Mardi Gras float during the North Bay Mardi Gras Association Parade of 2004. "Throw me something Mister—and Mrs.!" (Courtesy Oliver Diaz Sr.)

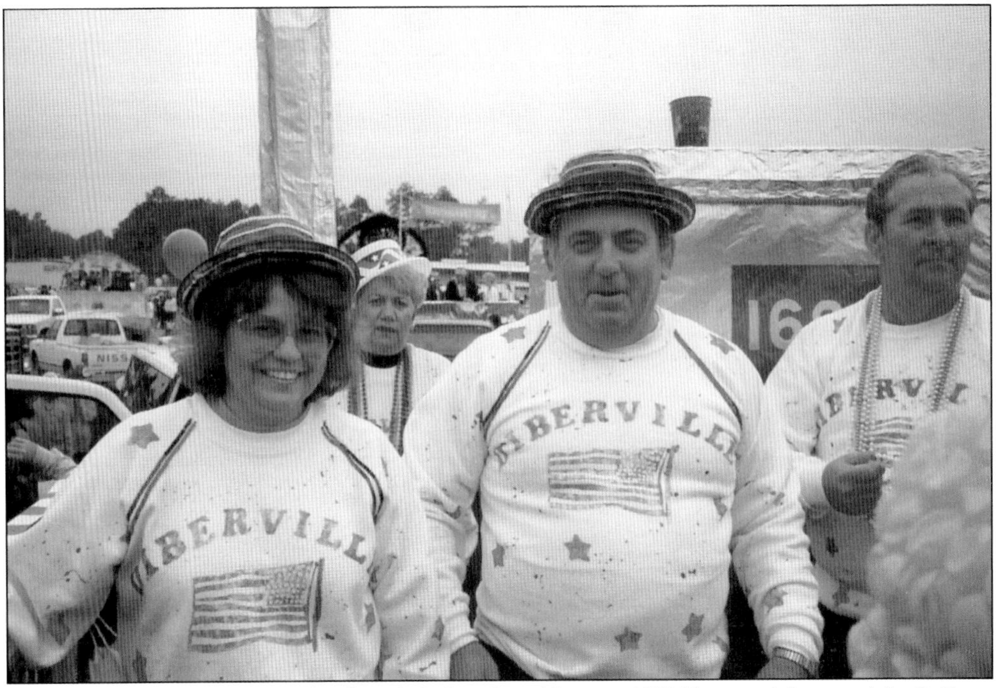

City councilmen Tom Moore (with wife Delores) and Leonard Wolfe are celebrating Mardi Gras. Tom managed the local branch of First Mississippi Bank; Delores was a schoolteacher; and Leonard owned and operated a local TV service-repair company. (Courtesy the City of D'Iberville.)

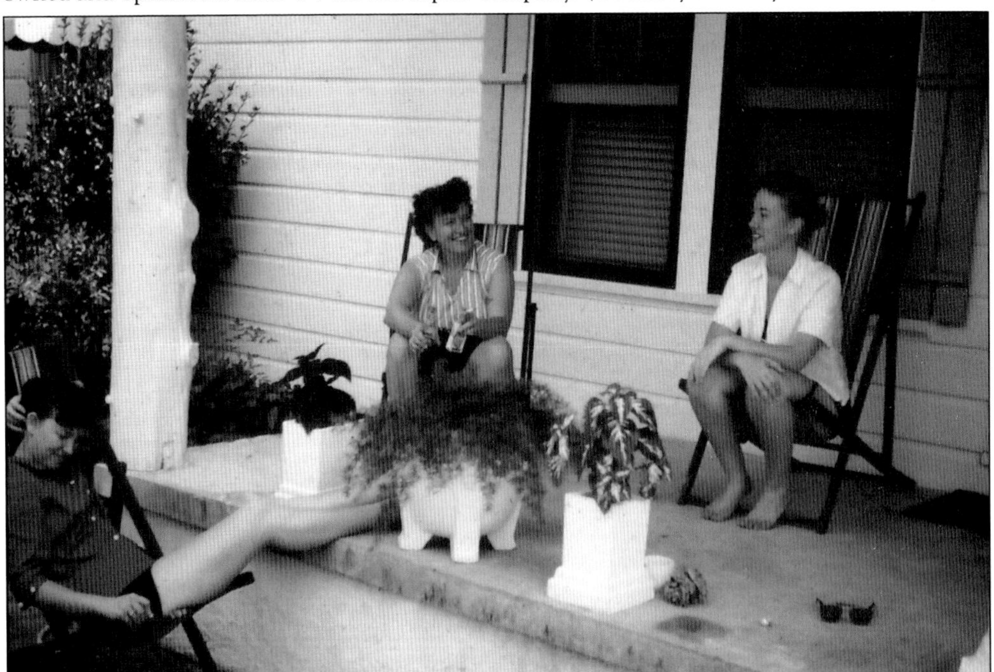

Alnida Walton and her daughters Wanda and Nickie relax at home, which is on the site of the old racetrack, where Race Track Road got its name. After 16-year-old Randy Quave died when thrown from a racehorse on December 2, 1902, the track was closed forever. (Photograph by author.)

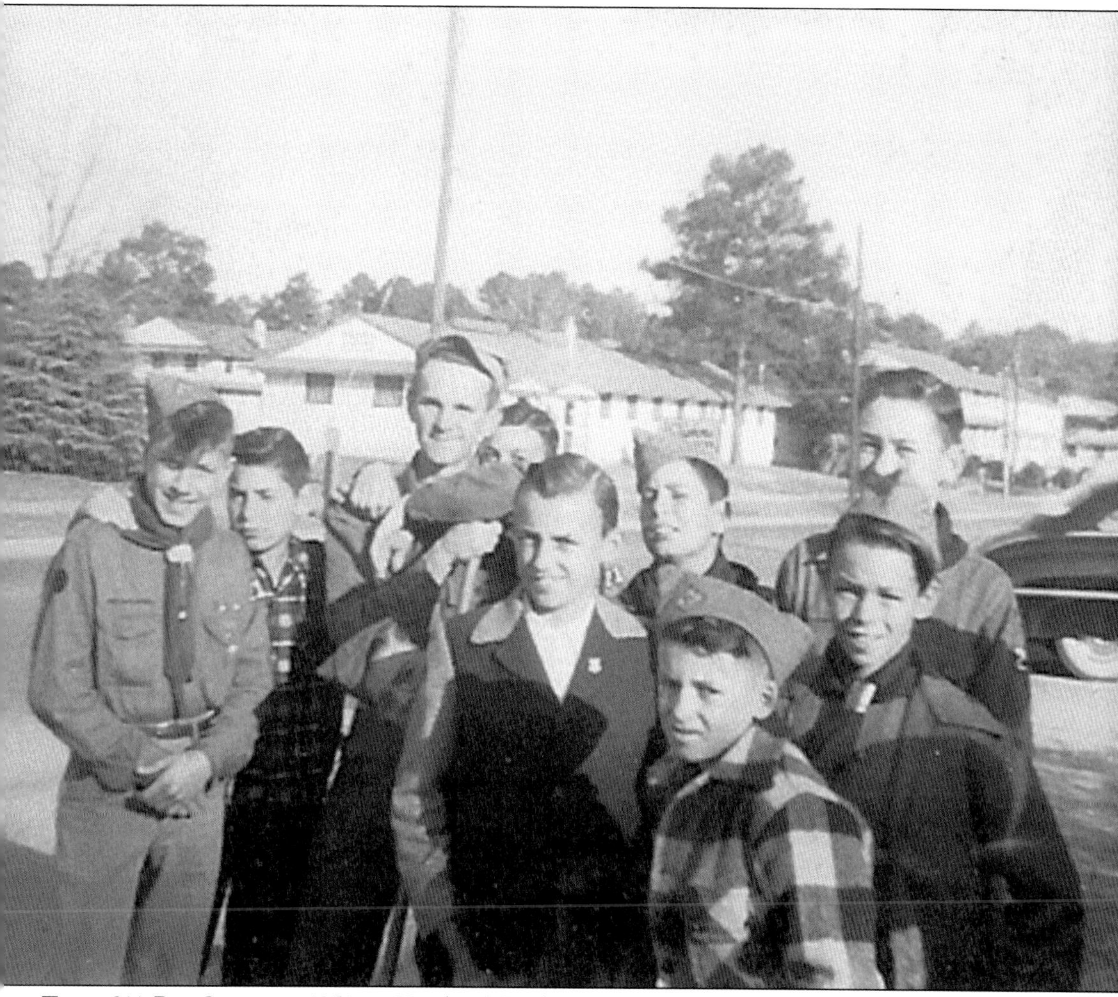

Troop 211 Boy Scouts in 1951 on Keesler AFB during Scout Week included, from left to right, Bernard Talley, J.P. Poulos, airman unidentified, Jackie Tiblier, Raymond Poulos, Vincent Trochesset, Billy Kornman, Tommy Moran behind Billy; the scout behind the airman is unidentified. This photograph was taken by the SPL of the troop, Dale Greenwell. (Photograph by author.)

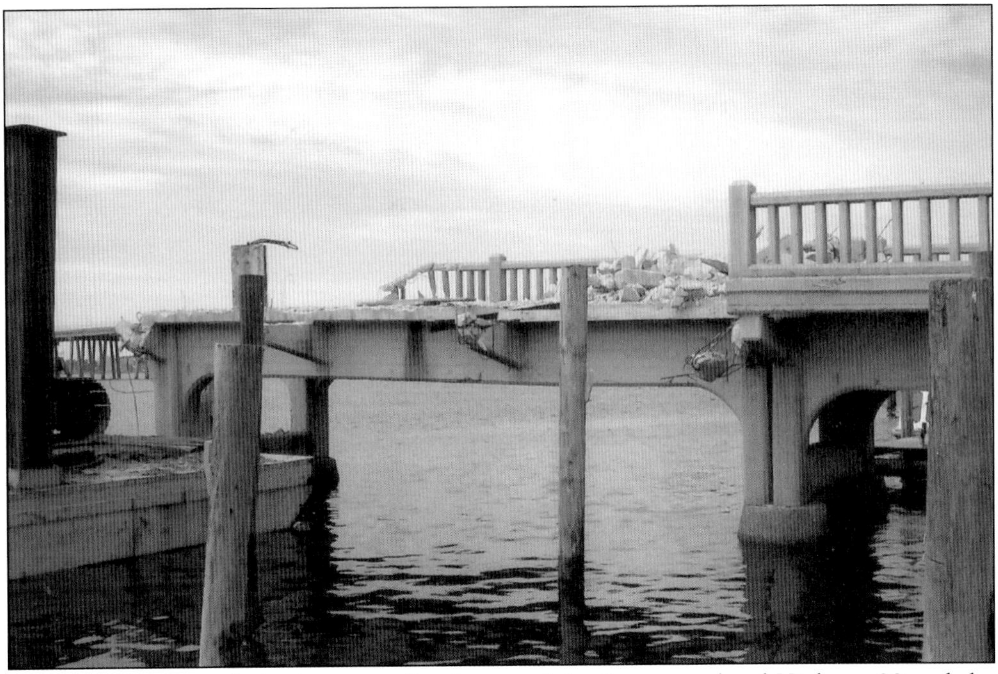

The second D'Iberville bridge, immediately east of the first, completed Highway 90 and the Old Spanish Trail, which runs between the Atlantic and Pacific coasts. Dedicated January 26, 1926, it is 3,400 feet long. It was replaced by Interstate 110. The drawer had been removed. The Hurricane Katrina damages were great. In this photograph, the relic is being removed in 2012. (Photograph by author.)

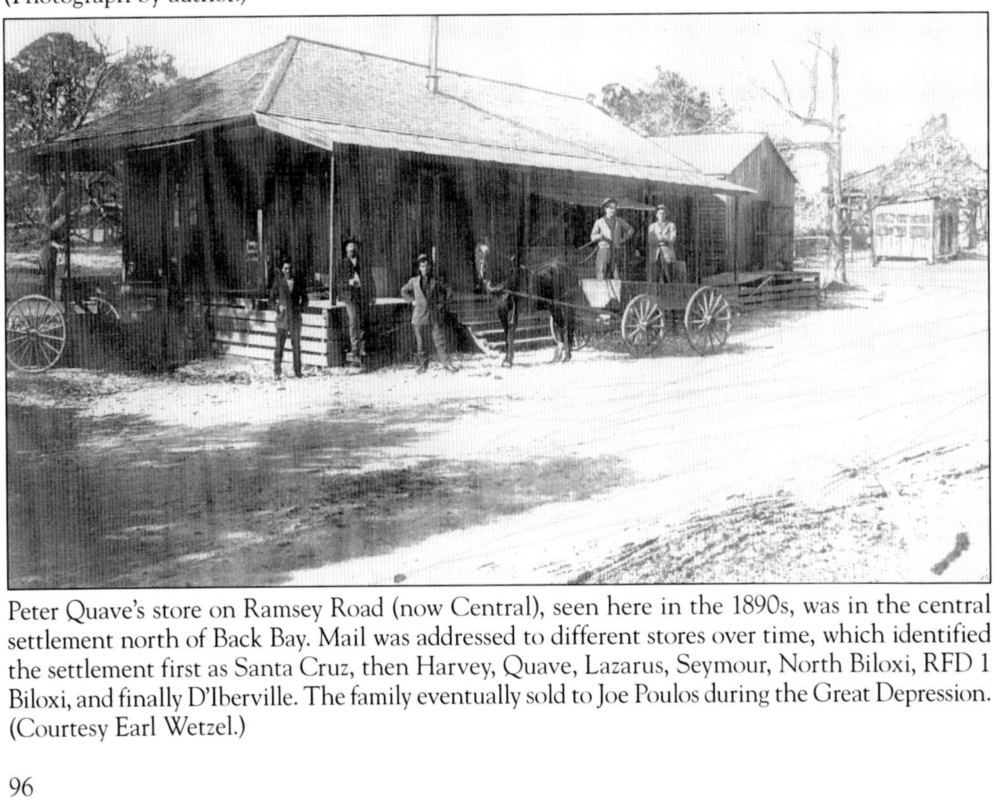

Peter Quave's store on Ramsey Road (now Central), seen here in the 1890s, was in the central settlement north of Back Bay. Mail was addressed to different stores over time, which identified the settlement first as Santa Cruz, then Harvey, Quave, Lazarus, Seymour, North Biloxi, RFD 1 Biloxi, and finally D'Iberville. The family eventually sold to Joe Poulos during the Great Depression. (Courtesy Earl Wetzel.)

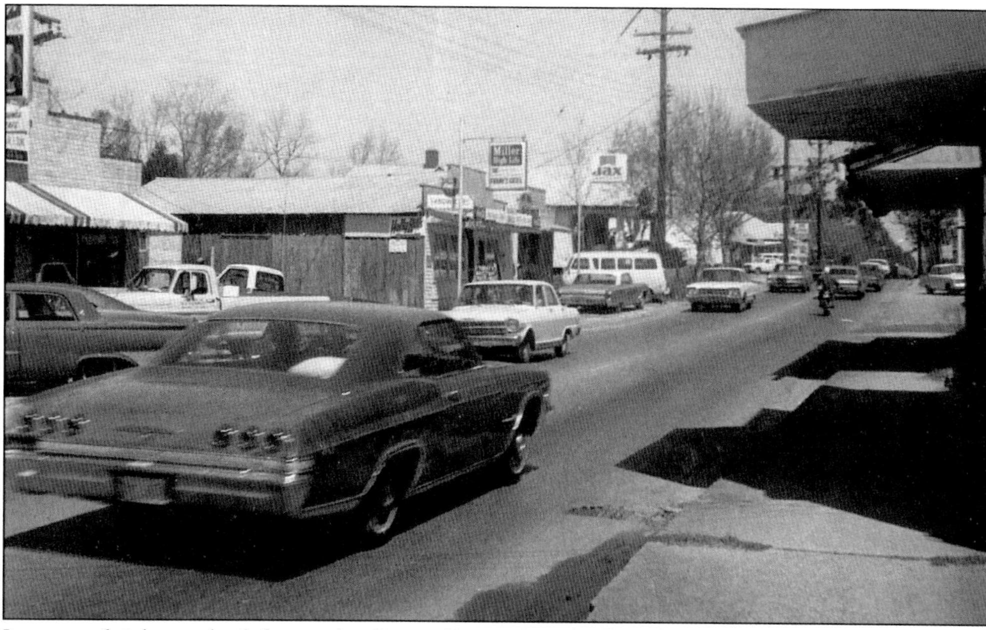

Just out of sight to the left was the Quave Store, described in the previous caption. The Poulos family used it as a residence until their own was completed. Next door was their pecan business. In the 1940s, they remodeled for Rip's Grill, the most popular café on the bay. Around 1950, they sold to Benny and Velma Fournier, who continued Rip's Grill until around 1961. They sold when the business district on Central began shutting doors. (Photograph by author.)

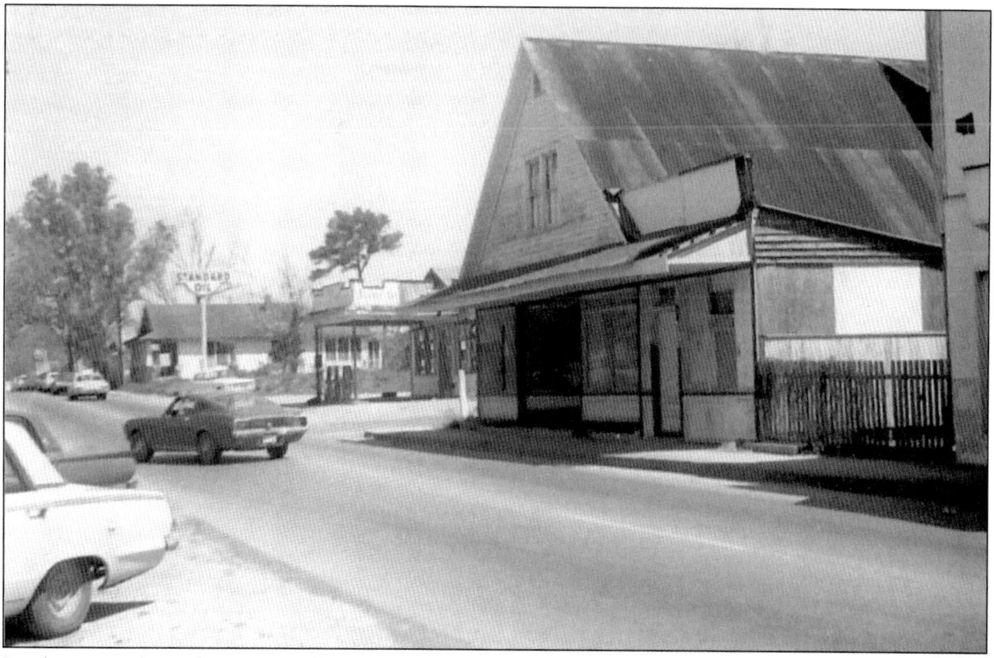

Looking northward on Central is Madeline Quave's Farmers Cash Store, once the mecca for dry goods (clothes, shoes, etc.) from 1917 thru the 1950s. A barbershop was added in 1920, before a theater and deli were added. By the 1960s, all were closed due to the business area moving north and away from hurricanes. (Photograph by author.)

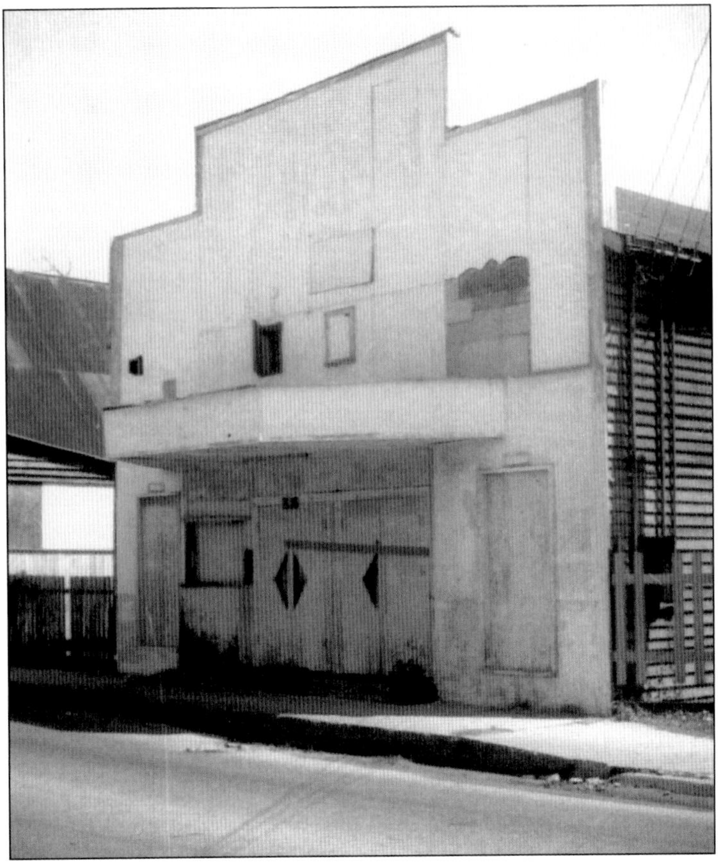

This Dixie (Star) Theater, owned by Ramon Quave and managed by his daughter, Madeline, was built in 1921 and used as both a dance hall and silent film theater, with furniture arranged accordingly. The Dixie was for silent films. When "talkies" arrived, rows of seats were installed. Henry Myers, then C.F. Gollott, leased it as the Star Theater until the town began moving northward in the 1960s. It was the only movie theater north of the bay. (Photograph by author.)

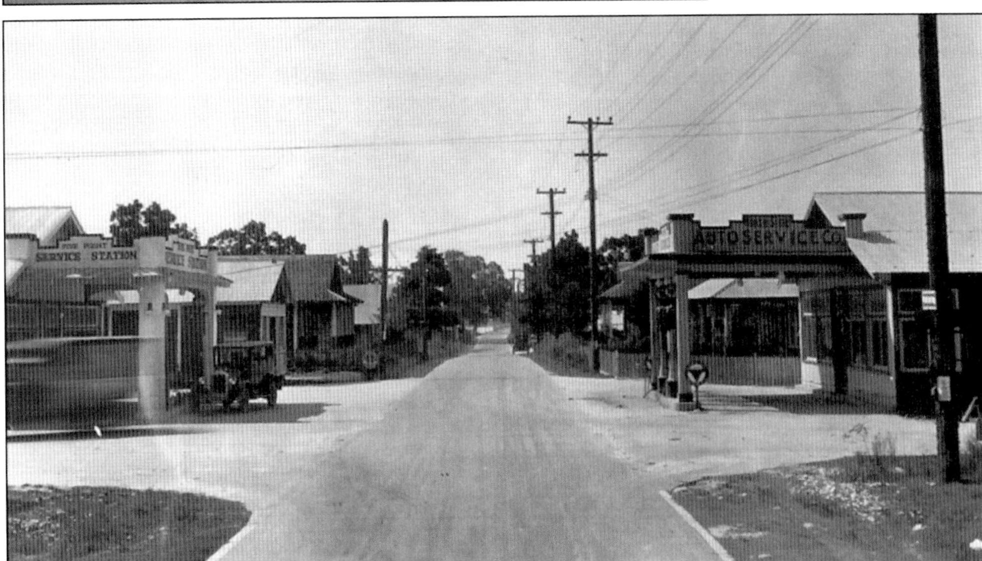

This 1926 view is from the north of "Five Points." The name came from the five roads meeting there: Ramsey (north and south), Race Track, Cedar Lake and Ocean Springs. The new concrete bridge across the Bay, the last link in the Old Spanish Trail, required a paved highway through D'Iberville to Ocean Springs. (Courtesy Tay Greenwell.)

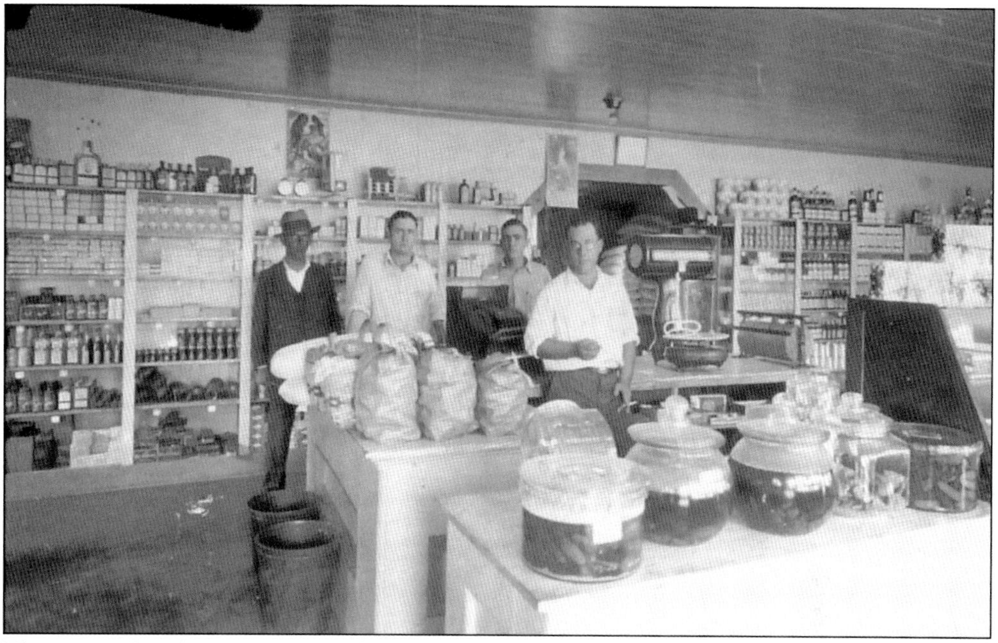

The men in Laz Quave's store, in this 1930s photograph, are (front center) Raymond. L. Quave; (in the background) from left to right, Thomas Fountain (of Fountain's Barber Shop), Jules Santa Cruz (partner of North Biloxi M & SS), and Clarence Ladnier. Laz and Clarence were grandfathers of Mayor Rusty Quave. (Courtesy Paul Fayard.)

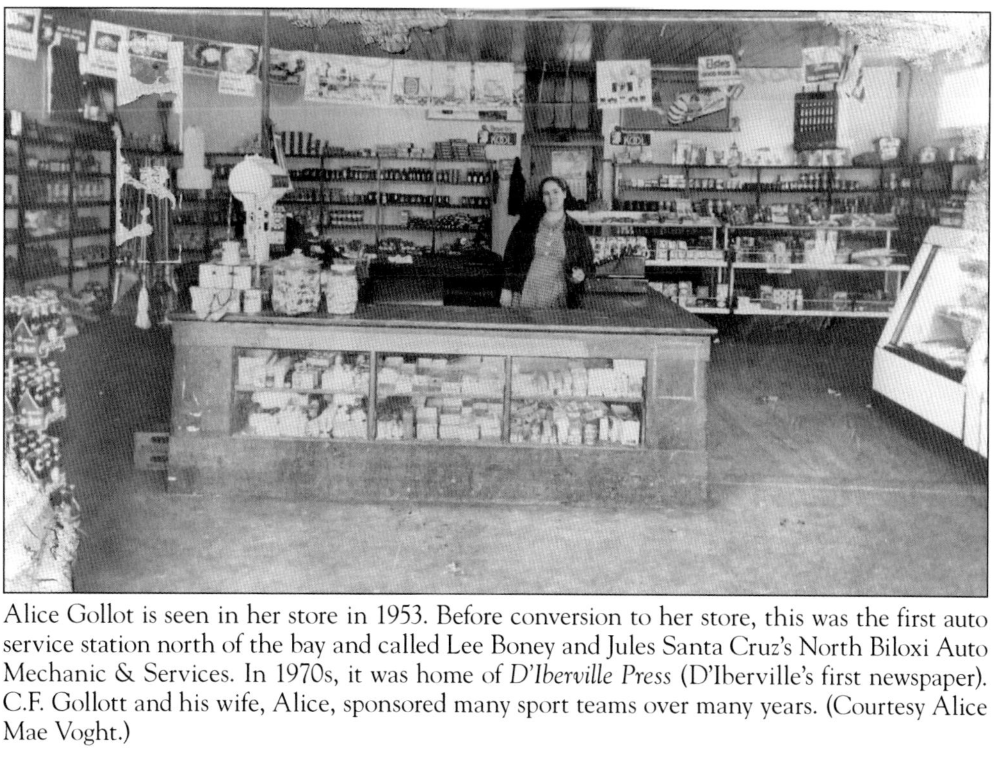

Alice Gollot is seen in her store in 1953. Before conversion to her store, this was the first auto service station north of the bay and called Lee Boney and Jules Santa Cruz's North Biloxi Auto Mechanic & Services. In 1970s, it was home of *D'Iberville Press* (D'Iberville's first newspaper). C.F. Gollott and his wife, Alice, sponsored many sport teams over many years. (Courtesy Alice Mae Voght.)

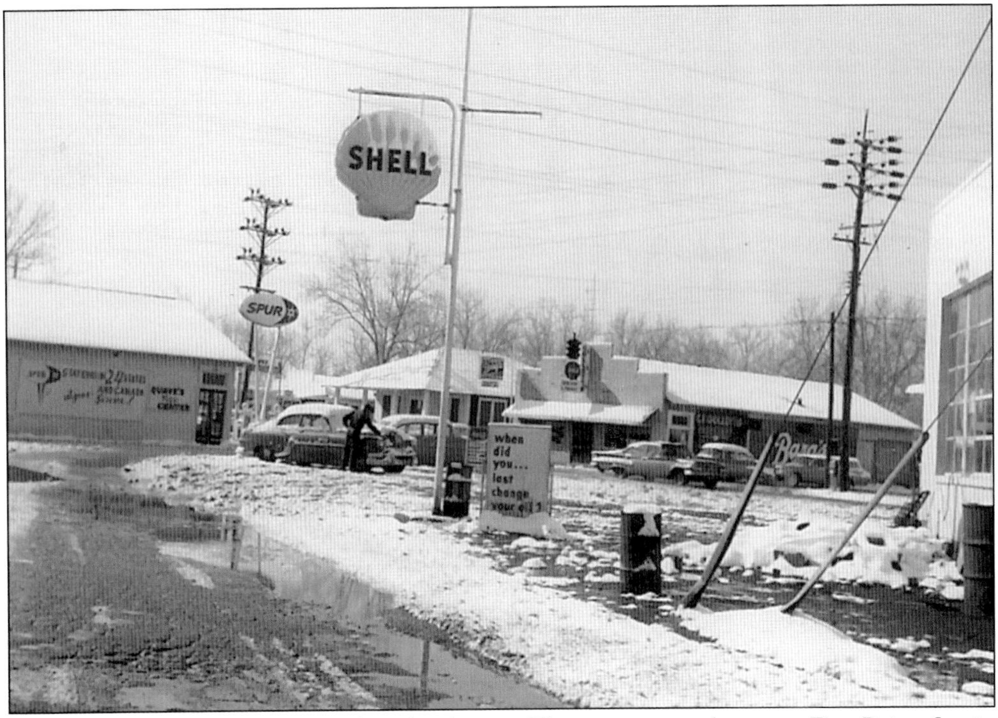

In 1965, people awakened to a white landscape. This view is southwest to Five Point. Ice in ditches from October to March was less common than a decade earlier. This was the first snow in D'Iberville since 1953. To the right is Alice's Grocery, where Lee's Auto Service was located in the 1920s and 1930s. (Photograph by author.)

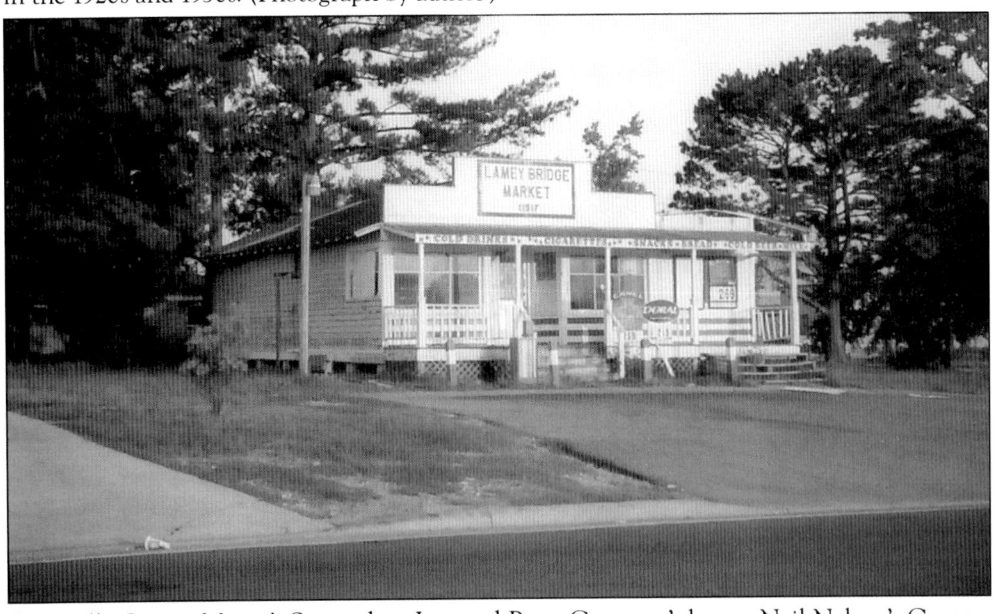

Originally George Moran's Store, then Lee and Patsy Cannette's home, Neil Nelson's Grocery moved to Central to become Lee's Place (tavern-pool hall), and after a fire and repairs was sold to Neil and moved to Lamey Bridge Road as a grocery store. Today, Walgreen's Pharmacy occupies the site. (Photograph by author.)

Pete Ferguson's Service Station is on the old highway (now LeMoyne Boulevard). The original road (between D'Iberville and Ocean Springs) was dirt. In 1926, it was straightened and paved, completing the Old Spanish Trail. In the 1970s, it was five laned. This station, still in the family, serves as a mechanic and paint business location. (Courtesy Tom Ferguson.)

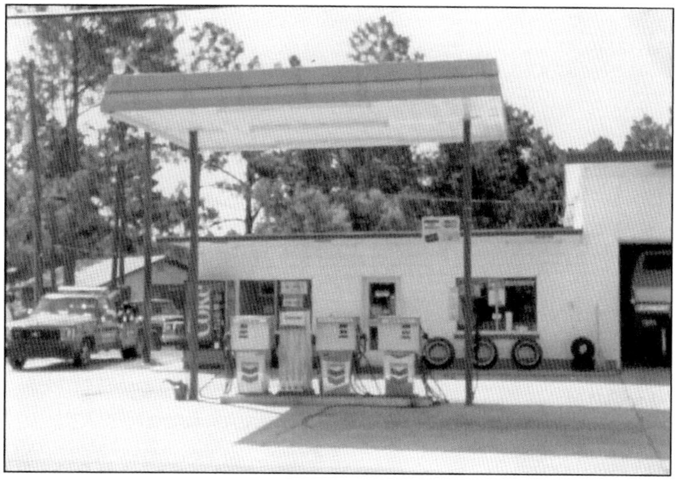

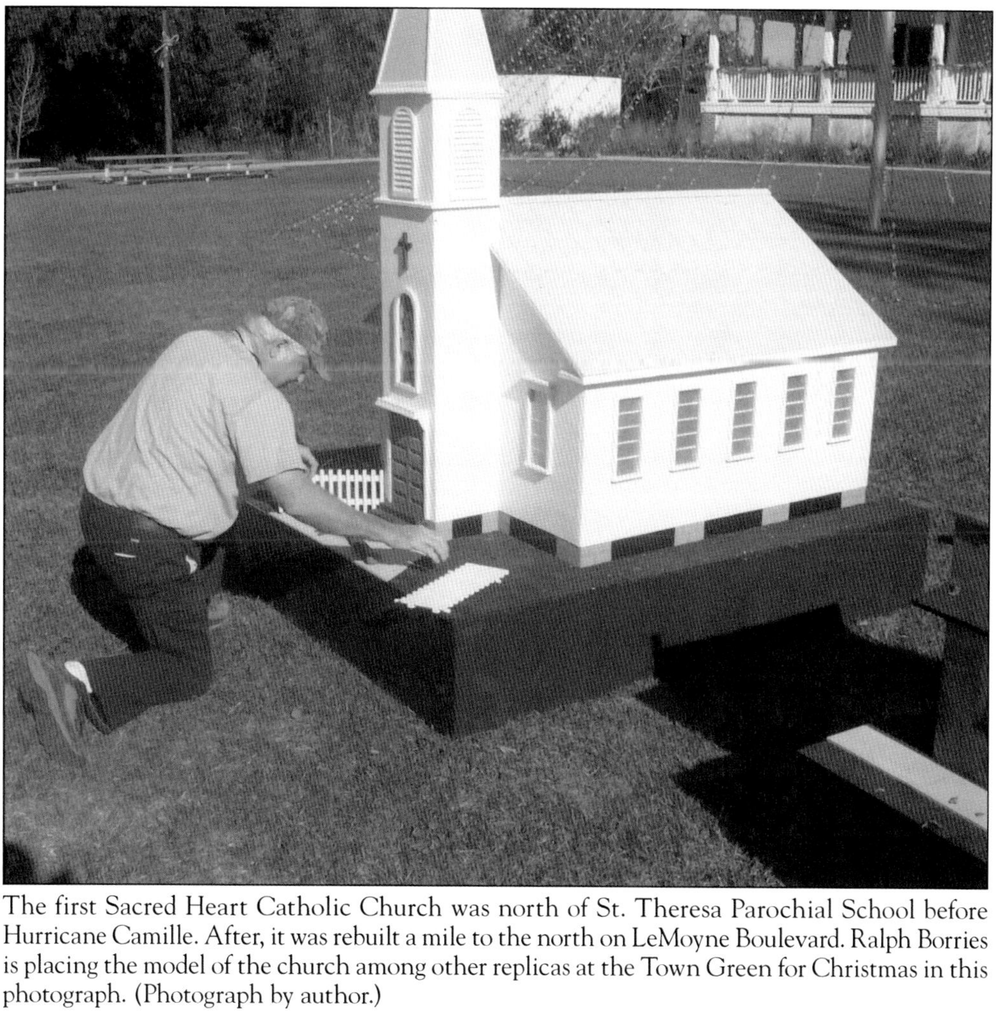

The first Sacred Heart Catholic Church was north of St. Theresa Parochial School before Hurricane Camille. After, it was rebuilt a mile to the north on LeMoyne Boulevard. Ralph Borries is placing the model of the church among other replicas at the Town Green for Christmas in this photograph. (Photograph by author.)

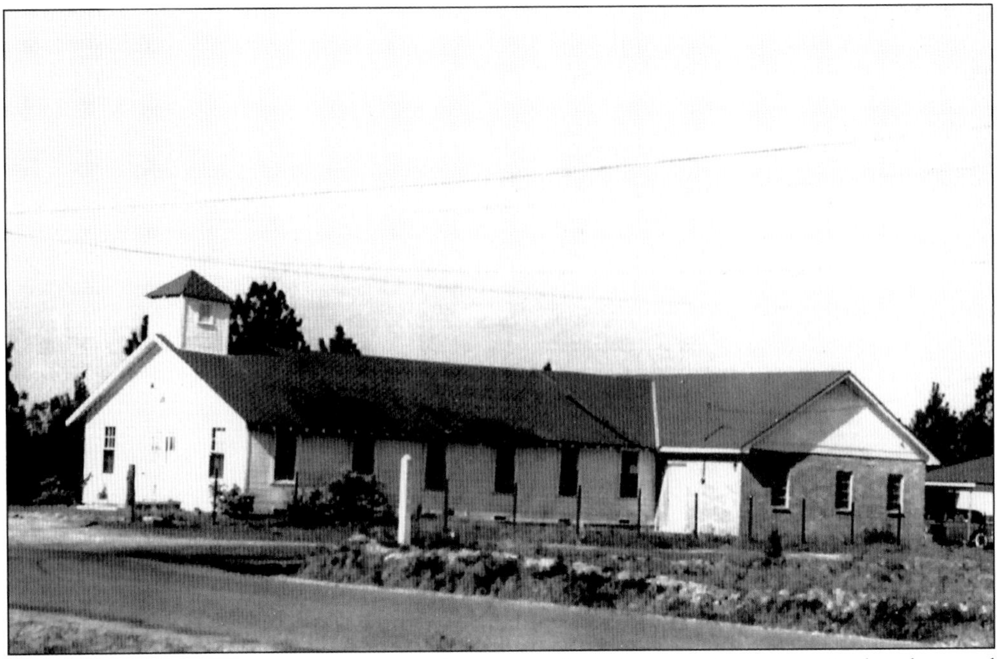

The Big Ridge Baptist congregation, after four years of religious meetings, organized and erected this church in 1946, under the leadership of Rev. Thomas Blass and his assistant, Rev. W.C. Wyatt. The facility has experienced exceptional growth, with many functions, including Bible studies, in the complex today. (Courtesy Linda Santa Cruz.)

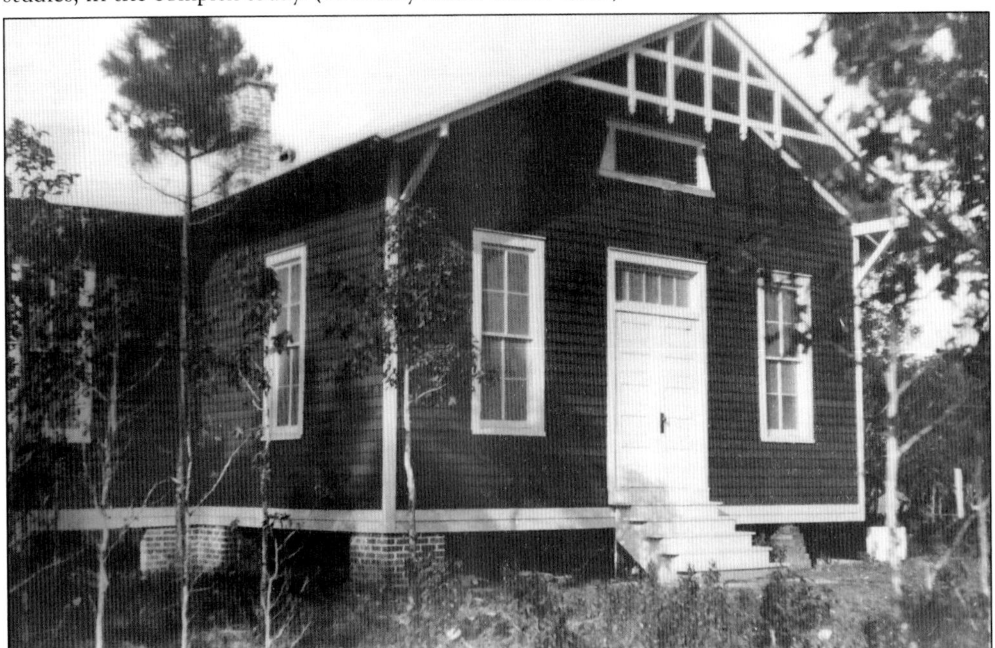

Under the leadership of Rev. W.W. Moore, the congregation, which evolved after the first gathering in 1914, built the North Biloxi Methodist Church on Race Track Road in 1921. Eventually, the growing congregation required more space. It relocated to Popps Ferry Road and is now a large institution of exceptional design and staff. (Courtesy Dot Ellis.)

Nine

Schools and Sports

Academia was not absent in the bay area before schoolhouses. There were private academies across the coast, but they cost money that few could afford. On the north side, there were many literate folks; the fine penmanship and school records predating World War I confirm it.

During the War between the States, there were soldiers in Confederate uniforms writing home to loved ones, in handwriting no different from some of today, despite their limited hours with literate neighbors. Many immigrants were from cities far away who had learned the three Rs in schools or from private tutors.

The first school north of the bay started in 1875 in a one-room cabin with a teacher and at least a dozen students, ranging from age five to twenty, in attendance. School months fluctuated from four to six months, with grades offered from sixth then to eighth. In the early 20th century, schedules and grades extended to eight months and the tenth grade as schools consolidated. New schoolhouses included an office and a teacher, each with several classrooms. Soon, diplomas were going to graduates of the 11th and, finally, the 12th grades. By 1929, schools had become modern and included faculty, staff, teachers qualified for specific courses, and organized sports with coaches.

Before World War II, D'Iberville Consolidated School included first through twelfth grade, an auditorium, a gymnasium, and parking lots. Basketball was the school sport. Football and baseball became school sports in 1953, replete with cheerleaders and stands for the home teams and visitors. St. Martin High School, which had many championship basketball teams, began football in 1958.

Long before high schools had baseball, football, and track, there were softball and baseball teams in leagues with teams from other towns and cities. They were the principal public attractions. Horse and boat racing were the attractions before the 20th century. Race Track Road acquired the name because of horseraces before a crowded track on weekends throughout the year, until Randy Quave was thrown from a horse into an oak tree, which took his life in 1912 and ended racing in D'Iberville. Boat races in the bay eventually moved to the Sound off Biloxi's front beach.

D'Iberville and St. Martin schools have always been competitive, but never in a hostile manner. A principal reason is because the student bodies share ancestries and very close kinships. It was common for kin to be sitting together in the stands, laughing and talking about family activities they share while rooting for different players on the field or court.

Basketball and baseball participation did not end with a diploma. Independent leagues kept the same people competing long after graduation, usually as members of the same team. In the 1950s, C.F. Gollott sponsored the D'Iberville All-Stars, a team of men from D'Iberville, St. Martin, and Biloxi; a third were still in high school, and a third had families. Only an imaginary county line separated the related communities of D'Iberville and St. Martin.

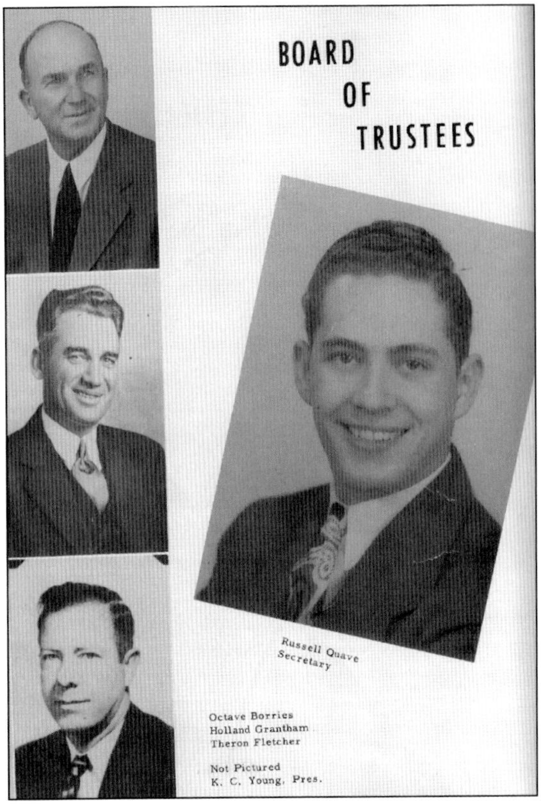

The 1955 D'Iberville School Board of Trustees had four prominent community leaders. On the left, from top to bottom, are Octave Borries, Holland Grantham, and Theron Fletcher; on the right is Russell Quave. (1955 D'Iberville School Annual.)

D'Iberville High School is seen here in 1961. Opened in 1925, it was named North Biloxi Consolidated two years later. It started with grades 1–8, then added two grades and finally had 12, all within a few years. Razed by fire in 1965, the replacement was a half-mile north, then several miles north to its present location. (Courtesy Donna Reed.)

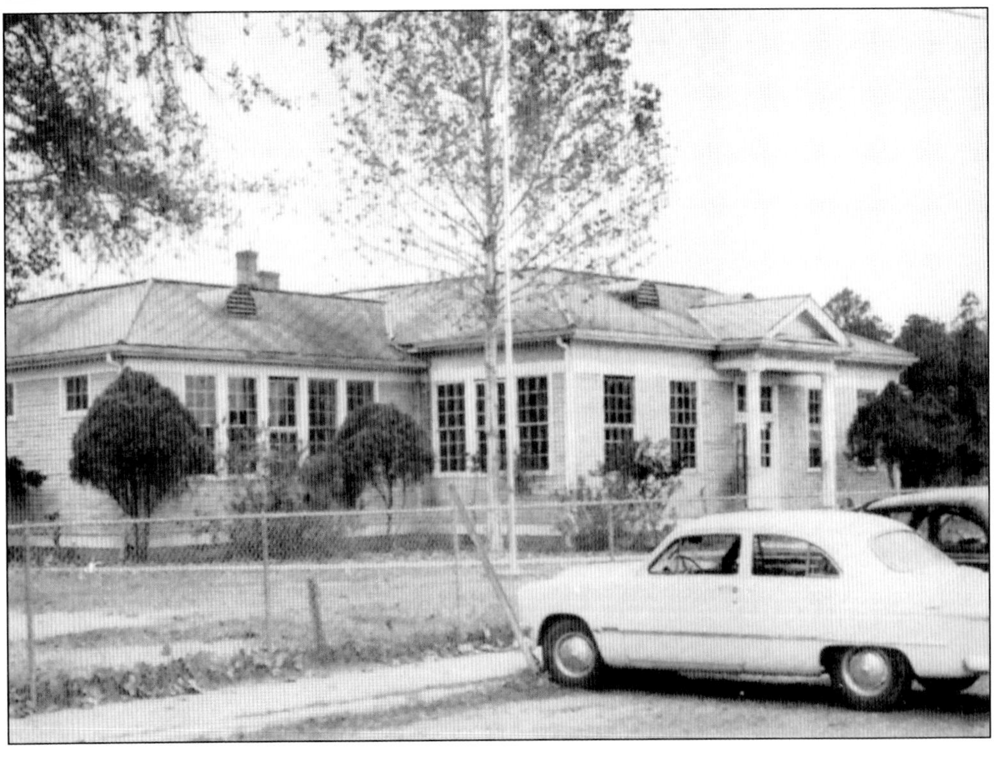

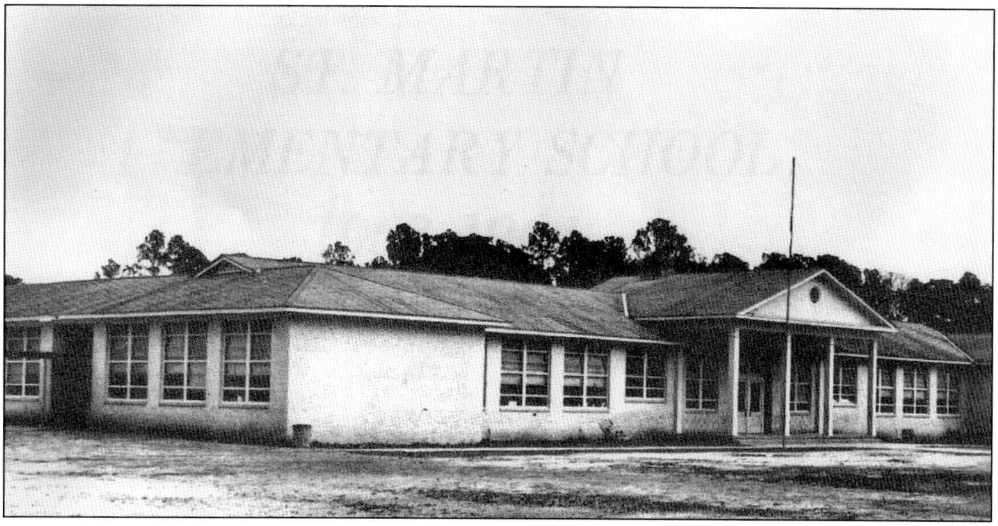

Prior to Camille in 1969, St. Martin elementary through high schools were on the north side of Old Hwy 90 (today's LeMoyne). In 1925, the small, scattered schools were consolidated to this location. Over time, it was enlarged, adding classrooms on the front lawn. The school moved north of Ocean Springs, where it is today. (Yellow Jacket Staff, 1964 coll.)

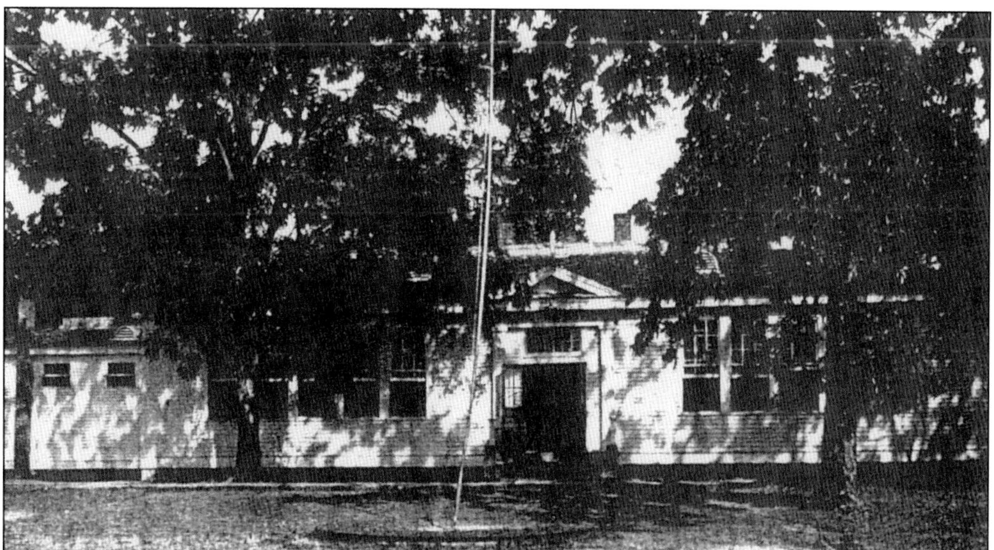

St. Theresa Parochial School's original two classrooms, auditorium, and stage were completed with the cornerstone of August 1, 1927, on the original Emanuel Sanchez home site (the house was remodeled for a convent). Widow Ellen McShane, of Biloxi, donated the land. An additional classroom was added in 1931. (Courtesy of Paul Fayard.)

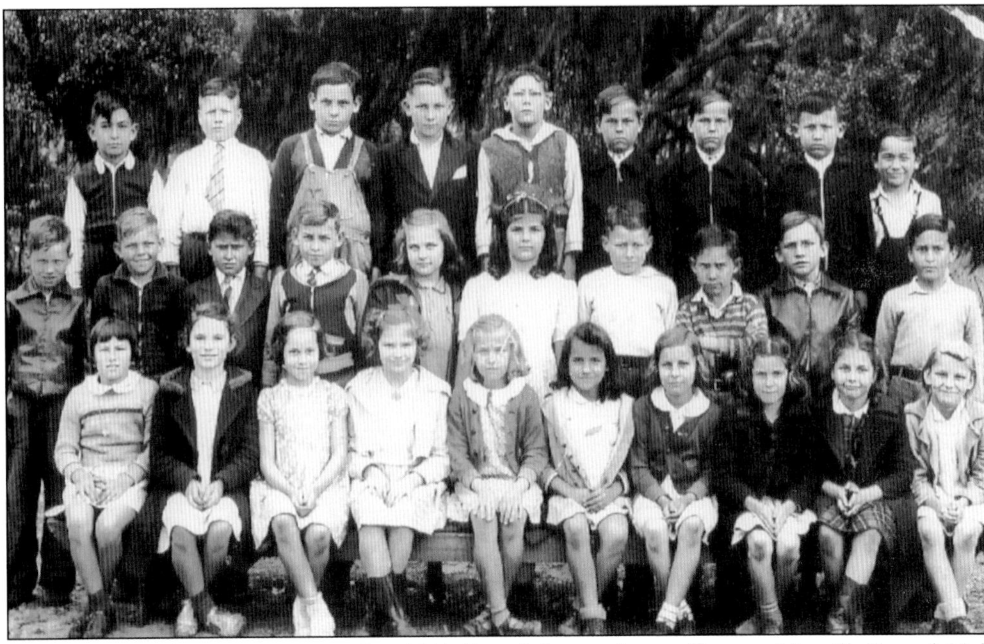

St. Theresa grades 6–8 are pictured in 1941. From left to right are (first row) Lucille Fayard, Nell Norton, Catherine Bosarge, Elaine Moran, Mary Catherine Lepre, Delores Tiblier, Iris Tiblier, Betty Jean Fountain, Delores Fountain, and Doris Tiblier; (second row) Jerry Richards, Donald Tiblier, J.C. Boney, Russell DeGeorge, Martha Cooper, Marie Cannette, Ferrell Bosarge, Alton Richards, Milton Tiblier, and Arlan Fountain; (third row) Rip Polous, Frank Byrd, Elwood Saucier, L.J. Fountain, Edward Lawrence, Melvin Fountain, Elvin Fountain, Jim Moran, and Fred Fountain. (Courtesy Catherine Lawrence.)

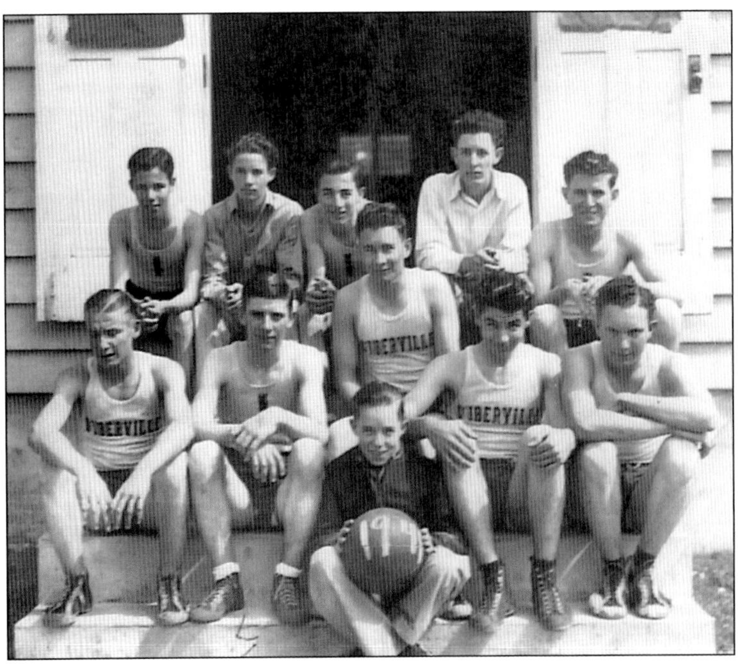

A 1941 D'Iberville High School scrap team included, from left to right, (first row) Neil McAllister, Lucius Hengen, Fred Husley, J.W. Fletcher, and Quintin Hengen; (second row) Perry Fountain, Arthur Trochesset, R.C.McMillan, and Lyle Fairley, and Fred Guilote. Junior Borries has the ball. Coach Homer Richards is not shown. (Courtesy Jackie Toncrey.)

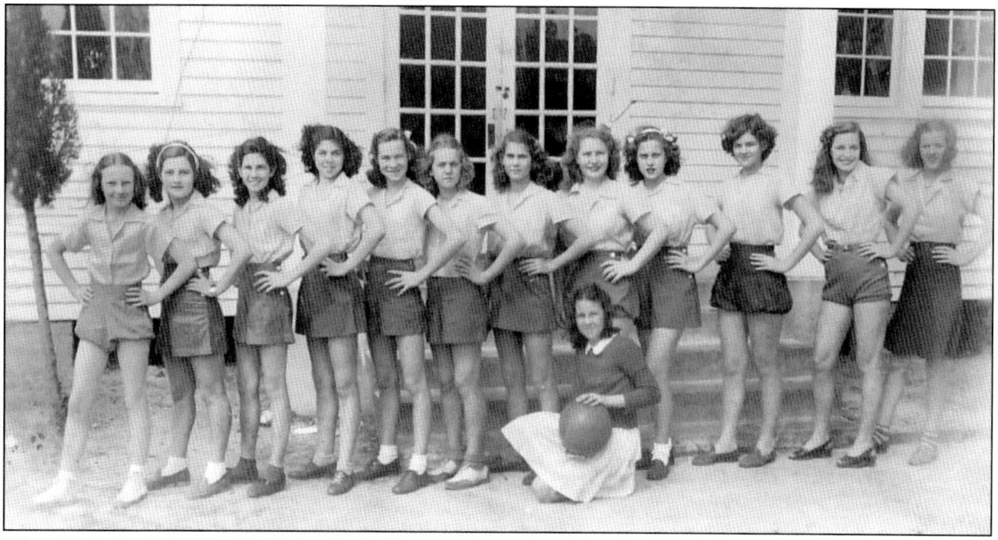

The 1949 St. Martin High basketball team included, from left to right, Betty Broadnax, Peg Wilkerson, Marietta Morris, Loraine Davis, Alice Byrd, Elba Seymour, Bobbie Bullock, Peaches Seymour, Katherine Krohn, Rosalie Flannigan, ? McClellan, and Dorothy Holley, in front. (Courtesy Kenneth Fountain.)

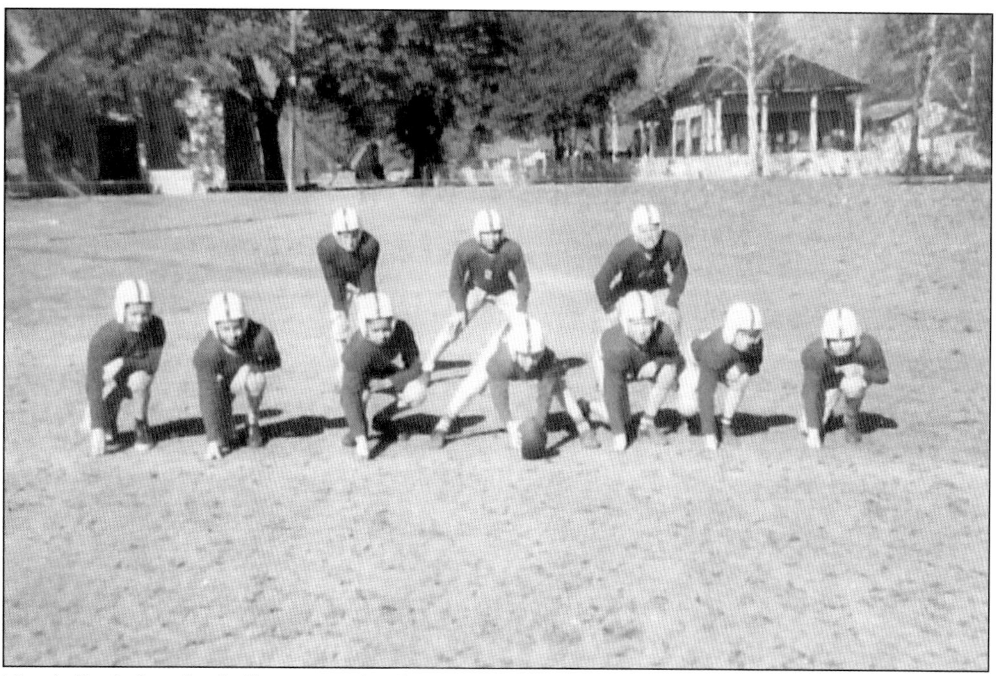

North Bay's first football team under Sister Owens of St. Theresa School is shown here. It was first coached by DHS freshman Dale Greenwell, then Rip Poulos. The team included J.P. and Raymond Poulos, Rudy and Carrol Ibele, Jackie Tiblier, Bernard Talley, Jerry and Edward Lapoma, Ashton Viator, Tim Greenwell, Carrol Batia, Steven and Richard Quave, and Ronnie Bosarge. (Courtesy Tim Greenwell.)

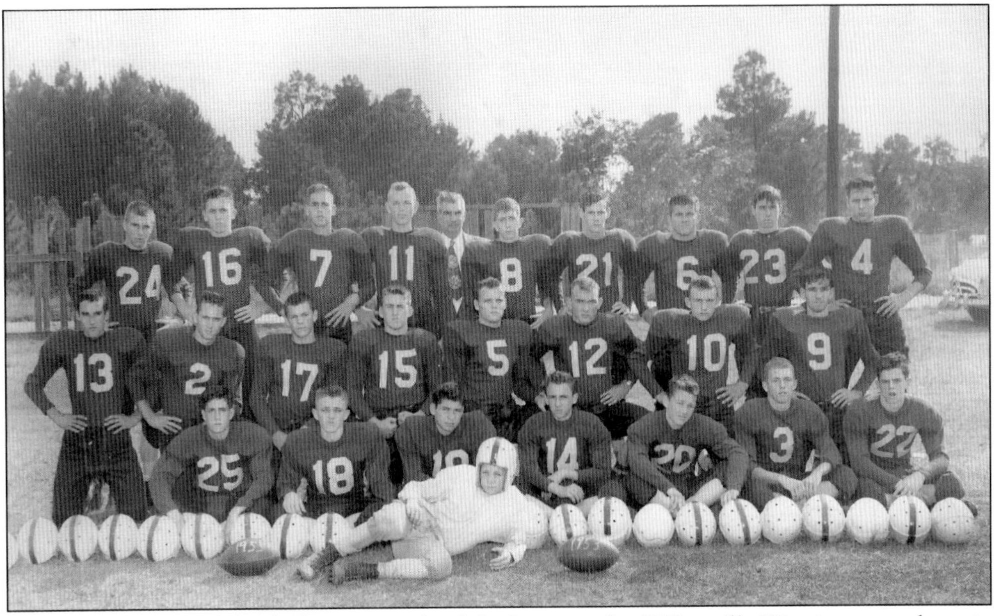

The first high school football team north of the bay was the D'Iberville Warriors, seen here in 1953. Pictured front and center is mascot Butsy Brombeau. From left to right are (first row) Orey Krohn, Frank Schnider, J.P. Poulos, Jack Tiblier, Ron Bosarge, Forest Eastham, and Jerry Mallet; (second row) Wallace Blanchard, Dale Greenwell, Mindon McMurran, Bob Degeorge, Leonard McMurran, Jerry Lawarence, Bill Raymond, and Larry Thompson; (third row) Bill Salters, Eugene Hart, Mike Fayard, George Dale Ladnier, Coach D.W. Salters, Harold Young, John Simmons, Gordon Etherton, Carl Pelez, and Buck Bosarge. (1954 DHS annual.)

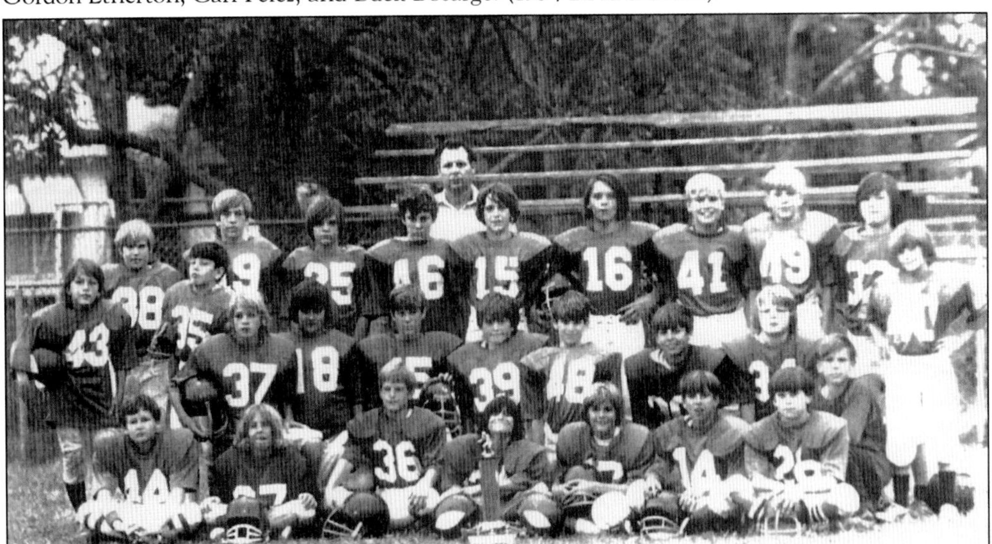

The 1974 Peewee football team was coached by Buck Bosarge. Pictured from left to right, top to bottom, are Chester Brooks, Joe Sharp, Tim and Don Parker, Jim Lawrence, Junior Clark, Scott Rector, Leo Bond, Dion Keel, Steve Benson, Ken Sharp, Darin Widel, unidentified, Greg Gilbert, Jerry Gandy, Mike Mullins, Mark Bosarge, Kim Wentzell, Doug Brashier, Tom Hebert, Glen Buck, Mitch Herrington, John Hardy, Tracy Burdine, Jeff Gehrmann, Mike Bosarge, and Ron Davis. (Courtesy Maxine Ramsey.)

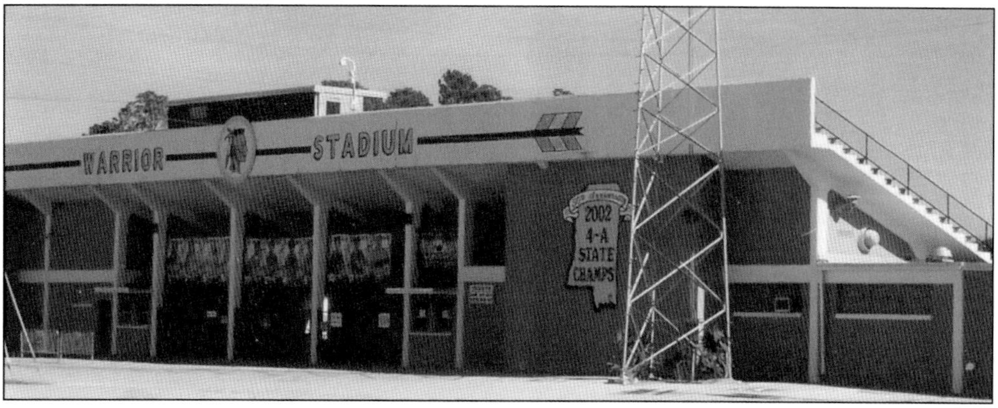

After the DHS fire in 1965, the school moved to Lamey Bridge Road. The first DHS stadium, Warrior Stadium, was erected east of the school. Prior to this, the Warrior football and baseball teams had used the field east of the original high school on Church. It had bleachers for about 200 and a wooden fence around it to keep cows out. (Photograph by author.)

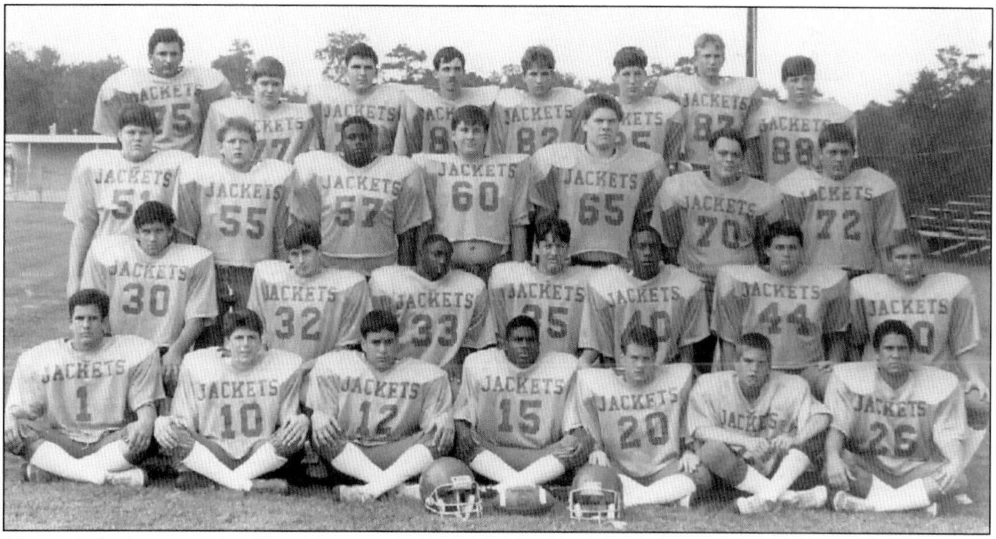

This 1993 photograph of St. Martin High's team does not identify the players by name. Football began there in 1958. (Courtesy *Bay Press*.)

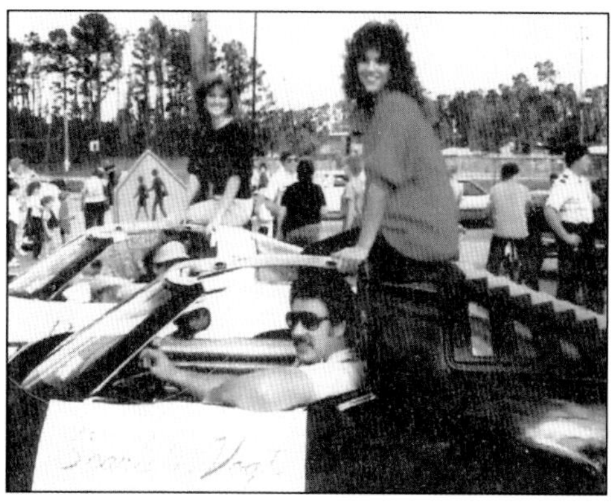

D'Iberville High's 1993 senior maid at Homecoming, Scarlett Voght, is in the foreground. Her sister Dana is in the background. The first Homecoming for DHS was in 1956; Rose Marie Scarbrough reigned. (Courtesy *Bay Press*.)

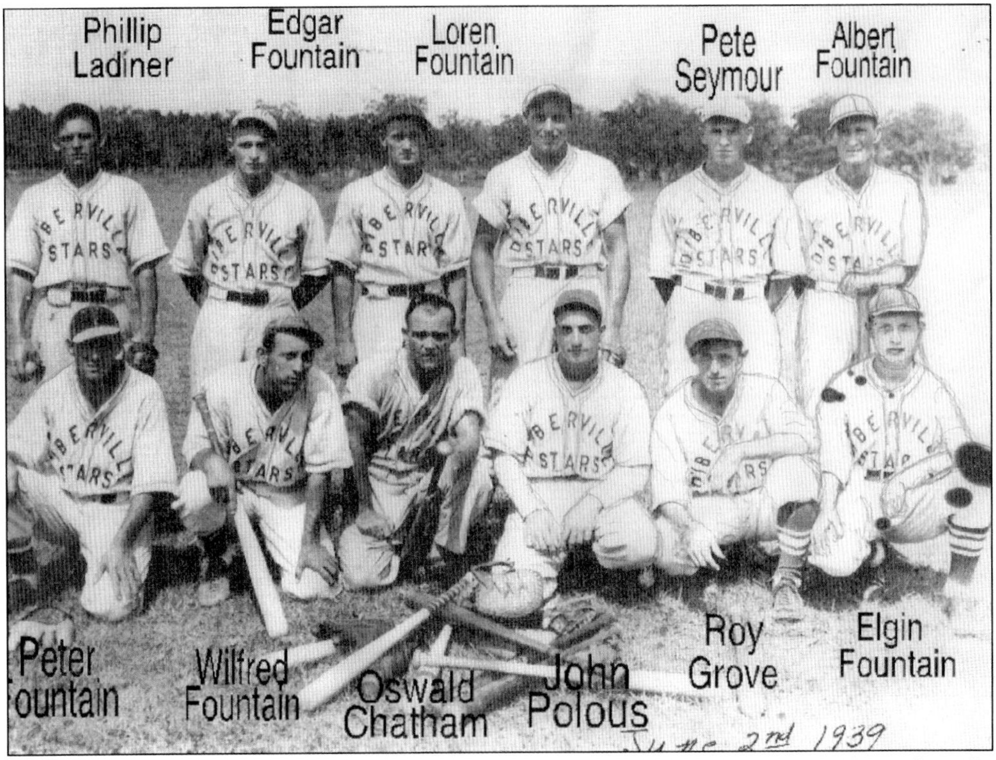

C F. Gollott sponsored independent baseball teams in local leagues for decades. The D'Iberville Stars team of 1939 is pictured here. The team was typically made up of high school, college, and married men, and they were always in the top of the league. (Courtesy Alton Richards.)

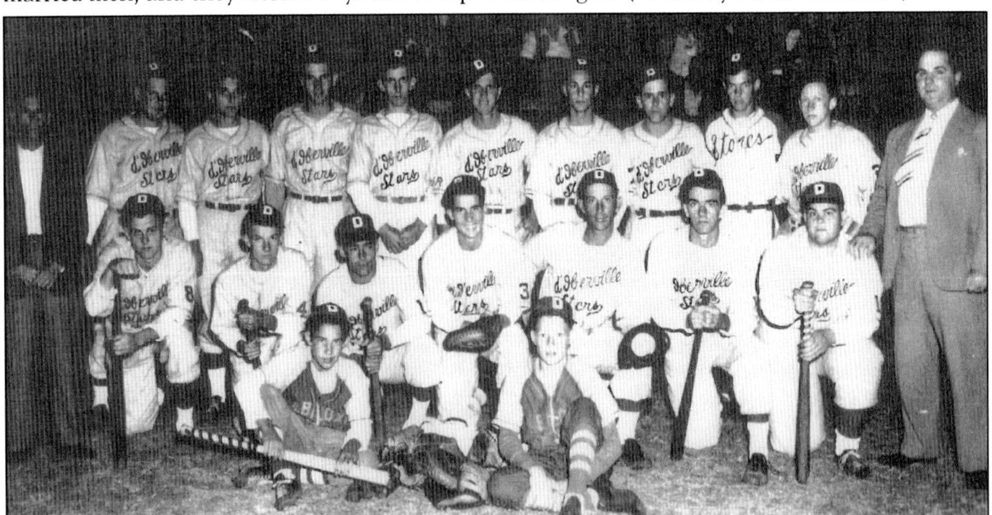

The D'Iberville Stars softball team is pictured in 1948. From left to right are (sitting) batboys Alton Richards and Ferrill Bosarge Jr.; (kneeling) Malcolm Pyron, Roy Gilmore, R.D. Etherton, Elvis Fayard, Elgin Fountain, Emile Tiblier (pitcher), and Dalton Ladner; (standing) Harry Fountain (coach), Chalmas Johnson, Roy Smith, J.W. Fletcher, J.W. Tiblier, Jack Delahoussey, E.J. Rodriguez (manager), Terry "KO" Etherton, Lindy Ladnier, Charles Bosarge, and C.F. Gollott (sponsor). (Courtesy Jane Rogers.)

Ten

THE BIRTH OF A CITY

Several years after World War II, when the local economy stabilized and men who had gone to war as boys returned to night school to continue where they had left off, a sense of business leadership evolved on both sides of the county line. Collectively, men joined a common cause, one to promote a sense of direction through a common business organization. The LeMoyne Business Men's Club was the first to introduce a desire to form a single community engulfing old St. Martin, D'Iberville, and fringe areas such as Cedar Lake.

When they began talking of incorporating those areas into one, there was some resistance from the general public—not against the purpose, but of a government controlling their business freedoms. Incorporation ideas were tabled.

In the 1980s, when the City of Biloxi considered expanding its borders, the folks on the north side rolled up their sleeves. A group of wise business people and alarmed citizens went to war for the rights of the north side to manage its own interest. The most interested among them organized and led the fight for a city free of another's rule. The issue went to court, and Biloxi lost. However, D'Iberville's borders were limited, giving Biloxi a shot at expansion on the north side, which they won in a later court battle.

On February 10, 1988, the City of D'Iberville was born. The organization responsible became the interim council and consisted of the following: Mayor Jerry Lawrence, Oliver Diaz, Linda Davis, Barney Scarborough Sr., Leonard Wolfe, and Tom Moore. Audrey Lamey was employed as the city manager. They met in a trailer next to People's Bank. After the first election, they met on the top floor of the bank. Eventually, the first city hall was completed. With limited tax dollars, the council turned to the county for help in the beginning. The district's county supervisor, Bobby Eleuterius, led the way for municipal paving, drainage, waterworks, and sewage.

Looking back in time, the bridges across the bay were the steppingstones into the future. Highway 90 from Ocean Springs, through St. Martin and D'Iberville to the bridge into Biloxi, was the backbone of development. The first high schools and most commercial development were on that route after 1926. Five Points to the bridge included a seafood factory, two taverns, three cafes, a general dry-goods store, two service stations, a doctor's office, drug store, pool hall, three grocery stores, bakery, dry cleaners, shoe repair shop, barbershop, pecan shop, and 11 homes. A public bus from Biloxi included an hourly run through "North Biloxi" (D'Iberville and St. Martin), a nickel each way for children and a dime for the rest.

Back Bay, or North Biloxi, was just a generation away from becoming the city known today as D'Iberville. The old town is just a fading memory.

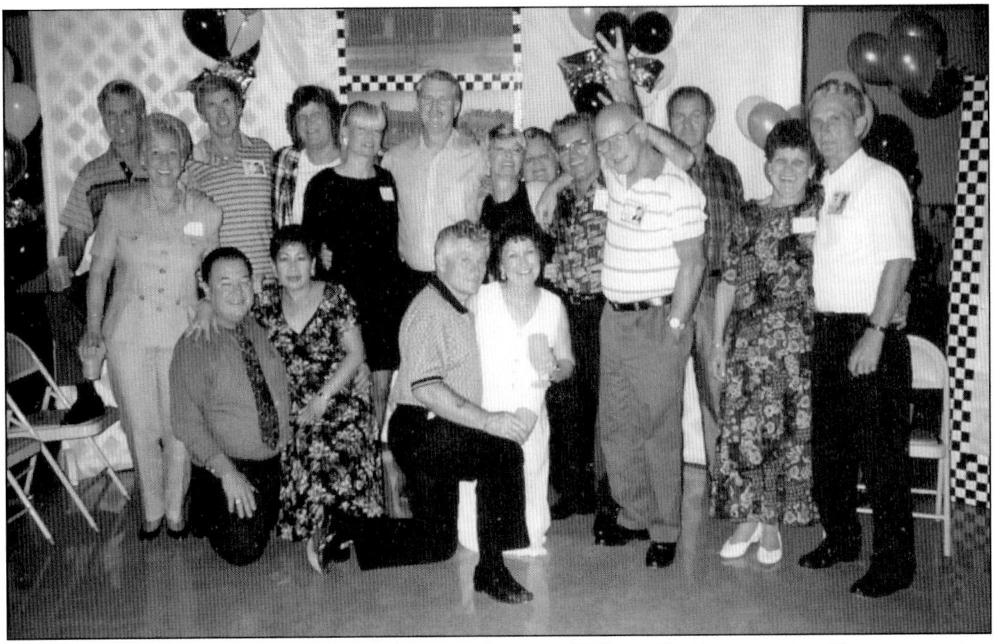

The 1993 Reunion Committee, seen here at the new D'Iberville Community Center, consists of alumni from the original D'Iberville High School, which was destroyed by fire in 1965. (Photograph by author.)

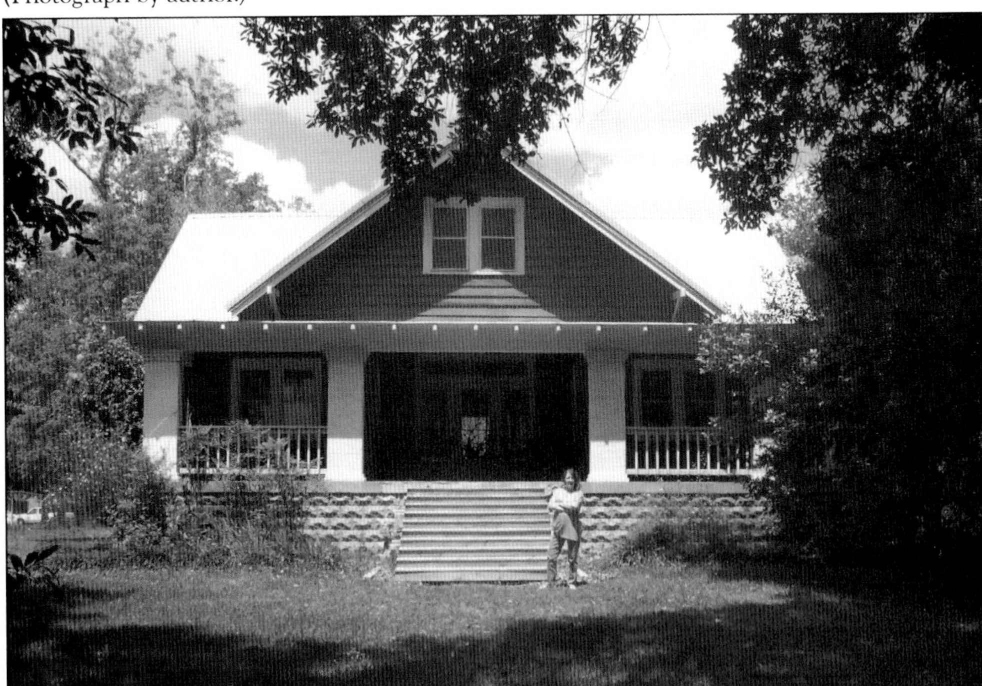

A reminder of the Prohibition era, the Boswell residence on Big Ridge Road was once, under a previous family, a private place for parties when alcohol was illegal. The house still has the concrete cellar and a trap door where booze was passed up behind the bar to keep the party going, though there is none of that today. (Photograph by author.)

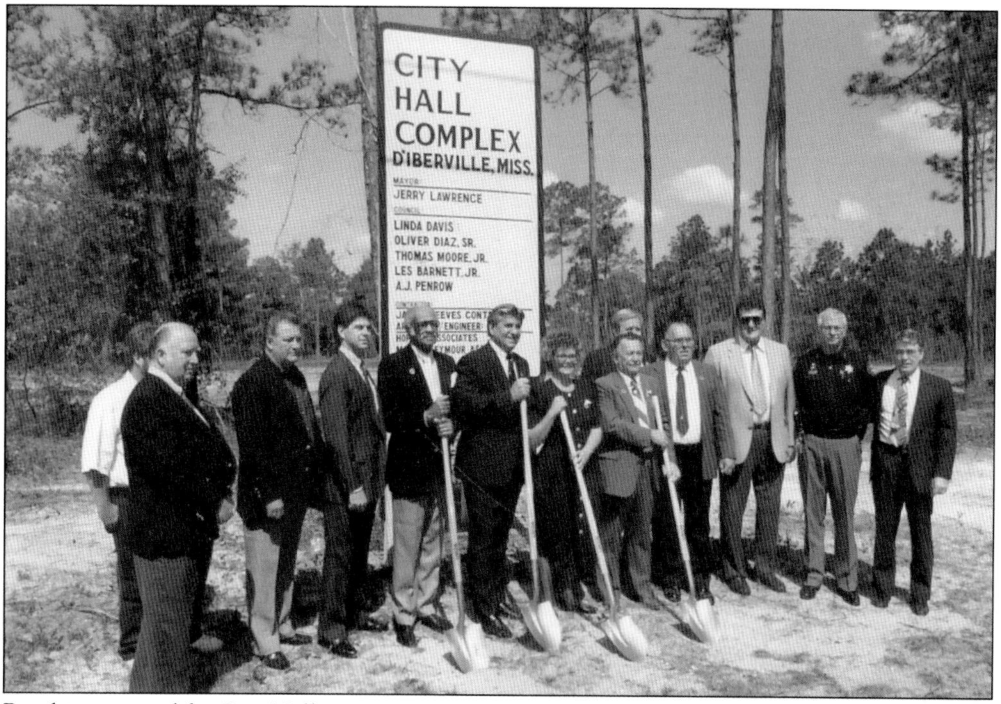

Breaking ground for City Hall in 1992 are, from left to right, Mark Seymour, Bobby Eleuteris, Les Barnett Jr., A.J. Penrow, Oliver Diaz Sr., Linda Davis, Mayor Jerry Lawrence (Al Santa Cruz is behind him), Thomas Moore, Jim Wetzel, Sheriff Joe Price, and Gerald Hopkins. (Courtesy the City of D'Iberville.)

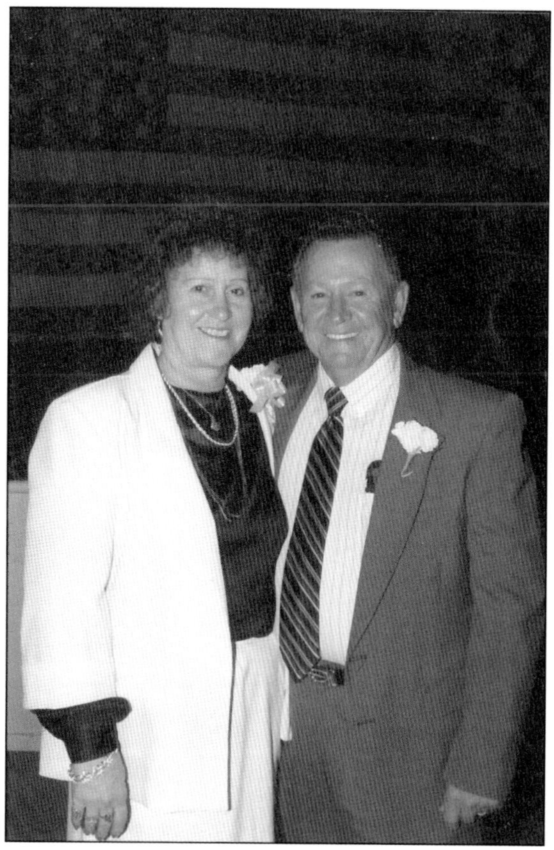

Before becoming mayor, Jerry Lawrence, seen here with his wife, was an organizer of the D'Iberville Civic Development Society that fought for the community's right to incorporate rather than be annexed by the City of Biloxi. The city's library is named for him. (Courtesy Catherine Lawrence.)

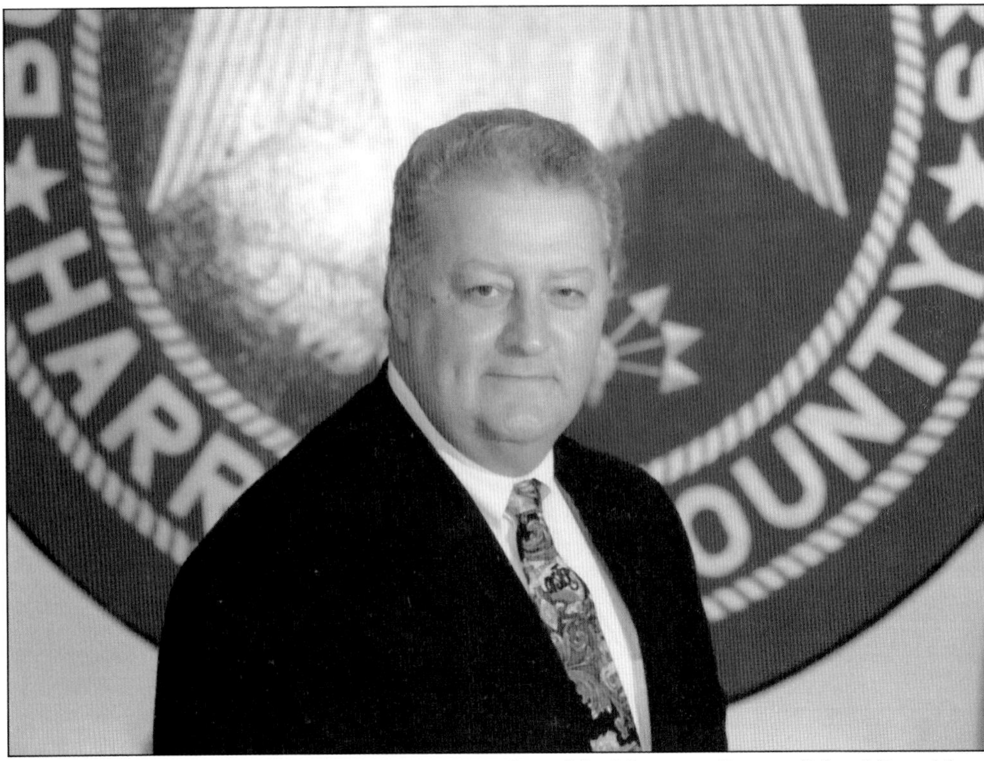

Bobby Eleuterius served the community as a member of the Harrison County School Board from 1974 to 1983, then as a member of board of supervisors from 1984 to 2008. After retirement, he accepted the position of D'Iberville city manager. (Courtesy Nancy Eleuterius.)

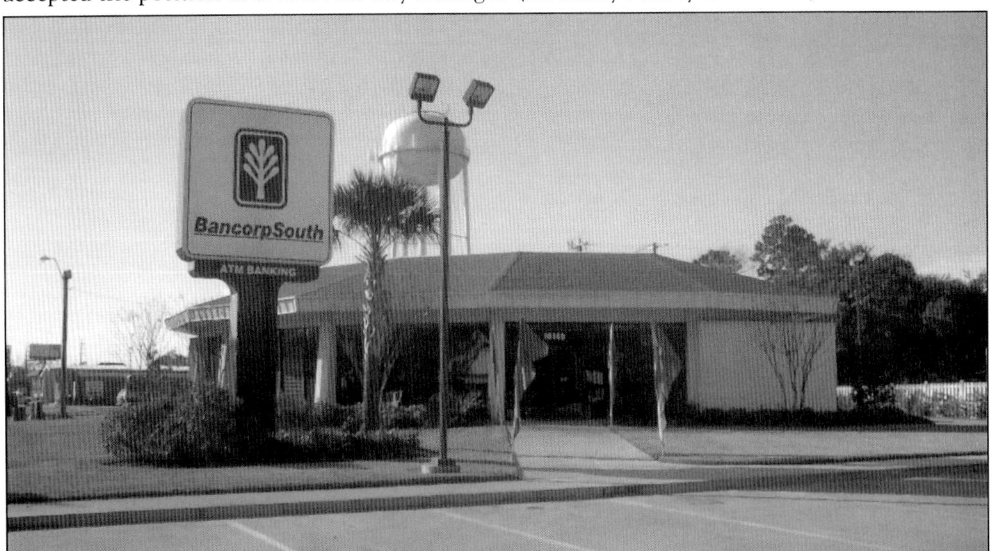

Russell Quave, father of current mayor Rusty Quave, managed the first banking facility in the town, a small branch of the First National Bank of Biloxi, located in a building owned by Bay Gollott. In 1972, the building shown here was completed and the bank's name changed to First Mississippi Bank, now BancorpSouth. (Photograph by author.)

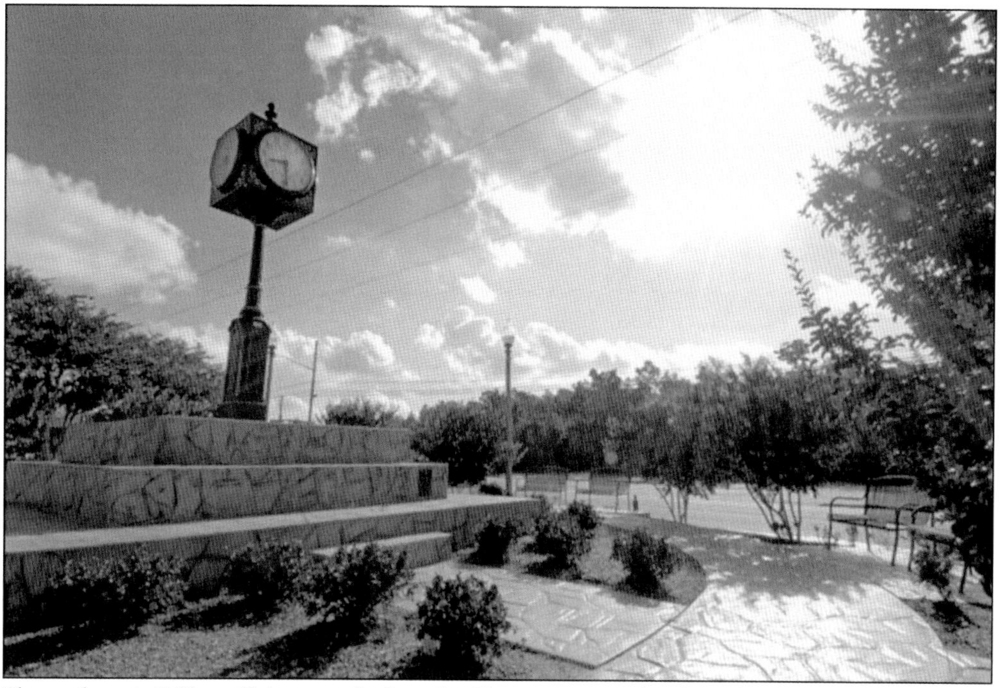

Shown here is D'Iberville's town clock at the Y-intersection of D'Iberville Blvd, Central Avenue and Ramsey Bridge Road. This point was an intersection of Ramsey Road, Grantham Lane, and Old Spanish Trail from 1926 to 1930. Grantham's Dairy was at the end of the lane. (Photograph by author.)

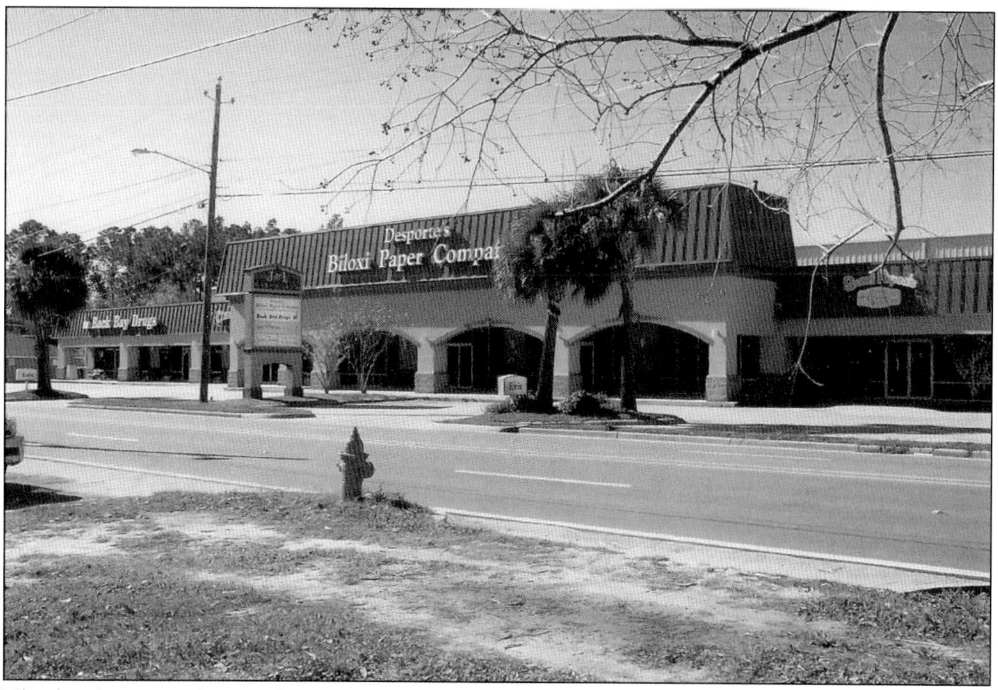

The first business plaza in the move north from the old town included J&L Plaza, Desporte's Paper Company, Back Bay Drugs, Celebrations, and Sweet Repeats. (Photograph by author.)

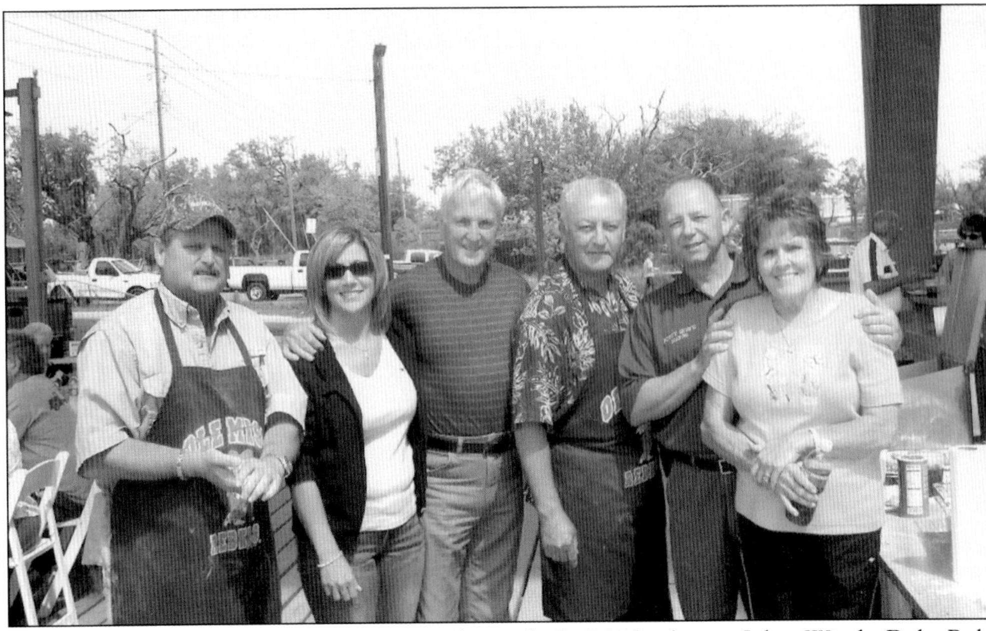

Pictured at Harvey and Rose Saujon's party beneath the I-10 bridge are John, Windy, Dale, Bob, Rusty, and Gloria. More than 100 friends gathered for the seafood dinner celebration. Harvey and Rose passed away shortly after. (Photograph by author.)

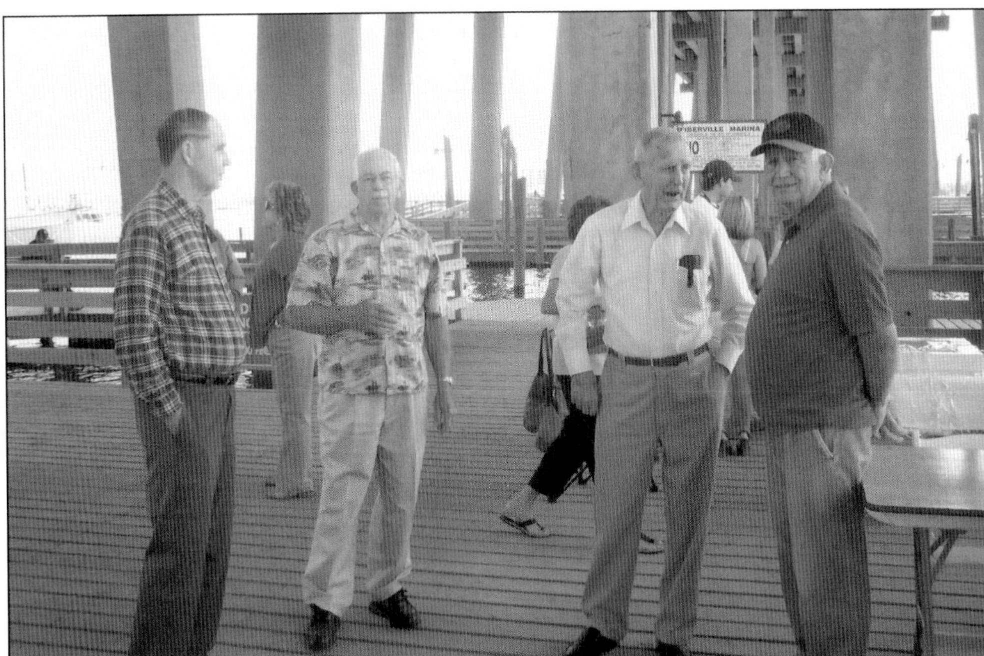

Paul Fayard, Ken Fountain, Harvey Saujon, and Jerry Taranto are a few of those celebrating Harvey and Rose Saujon's 50th wedding anniversary by the city's marina in 2011. Harvey retired from a career with the Merchant Marines, which began in World War II. Rose served as a nurse in the same war. She later operated a hair salon until retirement. Both died shortly after their anniversary. (Photograph by author.)

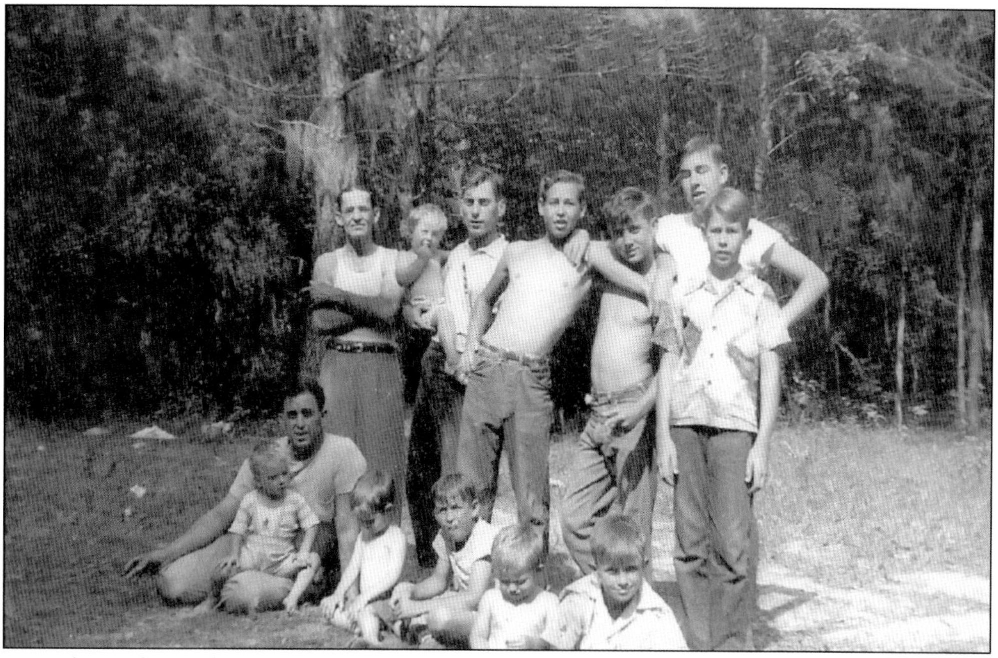

Some descendants of Joseph Boney are pictured at an outing on Lopez Point around 1947. Standing from left to right are Davis Fayard, C.J. in Carl Beaugez's arms, Mike Fayard, Dale Greenwell, and David and Paul Fayard; sitting are Sammy in Hugh Beaugez's lap, Greg Greenwell, Meck Boney, Mike Fayard, and Tim Greenwell. (Courtesy Tay Greenwell.)

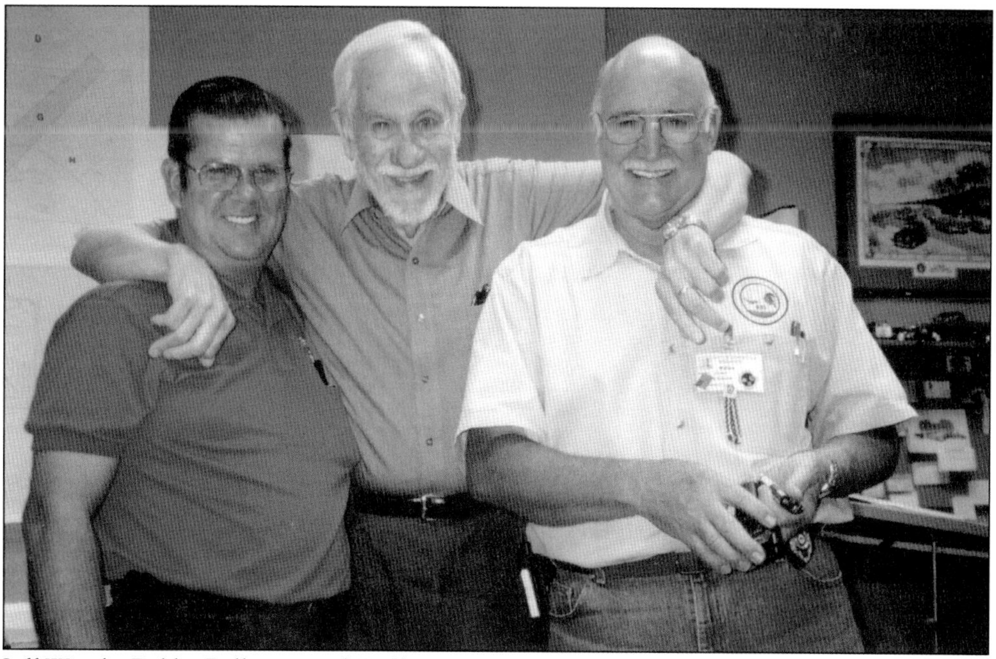

Jeff Woods, Bobby Bellman, and Wallace Freeman served the citizens for years, Jeff as a city-county liaison, Bobby as a city councilman, and Wallace as a building official. Even following retirement, the three continue to participate in public events and affairs. (Courtesy the City of D'Iberville.)

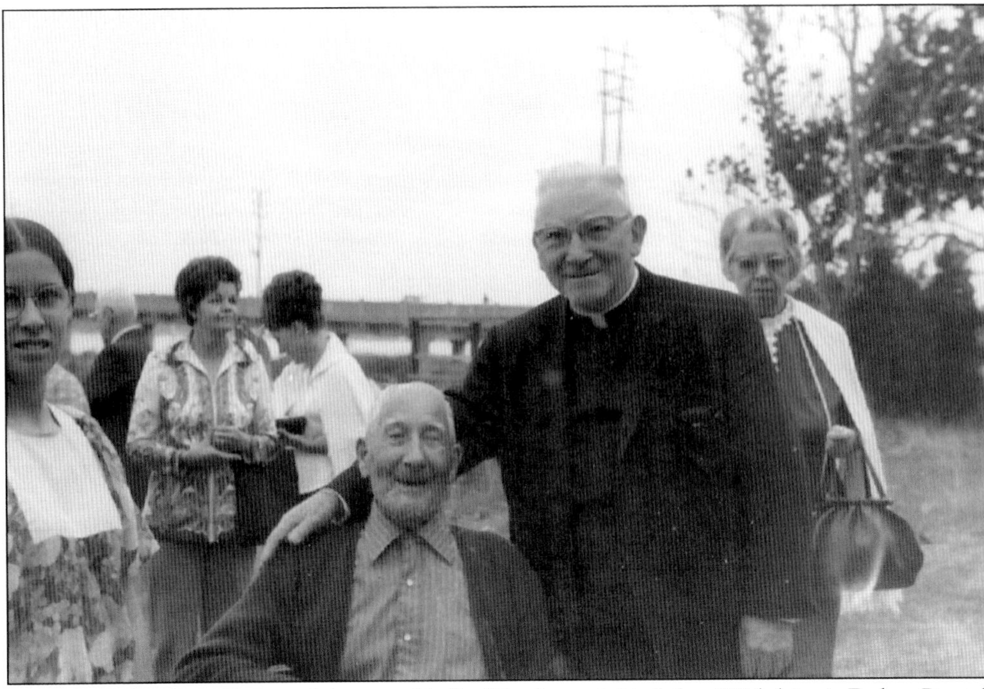

Residents of D'Iberville are celebrating Phillip Trochesset's birthday. With him is Father Patrick McAlpine of Sacred Heart Parish. They are on the site of the 19th-century Sanchez Chapel and St. Theresa Parochial School of the mid-20th century. Vada Talley and her daughter Stella Mae are in the background; the girl on left is unidentified. (Photograph by author.)

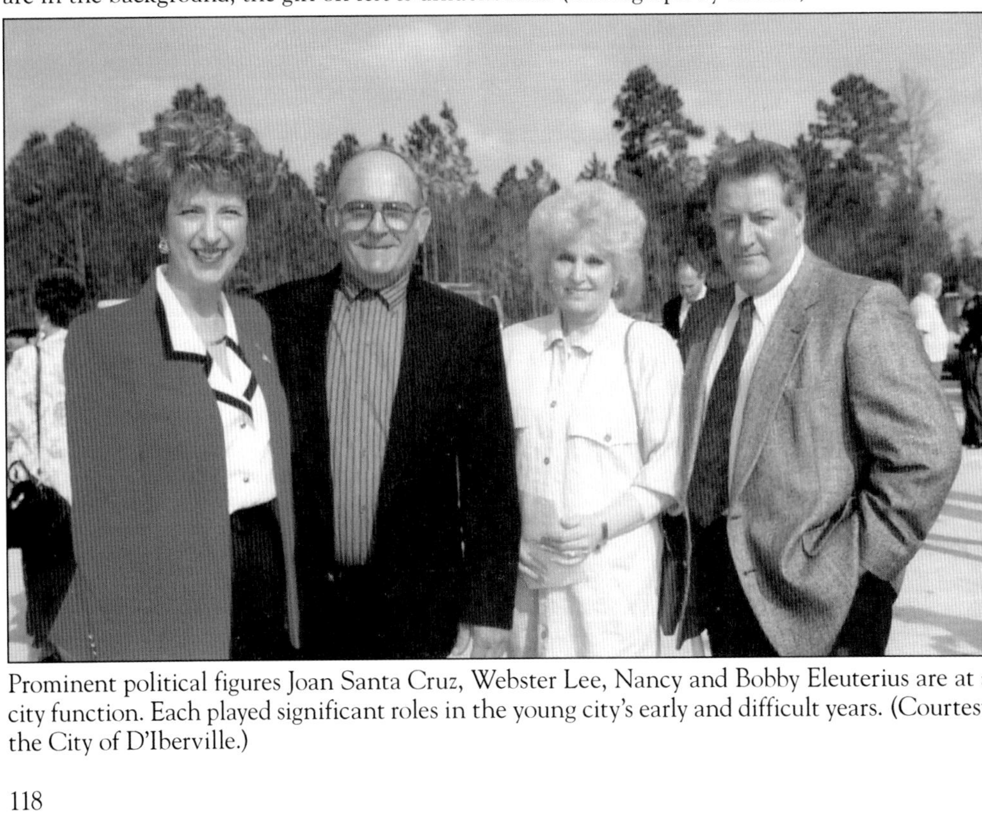

Prominent political figures Joan Santa Cruz, Webster Lee, Nancy and Bobby Eleuterius are at a city function. Each played significant roles in the young city's early and difficult years. (Courtesy the City of D'Iberville.)

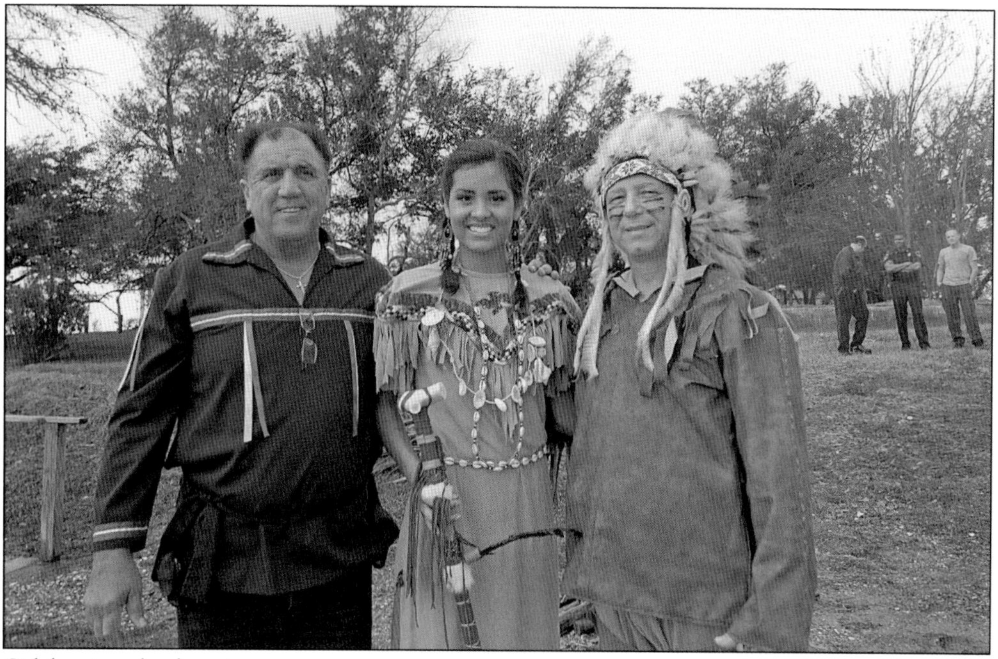

Celebrating the frontier past are Biloxi-Chitimacha chief Albert Naquin, Miss Mississippi Christine Kowalski, and Mayor Rusty Quave at the Fountain Beach Pavilion in 2010. The event marked the bay area's 311th anniversary. (Courtesy the City of D'Iberville.)

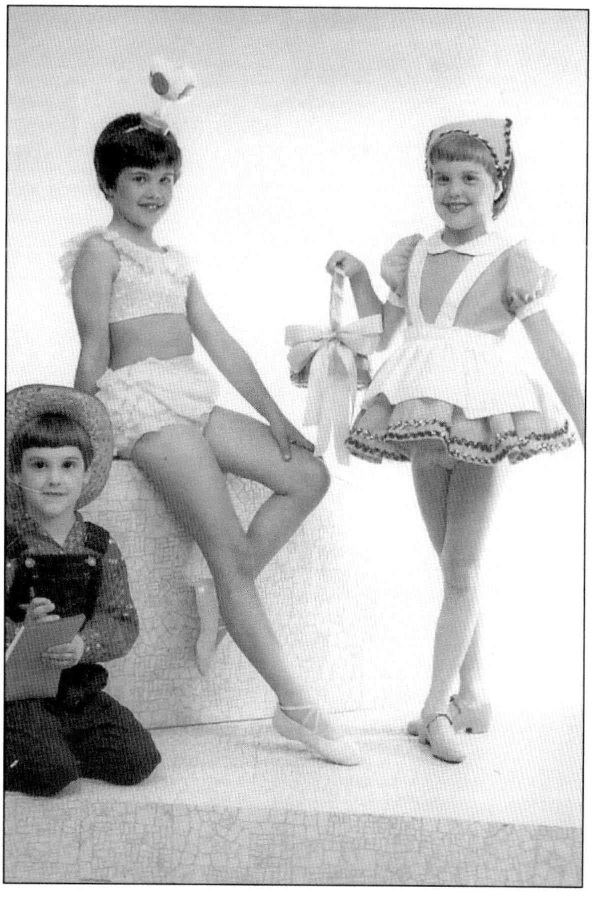

Scarlet, Dana, and Lance, children of Alvin and Alice Mae (Gollott) Voght, are waiting the signal to enter the stage during a performance in 1978. In a previous photograph, the two girls were riding convertibles in a DHS homecoming parade. Their talents only expanded from there. (Courtesy Alice Mae Voght.)

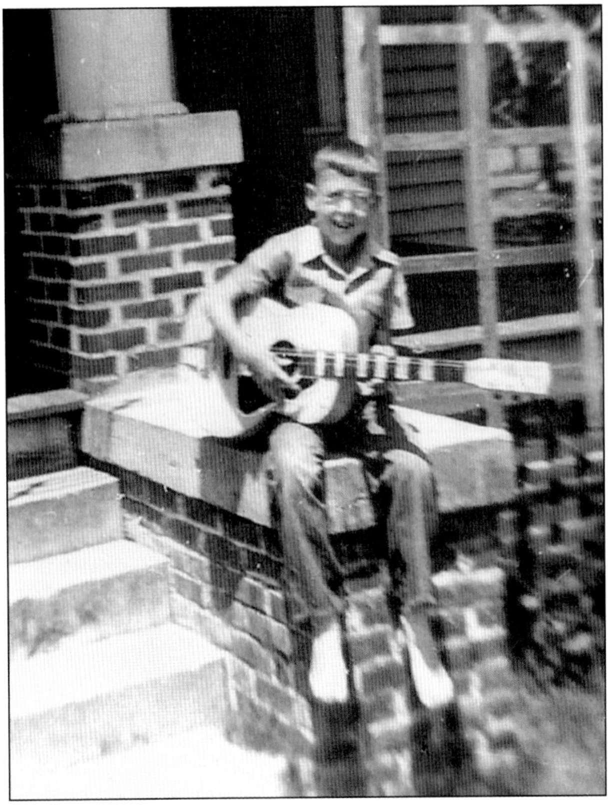

David Fayard is on Henry King's steps on Boney Road in 1941, singing to the neighborhood. One of Davis and Margaret's seven children, he is the only one with an interest in playing an instrument. (Courtesy Tay Greenwell.)

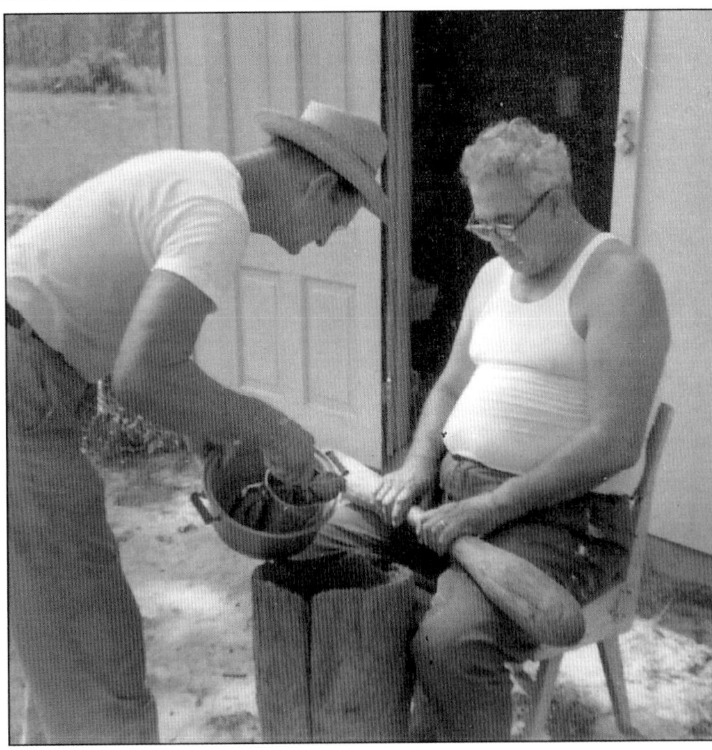

Maurice and Hugh Beaugez are seen with pestle and mortar in the traditional reduction of sassafras leaves to "gumbo filet." Tradition is that leaves are removed from the tree in May, dried in a dark shed, then pounded to powder in June. Their father was Paul Beaugez of St. Martin and their mother was Maggie Boney of D'Iberville (Photograph by author.)

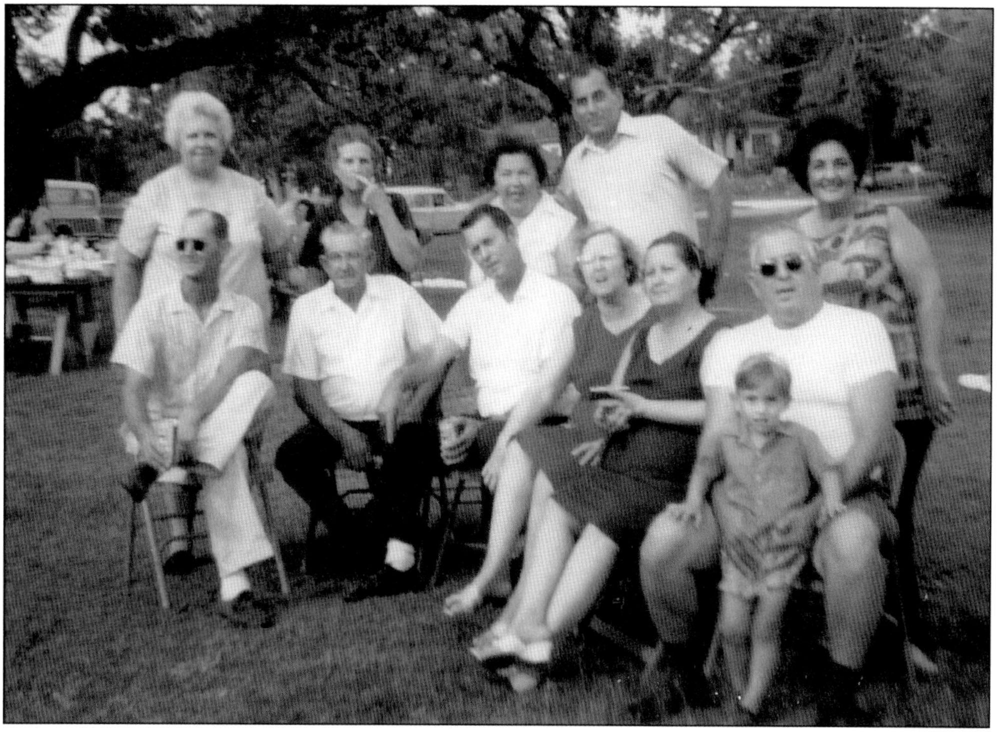

Pictured at the Beaugez, Boney cookout in the 1960s are, from left to right, (sitting) Maurice Beaugez, Arthur Boney, Walter Beaugez, Margaret Fayard, Martha Greenwell, Hugh Beaugez, and grandson; (standing) Irma Beaugez, Ellen Boney, Loraine Beaugez, Carl Beaugez, and Rose Beaugez. (Photograph by author.)

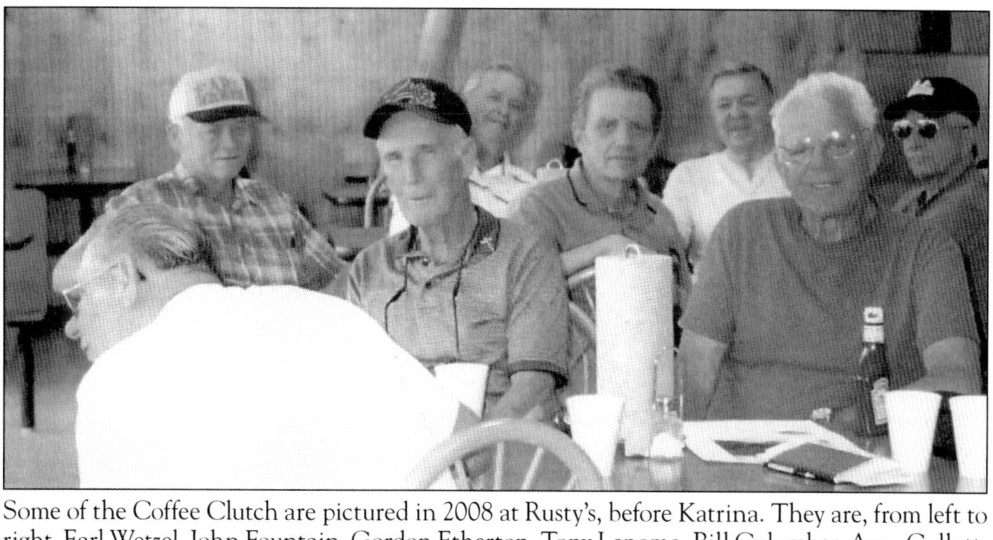

Some of the Coffee Clutch are pictured in 2008 at Rusty's, before Katrina. They are, from left to right, Earl Wetzel, John Fountain, Gordon Etherton, Tony Lepoma, Bill Culumber, Arny Gollott, Lell Thompson, and, with his back to the camera, Buck Bosarge. (Photograph by author.)

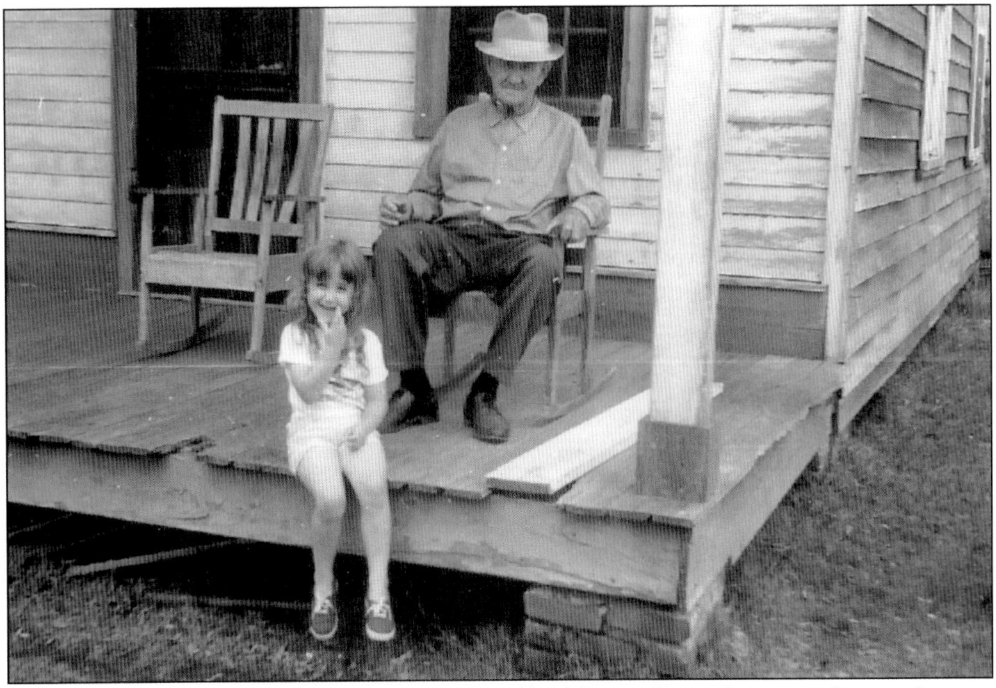

Fritz Boney and Michelle Greenwell are at the old Alphonse Boney home on Saucier Lane in 1968. Fritz and his brother Henry (a World War I veteran) were from Harrison County, never owned a vehicle, and walked everywhere. They lived at home all their lives and never married. (Photograph by author.)

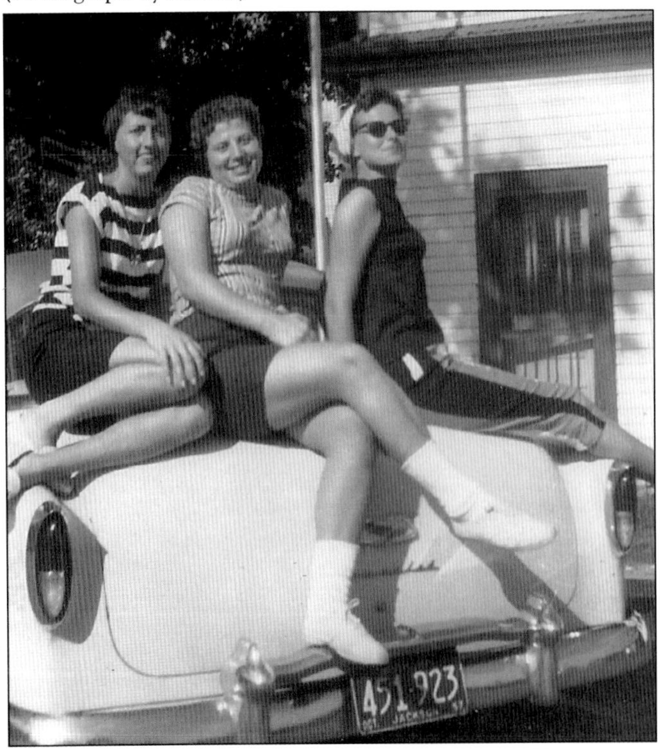

In the 1950s, Sylvia Terretta, Shirley Beaugez, and Tanya Greenwell—cousins, Reynoir Road neighbors, and St. Martin High schoolmates—are perhaps planning an evening getaway in this image. (Courtesy Cheri Rowan.)

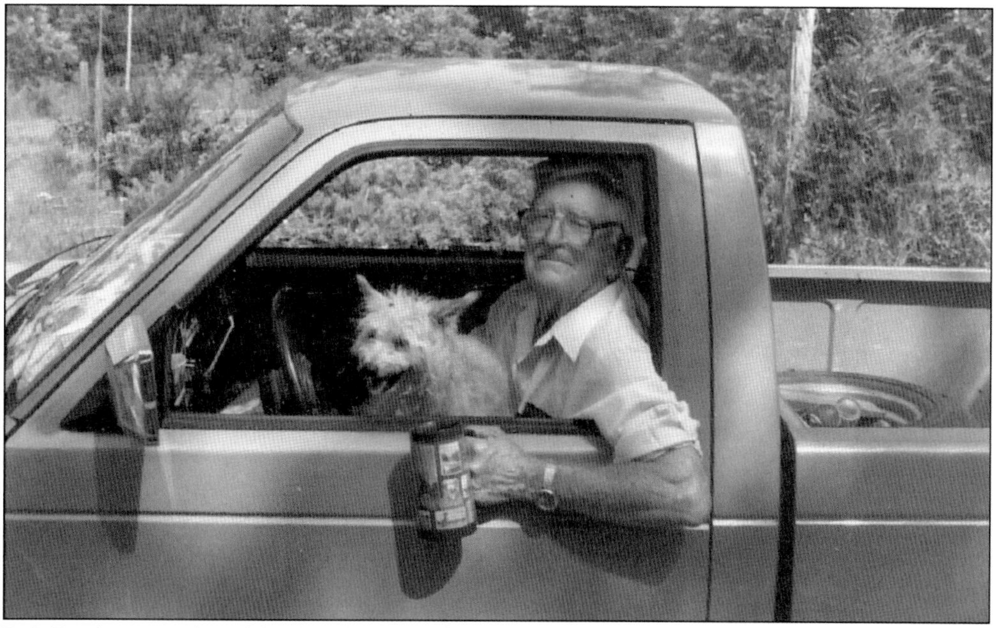

Bob Brodie, retired, and his best friend are on a typical ride-around. He and his brother, James, inherited Brodies Biloxi Nursery from their father and operated into their late senior years, with Bob's son, Jimmy, assisting. The nursery employed many schoolboys (including the author), as well as both black and white men. The boys learned what real work was about. (Photograph by author.)

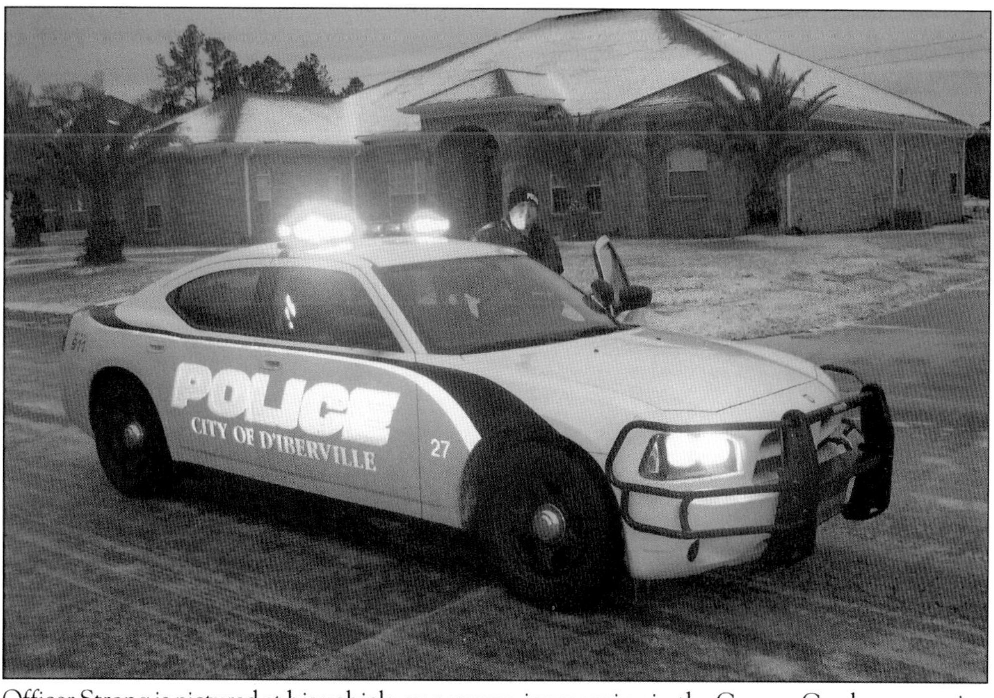

Officer Strong is pictured at his vehicle on a snowy, icy morning in the Cypress Creek community. His blue lights are warning drivers to proceed with caution—iced roads in D'Iberville are as rare as solar eclipses. (Photograph by author.)

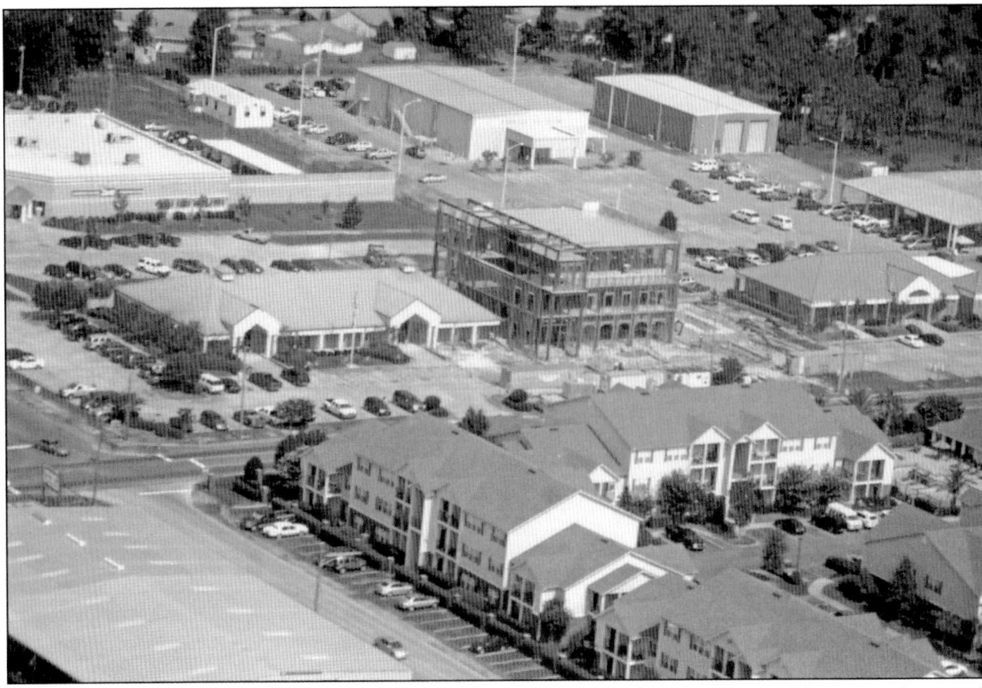

The post-Katrina city hall neighborhood includes a three-story steel frame addition on the north end of city hall. To its left is the Jerry Lawrence Library. Behind and north of the library is one of the city's public-service complexes. The post office is behind city hall and in front of Harbor View apartments (where 21 units were destroyed by arson in March 2014). (Courtesy the City of D'Iberville.)

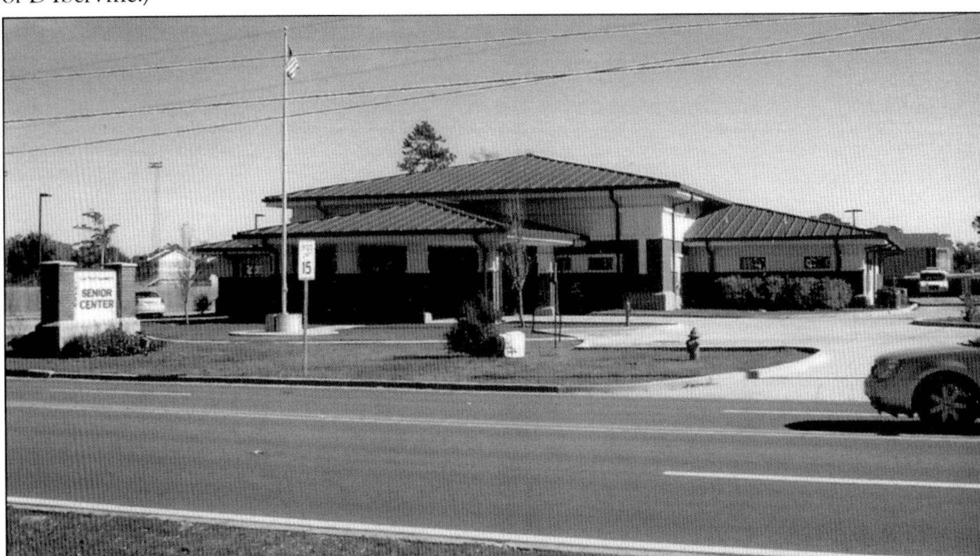

The Les Barnett Senior Citizens Center on Lamey Bridge Road is very popular with citizens of all ages. Art, exercise, entertainment, and community and institutional events have made the center very popular. It is named in honor of Les Barnett Sr., for his many years of selfless service to his fellow citizens. He and his wife operated Bay Furniture Co. for many years. (Photograph by author.)

The Moore House on Church Street was the last house to be removed from the planned casino strip that extends from the bay and includes the east half of the old town. The Moore family sold to Lindell Lepre Sr. in 1964. The house is about a century old. Lindell's son, Brian, is in the photograph. (Photograph by author.)

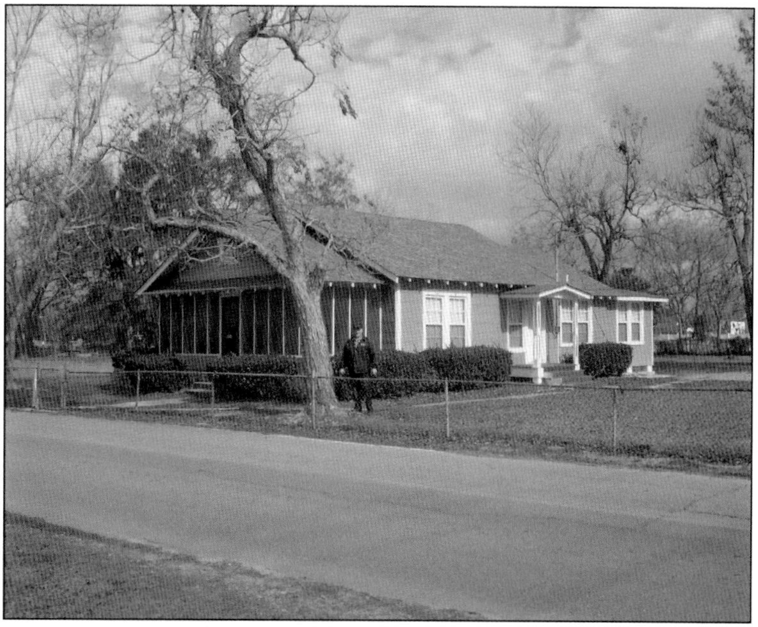

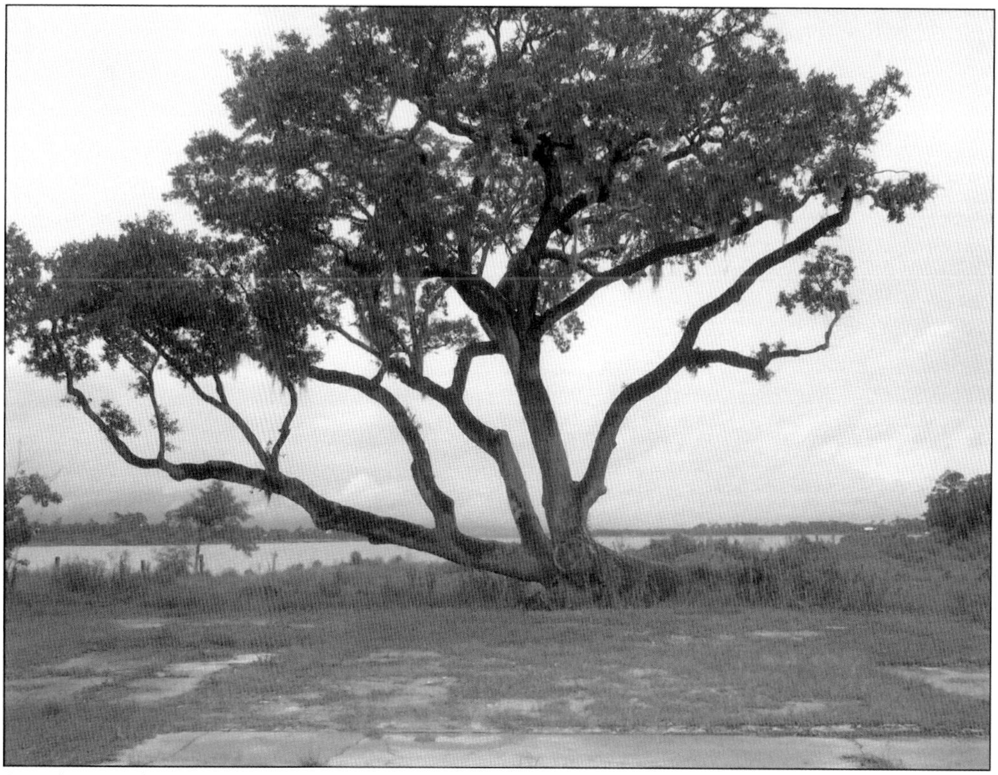

Seen here is the Harvey Oak. On this site Casimer Harvey erected his home, ferry landing, Flying Tiger tavern/grocery store, sawmill and boatyard. He competed with the small business area on Ramsey Road, which had a ferry landing and an intersection of five roads. However, when the bridge was built in 1901 on Ramsey Road, it killed his business opportunity. This oak was young when the hurricane of 1893 blew it over. (Photograph by author.)

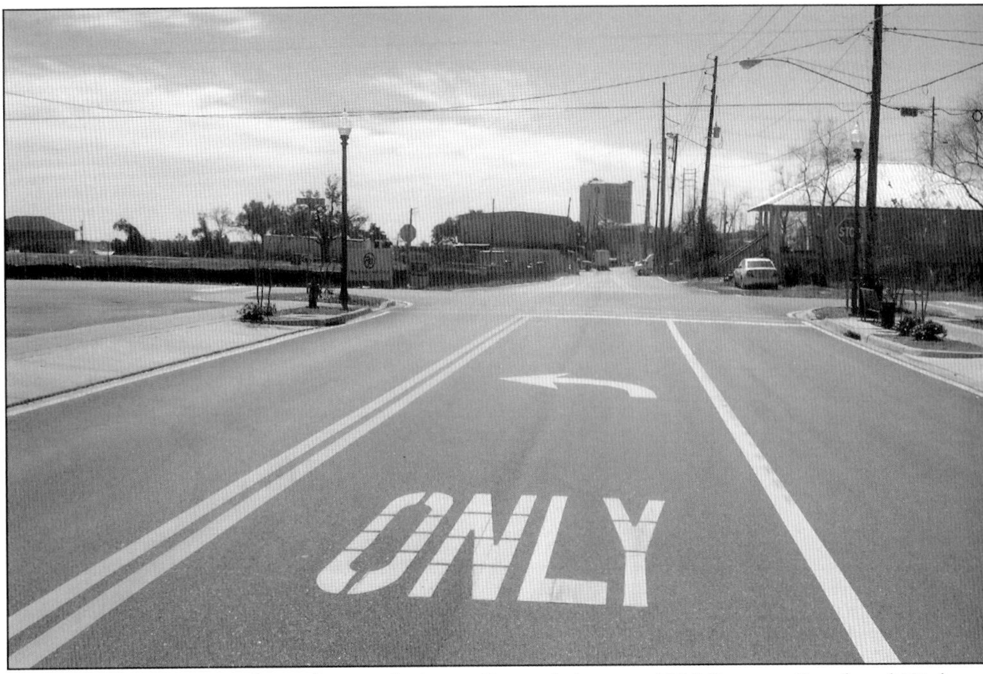

This view of Five Point from the north shows Central Avenue (Old Ramsey Road and Highway 90, then 15 and 67) after the old community was washed away in Hurricane Katrina.

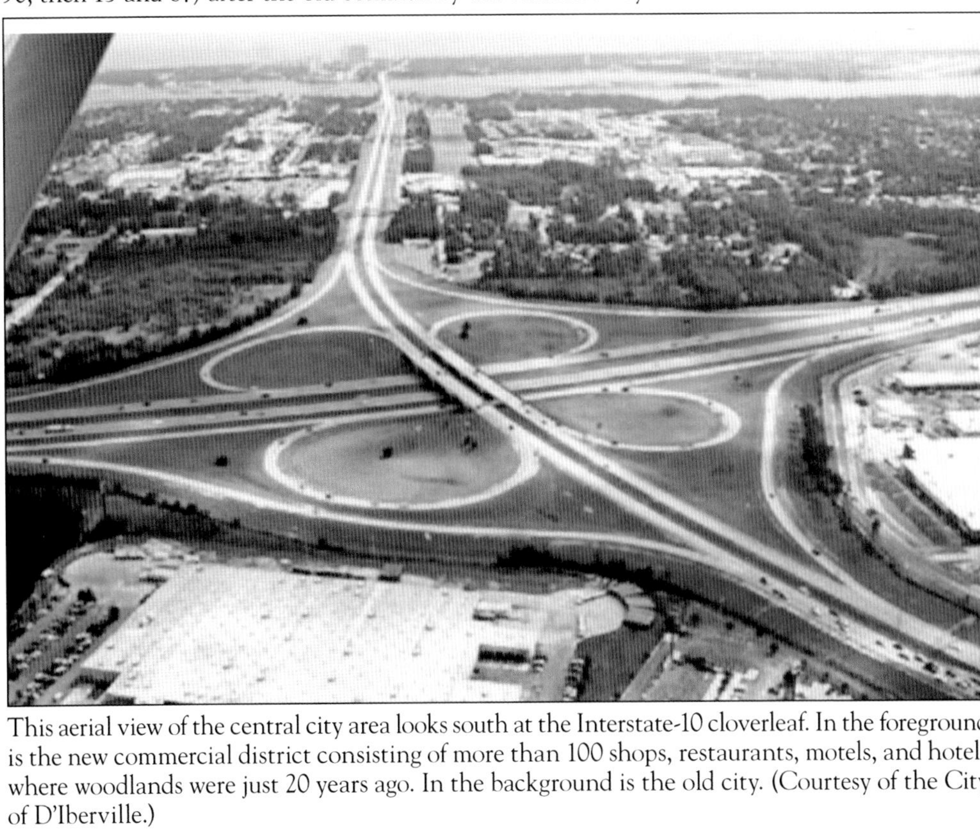

This aerial view of the central city area looks south at the Interstate-10 cloverleaf. In the foreground is the new commercial district consisting of more than 100 shops, restaurants, motels, and hotels where woodlands were just 20 years ago. In the background is the old city. (Courtesy of the City of D'Iberville.)

Martha (Beaugez) Greenwell, the author's mother, is shown here in her early 20s. An artist of many talents, her education ended with high school on the eve of the Great Depression. She loved writing romance novels that were read only by her friends. They are being considered for publication. Her ashes were scattered in Back Bay, as promised.

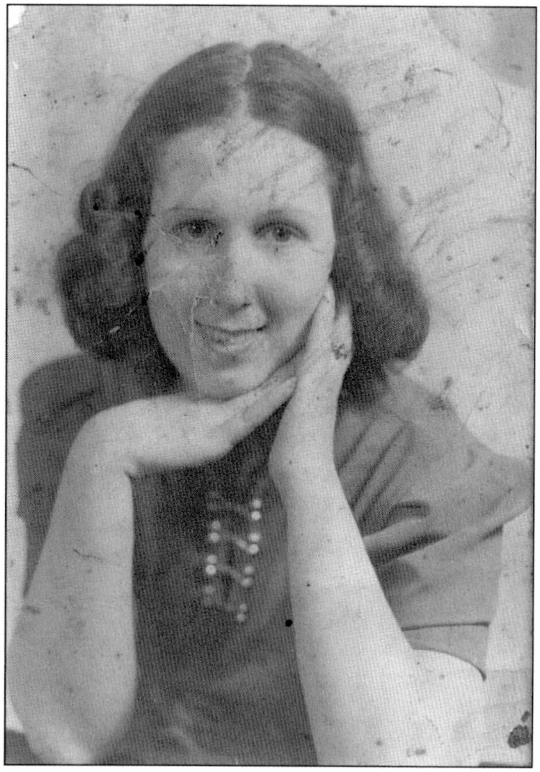

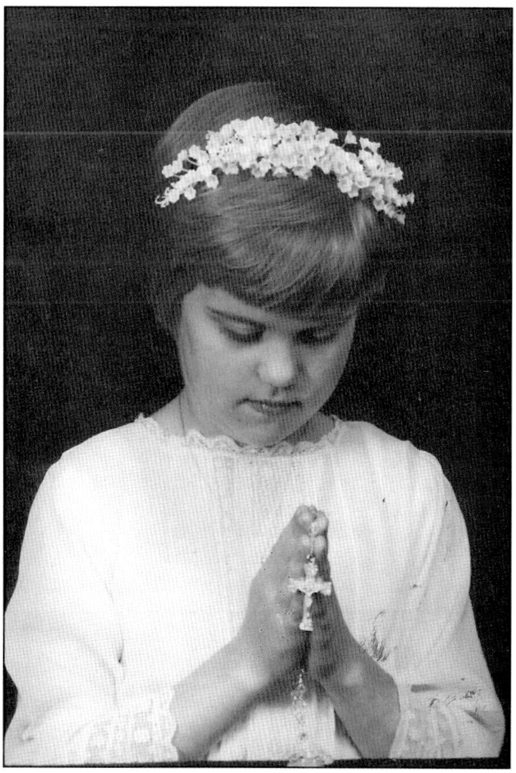

On a Sunday morning in the 1970s, at Sacred Heart Church, Dana received her First Communion.